The New Eastern Europe
and the World Economy

Eastern Europe After Communism

Sabrina Petra Ramet, *Series Editor*

Since the collapse of communism throughout Eastern Europe, 1989–1990, the societies of the region have begun searching for new social and political formulae, setting new tasks, and facing new challenges. New social forces have arisen, such as nationalism and chauvinism, and preexisting social institutions and groupings, such as the churches and feminist groups, have intensified their activity. Above all, Eastern Europe is dominated, in the years following the collapse, by the twin tasks of democratization and privatization, tasks that are complex and multifaceted, with consequences that reach far beyond the formal goals associated with these processes.

This new series is designed to provide a set of windows on the changing realities of Eastern Europe and to chart these societies' courses as they attempt to deal with the legacy of communism and the problems of transition. This volume tackles the economic challenges facing all of Eastern Europe. Future volumes will examine the security context and offer perspectives on each country in the region.

Books in This Series

The New Eastern Europe and the World Economy, edited by Jozef M. van Brabant

FORTHCOMING

Beyond Yugoslavia: Politics, Economics, and Culture in a Shattered Community, edited by Sabrina P. Ramet and Ljubisa Adamovic

Albania and the Albanians, Elez Biberaj

The New Eastern Europe and the World Economy

EDITED BY

Jozef M. van Brabant

WESTVIEW PRESS

Boulder • San Francisco • Oxford

To my three ladies: Anja, Katja, and Miyuki

Eastern Europe After Communism

Copyright © 1993 by Westview Press, Inc.

Published in 1993 in the United States of America by Westview Press, Inc., 5500 Central Avenue, Boulder, Colorado 80301-2877, and in the United Kingdom by Westview Press, 36 Lonsdale Road, Summertown, Oxford OX2 7EW

A CIP record for this book is available from the Library of Congress.
ISBN 0-8133-1523-9

Printed and bound in the United States of America

The paper used in this publication meets the requirements
of the American National Standard for Permanence of Paper
for Printed Library Materials Z39.48-1984.

10   9   8   7   6   5   4   3   2   1

Contents

Preface

Although this volume is directed at analyzing critical elements of the transitions in the former planned economies of Europe, its ultimate gestation became in part a victim of that very transition. Not that I would claim intervention on the part of the policy makers of one transition process or another. But the demands on the scarce time of a comparatively small number of specialists who could dissect the defects of central planning and its legacies, and bring that knowledge to bear for an insightful treatment of what is likely to happen in external relations under conditions of transition did have its negative impacts both on the conceptualization and the final production of the book.

This volume is one of the series *Eastern Europe After Communism*, under the general editorship of Sabrina Petra Ramet. When first conceived in late 1988 under the editorshop of Vladimir Sobell, this volume had a dual focus. On the one hand, it was intended to examine opportunities for prospectively improving regional economic cooperation in the eastern part of Europe, given ongoing tinkering with the administrative planning systems in place and the significant ferment about socialist economic integration that had been crystallizing from the mid-1980s on. On the other hand, it was to assess how these emerging trends could inhibit or complicate the association of the still partly planned economies through formal ties with the multilateral economic organizations and less formal relations, through trade, financial, and factor mobility with the western economies.

The marked changes that occurred in Eastern Europe in late 1989 and early 1990 made it imperative to reconceive the entire purpose of the volume, almost from square one. Mr. Sobell withdrew from the project and I was entrusted with that new task. Rather than continue to focus on how transforming planning systems could be rendered compatible with various international economic regimes or established trading, pricing, financing, and investment practices, it was decided that the central emphasis of the volume should be on looking forward, towards the implications of the various transitions for the near-term and eventual position of these economies in the global economic environment as best as one could grasp emerging trends.

As a result, a completely new outline and list of contributors was assembled. Unfortunately, because of the demands on the time of several individuals who had initially pledged to contribute a paper against a fairly tight delivery deadline, they felt compelled to withdraw from the project unless successive claims for more time in order to ready the manuscripts could be extended. I labored between disappointing those who contributed on time, or at least within tolerable delays, and others who would have wished to delay publication for another 3 to 6 months. In the end, I decided to assemble the product and ready it for publication with fewer contributors than had originally been envisaged.

Under the circumstances, I would be remiss if I did not take this opportunity to express my sincere gratitude to all those who have borne with me throughout this project and who have taken my repeated prodding, cajoling, and at times (mostly friendly) threats with a sense of forbearance and good humor.

I have edited this volume on my own time. Nonetheless, as staff member of the Department of Economic and Social Development of the United Nations Secretariat in New York, I should like to stress that the views advocated and the analyses presented here by any of my colleagues or myself do not reflect views that any of the United Nations' organs may have on the matter. Each of the authors is responsible for the printed contributions and where I as editor have added or subtracted from the delivered manuscript, ultimate responsibility is mine only.

And a final word of thanks to my three ladies, especially Miyuki, my nearly silent and understanding partner, through thick and thin, for about a quarter century.

Jozef M. van Brabant

Abbreviations

BIS	Bank for International Settlements
BTPA	bilateral trade and payments agreements
CAP	Common Agricultural Policy
CEPU	Central European Payments Union
CIS	Commonwealth of Independent States
CMEA	Council for Mutual Economic Assistance
CoCom	Coordinating Committee for Multilateral Export Controls
ČSFR	Czech and Slovak Federal Republic
EBRD	European Bank for Reconstruction and Development
EC	European Communities
ECO	Economic Cooperation Organization
ECSC	European Coal and Steel Community
ECU	European currency unit
EFTA	European Free Trade Association
EIB	European Investment Bank
EPU	European Payments Union
FDI	foreign direct investment
FRG	Federal Republic of Germany
FTO	foreign trade organization
Fund	International Monetary Fund
GAB	General Arrangements to Borrow
GATT	General Agreement on Tariffs and Trade
GDR	German Democratic Republic
GSP	general system of preferences
G-7	Group of Seven
G-10	Group of Ten
G-24	Group of Twenty-four
IBRD	International Bank for Reconstruction and Development, *see also* World Bank
ICSID	International Center for the Settlement of Investment Disputes
IDA	International Development Association
IEO	international economic organization

IFC	International Finance Corporation
IMF	International Monetary Fund, *see also* Fund
MFA	Multi-fibre Arrangement
MFN	most-favored nation
MIGA	Multilateral Investment Guarantee Agency
NIE	newly industrializing economy
ODA	official development assistance
OECD	Organisation for Economic Co-operation and Development
OPEC	Organization of Petroleum Exporting Countries
PET	planned economy in transition
PHARE	*Pologne/Hongrie: assistance à la restructuration économique*
RCA	revealed comparative advantage
RCD	Regional Cooperation for Development
SDR	special drawing right
SITC	standard industrial trade classification
SOE	state-owned enterprise
TNC	transnational corporation
TR	transferable ruble
USSR	Union of Soviet Socialist Republics
VER	voluntary export restraint
World Bank	International Bank for Reconstruction and Development together with the International Finance Corporation

1

Introduction

Jozef M. van Brabant

The *annus mirabilis* in Eastern Europe and subsequently the disintegration and dissolution of the Soviet Union undoubtedly rank among the epochal events of the 20th century. Their far-reaching, pervasive ramifications will be felt for decades to come. Not only have the most overt emanations of the old antagonism between socialism and capitalism now been obliterated, or at least put to rest, but the east-west conflict with all of its conventional Cold War overtones is a nightmare of the past. The remaking of the societies in the eastern part of Europe, stretching from Germany's newly regained eastern borders all the way to the Pacific, or wherever Europe's eastern border will eventually be drawn, holds promising opportunities in terms of infusing more buoyant economic growth in the region; improving the area for fruitful interaction between east and west, and indeed directly and indirectly with the south as well, through trade and finance; and in better coming to grips with an ever more complex global economy.

But the transitions in the East also harbor considerable dangers and costs for years to come, with the latter possibly exacerbating the former. East is the preferred designation here to delineate all the former planned

---

Principal Economic Affairs Officer of the Department of Economic and Social Development of the United Nations Secretariat in New York. The opinions expressed here are my own and do not necessarily reflect those that may be held by the United Nations in general and its Secretariat in particular.

economies of Europe and the successor states to the Soviet Union as well as Yugoslavia and its successor states. They are also referred to as the planned economies in transition (PETs—no pun intended). I have justified the use of this term at some length elsewhere (Brabant 1992g). Undoubtedly the most profound effects of the revolutions in the East will be felt for years to come in each of these countries and among them, rather than in most countries previously classified with various southern or the western economic and political groupings.

The Principal Themes Addressed

This collection cannot come to grips with all facets of the momentous changes under way in the various transition economies, of course. And it certainly was not meant to address such a comprehensive agenda. Its focus is indeed chiefly elsewhere, namely the positioning of the new Eastern economies in the global economic context. This has certainly been a basic preoccupation of those managing the transitions and of key leaders of the western world—in national governments as well as in regional and international organizations concerned about assisting these economies, if only to prop up the fragile sociopolitical framework in which the transitions necessarily must mature, and thus improve upon the degree of stability that these countries can hope to achieve by themselves.

Much less attention has been paid to the opportunities for fruitful economic cooperation among the PETs themselves. There are many reasons for this apathy. Some can be perfectly explained in economic terms. But a good deal of what is hindering economic interaction among these countries is due to metaeconomic posturing and, at least for a while, rather myopic ways of looking at the opportunities at hand by western governments and the regional and international organizations involved in raising and delivering assistance to the transition economies according to a format they themselves have chosen to conceptualize.

It was against this background that the four themes of the present volume were conceived: economic liberalization in foreign sectors; the disintegration of the trade payment, pricing, and settlement systems among the PETs in the postwar period; accession to and active participation in the key organizations entrusted with international financial, monetary, and trading regimes; and ways and means of alleviating the adjustment costs being incurred as a result of or in conjunction with ongoing transition policies.

Before any of these broad themes about desirable changes in the Eastern economies can be properly addressed, however, it is important to be fully cognizant of precisely what is being changed. Likewise it is critical to be aware, even if only approximately, of how fast political intentions regarding desirable sociopolitical and economic mutations can be completed. There are several reasons for this state of affairs aside from the prevailing political will and the associated sociopolitical consensus. In addition, there are many legacies of the old regimes that impinge upon what can be accomplished at any given point of time during the transition, particularly its first critical phases. The latter include not only the hysteresis effects of more than four decades of communism in Eastern Europe and over seven decades in the former Soviet Union. They should also include coming to grips with the specific features of these societies seen from within a broader historical perspective.

Legacies of the Past and Economic Transformation

Being as completely as possible in the picture about the constraints on the transformation processes in the Eastern economies is critical not only in assessing the art of policy making. Such comprehensive knowledge would also appear critical in ensuring that the envisaged goals of political democracy and market-based allocation of resources can be carried out without generating highly dysfunctional side effects that themselves may undermine the very process of moving forward with the unavoidable structural mutations of these societies. These may at times threaten to usurp the dynamics of the transformation process itself. Hence, being aware of the limits of the adjustment costs that can be tolerated, even though these boundaries themselves may be shifting over time in various ways, would seem a critical variable in designing the comprehensiveness, speed, and sequencing of the associated policies.

Unfortunately, the legion of advisers that have jumped into the fray about transition modalities in the Eastern economies as well as the agencies newly appointed to deliver and conceptualize assistance have all too often departed from the notion that, once the communist yoke jettisoned, t ιe Eastern economies would quickly revert to a western-style democracy and a market-driven economy. Particularly inappropriate have been assumptions that these economies would be characterized by proper, fairly rapid adjustments of demand and supply in all markets—goods and services as well as production factors—under impact of competition. That drive would presumably emanate, if not from within these economies then from without.

Coming to grips with the legacies of the past evolution of the Eastern economies individually and in their regional concert, including in the context of the former Council for Mutual Economic Assistance (CMEA), could easily have justified a weighty tome all by itself. But the purpose of the present collection is not to provide an exegesis of the Eastern economies and societies, say, in the twentieth century. Instead, this volume purports to be forward-looking, dissecting as best one can the foreign economic implications of the mutations in the East. As a result, a hard choice had to be made.

It was in the end decided to leave the study of the past up to each reader's proclivity towards exploring the, often admittedly abstruse, literature on these economies. Perhaps János Kornai's (1992) recent attempt to come to grips with the socialist economic system offers a convenient point of departure for this exploration and enhanced understanding of the past. But I readily admit that a definitive account of the pervasive transformations that the communist system exerted as well as of the immanent features of what some commentators have called the *Mitteleuropa*-syndrome remains to be written. It should be a fascinating eye-opener, but its potential interests can alas only be pointed to in this volume.

Certainly, each chapter in one way or another touches upon the lingering consequences of postwar developments in the East. A rounded picture of the past would have been useful. It would on the one hand have clarified the system of the centrally planned communist society envisaged in the 1920s in the Soviet Union and the 1950s throughout the former Soviet bloc. Even more important, it should have illuminated the process whereby the partially realized blueprint from the 1960s on began to degenerate into a system of largely administrative regulation. This was not a system that was overwhelmingly dominated by caprice or voluntarism. On the contrary, the existing socialist system had its immanent logic. Originally it sought to improve, among other things, the allocation of resources both on the production and the distribution sides of the ledger of economic activity. Especially since the mid-1970s, however, this motivation of economic policy became ever more remote to actual decision making. This has had its own implications for human behavior in general as well as the way in which the institutions of the market in the broad sense can be realized in the East in the near term. Yet, the realization of these institutions is by all counts a *conditio sine qua non* for ensuring the proper functioning of the market mechanism. In other words, heeding the lingering defects of past policies and experiences in as comprehensive a setting as possible is a key determinant of the eventual magnitude of the success of economic transformation of the Eastern societies and how quickly this stage will be within reach.

Foreign Trade and Exchange Liberalization

As planned economies, the countries of the eastern part of Europe shielded themselves from much of the world economy. Although various changes occurred in this policy stance in the postwar period, by the time the East's revolutions careered around the corner, these economies remained separated from the world economy in a number of respects. One was in pricing, domestic pricing being pursued with a great deal of domestic policy autonomy. This could be preserved in part because the economy was buffered against foreign competition and domestic economic agents were not given any other incentive either to compete in the global economic framework or to ensure that the planned economies remained potentially competitive, even if for now they were to shun more active integration into the world economy.

Of considerable importance was also the existence of their own payment, pricing, and settlement regimes within the context of the CMEA. All these provisions were integrally anchored to the so-called transferable ruble (TR)—the unit of account in most economic interactions among nearly all of the former planned economies. Another important variable that shielded these economies was inconvertibility of the domestic currencies in virtually all senses in which the notion of currency convertibility can usefully be considered (Brabant 1987a, pp. 357-82).

The liberalization of the systems of foreign trade and payments has, therefore, been one of the most obvious priority concerns about transforming the Eastern economies and merging them into the global context as both a means as well as an objective of domestic economic restructuring. The manifold issues involved are examined notably in the chapters

by Jozef M. van Brabant, and Ben Slay, while Giovanni Graziani address-
es the problems of cooperation and competition in international markets
that are bound to accompany the restructuring of the smaller Eastern
European PETs.

Quo Vadis Intraregional Economic Ties?

One of the important markers of the division of the world economy after
World War II was the establishment of the CMEA in 1949 and the decision of the planned economies either not to join the multilateral economic
organizations created in the second half of the 1940s or, in some cases
(China, Cuba, Czechoslovakia, and Poland) to quit. Although economic
integration was never effectively pursued within the CMEA framework,
both because that context was not conducive to integration and, more
important, the member countries did not seek to dovetail their economies
in any intricate way, the CMEA's rather unusual trade and payment
arrangements were nonetheless of critical importance in two respects.

One was that it enabled sizable volumes of trade to be cleared at
rather unorthodox conditions. It notably afforded a fairly extensive exchange of raw materials and fuels, chiefly from the former Soviet Union,
for manufactures, chiefly from the smaller Eastern European countries;
but the buoyancy of this exchange came under increasingly adverse
pressures, beginning with the latter part of the 1970s.

Moreover, the CMEA as a framework for regional economic cooperation, just like the member economies, provided captive markets. These
were certainly poorly interlinked and oftentimes not really justified on
any solid efficiency grounds. Nonetheless, they implied a special type of
regional production specialization that could be accommodated within the
planning context; but the arrangements built upon these special provisions could not possibly survive open competition.

With economic liberalization of the Eastern countries, the future of the
CMEA came into jeopardy. And from a political point of view, wide layers
of the populations of the smaller Eastern European countries perceived
the organization, and even more of what it stood for, as an instrument of
Soviet hegemony in the area. The utter destruction not only of the CMEA
as an organization but also as a framework of cooperation, including the
structures that depended on at least the earlier framework, was, thus,

being avidly coveted by the new leaders of the East. Perhaps somewhat unexpectedly, they succeeded in doing so in record tempo.

Although conditions for economic cooperation among the CMEA countries could have been modified in such a way that buoyant exchanges among the PETs would have become gradually unraveled and new paths for economically warranted trade specialization would have been exploited, this simply did not happen in the haste of obliterating all vestiges of what could remind those entrusted with the management of the transition of the past.

A second theme of the volume is, therefore, the disintegration of the postwar intragroup trading arrangements of these countries and whether there is any room worth exploring for engineering a revival of intragroup trade that would at this juncture be justified chiefly on economic grounds, and thus could perhaps be argued more positively also on political and ideological grounds.

The topic is first broached in the chapter 3 by Jozef M. van Brabant, but subsequently deepened in that by Harriet Matejka. The two chapters offer seemingly contrasting, and perhaps even conflicting, solutions to the quagmire in which the PETs find themselves. In fact, the two views are complementary rather than contradictory.

Matejka by and large focuses her analysis on whether, from a theoretical point of view, it makes sense to pursue any formalized form of economic cooperation among the PETs. Her answer predictably is negative. Because the broad institutions of the market are not yet in place in any PET, it is impossible to predict sensibly whether any formal discriminatory trade and/or payments arrangement would, or even could, be beneficial for the cooperating partners themselves, let alone have positive implications for global economic welfare.

Van Brabant in contrast focuses on whether one can argue, on logical grounds, that it might be beneficial to tackle issues of regional economic cooperation even prior to the completion of the basic institutions of the market. After all, policy makers cannot afford to simply sit around and wait for the institutions of the market to emerge or to be laid. The logic would be in the contingent probability of lessening the economic, political, and possibly even social costs of the transition through concerted cooperation. But this can be correct only if there is in place credible government in the various potential cooperants. A critical variable in this approach is the supervision to be exercised under an international authority bent on facilitating the emergence of market mechanisms in the Eastern countries at the earliest possible opportunity without jeopardizing the transitions themselves as a result of sociopolitical disaffection, which is an inevitable concomitant of pervasive structural change.

The PETs and International Economic Regimes

As already mentioned, for a long time after World War II the former planned economies, excepting Yugoslavia, shunned the international economic organizations (IEOs) in place (particularly the General Agreement on Tariffs and Trade [GATT], the International Monetary Fund [IMF], and the International Bank for Reconstruction and Development or [IBRD or World Bank]). But they also looked askance at the emerging regional economic blocs in Western Europe, most notably the European Communities (EC) and, to a lesser extent, the European Free Trade Association (EFTA).

Certainly, changes in attitudes had taken place over time and even some of the CMEA countries had gingerly joined some of the multilateral economic organizations well before the revolutions of the late 1980s tolled the end of postwar communism. But they never fit comfortably within the framework of the international economic regimes that these organs were designed to serve. The reasons are complex (Brabant 1991c). The very fundamental differences in the nature of a planned economy as compared to one based on market-regulated allocation of resources explain in part why the Eastern economies could be fused into the international organizations only in an awkward manner. But there was also considerable reluctance to yield even nominal control over the national economies in most of the East.

This apathy—in some cases outright hostility—towards these organizations changed almost overnight with the onset of the political revolutions. And with the resolve to mutate towards market-based decision making and adopting the proper transition steps to reach operational market-based economic systems, the PETs eventually will fit almost fully into the scheme of things regarding international economic management. But they cannot do so immediately. This factor should be heeded in exploring the relationship between the PETs and the IEOs.

It is, therefore, useful to inquire into how these countries can play a constructive role in the organizations in place and whether it might be useful to revamp the organizations and the regimes they were intended to serve to improve global economic management now that virtually all countries are willing to join in the effort. Jozef M. van Brabant does so in chapter 5 with respect to the global economic organizations, placed fully against the backdrop of fundamental changes in the structure of the global economy as well as the urgent need to improve the effectiveness of assistance delivery to the PETs. Cooperation of the PETs with the EC is discussed in the chapters by Giovanni Graziani, largely from the point of view of access to market economies, and Harriet Matejka, largely from the point of view of the theoretical benefits and costs of regional economic integration schemes.

The PETs and International Assistance

From the very beginning of the political revolutions in the Eastern countries, it was clear to many, but by far not all, observers that moving to an open market economy and political pluralism would impose a sizable adjustment cost, material as well as otherwise. In retrospect, the magnitude of this cost and the duration of the economic recession, which has now turned into a veritable depression, were widely underestimated. Nonetheless, even at the lower level of adjustment cost that was initially anticipated, the international community stepped forward with all kinds of assistance with a view to alleviating the burdens of the transition.

It is now clear that the transitions in the East have been exacting a terribly toll in terms of adjustment cost and will continue to do so for quite some time. Various questions have arisen as to whether the populations at large of these countries will continue to be willing to shoulder this cost by supporting a broadly based, if perhaps only tenuous, sociopolitical consensus. The potential for reversals not only in economic policy but, perhaps even more, in the political transitions is presently considerable and daunting. The shaky popular and, in some cases, even intellectual support for economic and political reform that has endured since late 1989 appears presently to be fraying. This is dangerous and unhelpful for an orderly management of the global economy in general or the successful revamping of the Eastern countries in particular.

A natural question to ask, then, is whether the international community's generosity in terms of delivering financial, technical, and other assistance to the East has been useful to the shaping and implementation of transition policies. A concomitant, followup question, regardless of the answer to the first, is whether more could have been done and better assistance could prospectively be delivered in terms of obtaining greater efficiency and exerting a more streamlined influence on the transformation processes; and perhaps to have done so in a dovetailed manner. Also, this effort on the part of the international community has raised considerable apprehension, notably on the part of a number of developing countries.

Jozef M. van Brabant in chapter 5 examines the questions at hand largely from the perspective of how to improve the management of assistance policy formulation, delivery, and monitoring, given the global institutional framework from within which one most likely will have to operate for the foreseeable future. Actual delivery forms part of the concerns addressed in the chapter by Joseph E. Smolik. He deals more specifically with the volume and composition of assistance, and how effectively it has been delivered. Miklós Losoncz analyzes the potentially adverse impacts of this assistance for developing countries. As regards privately funneled assistance, both through trade and more formal forms of interfirm cooperation, the chapter by Wladimir Andreff covers the essential parts. He is specifically concerned with the potential contribution that the private sector in mature market economies may provide to firms in the PETs, aside from rendering foreign direct investment (FDI).

Adopted Conventions

To provide some constants in discussing an area of inquiry that is not only in the process of fundamental reconstruction but, throughout history, has rarely had clearly defined boundaries, I have attempted to streamline the arguments as follows. Unless the context indicates otherwise, as indicated, East (with a capital E) comprises all of the old and new European PETs as of the date of writing. Eastern Europe is as a rule reserved for the traditional planned economies of Europe, including the former Soviet Union. But when there is little room for misunderstanding, Eastern Europe refers only to the six or five smaller former planned economies (Bulgaria, Czechoslovakia, with or without the German Democratic Republic [GDR], Hungary, Poland, and Romania) depending upon whether reference is to the period prior to or beginning with 3 October 1990, when the GDR was formally melded into the Federal Republic of Germany (FRG).

An attempt was also made to separate the problems of the three Baltic republics (Estonia, Latvia, and Lithuania) that seceded from the former Soviet Union from those besetting the other successor states of the USSR, that is, Georgia and the states allied to some degree in the Commonwealth of Independent States (CIS). In discussing developments since late 1990, the three Baltic Republics, as well as Albania and Yugoslavia and its successor states, are included under the umbrella term Eastern Europe. To avoid confusion, however, I have attempted to ensure that the context makes it clear which Eastern Europe is being dealt with, just like in the case of whether or not the former Soviet Union is being envisaged.

Finally, when invoking the now defunct CMEA and its associated TR payment, pricing, and trading regimes, reference is chiefly to the former European members—Eastern Europe, as defined. But in some chapters related problems of the other countries that used to participate in the CMEA as full members (Cuba, Mongolia, and Vietnam), as an associate member (the former Yugoslavia), as cooperants (Afghanistan, Angola, Ethiopia, Finland, Iraq, Mexico, Mozambique, Nicaragua, and [Democratic] Yemen[1]), or as observers (mostly other developing countries that maintained some relationship, however unofficial, with the CMEA) are touched upon. The context makes it then clear that this wider circle of CMEA collaborators is under review.

---

[1] It was, of course, Democratic Yemen that had a cooperant status with the CMEA. It was never clear what happened to this when the two Yemens reunited in early 1991, prior to the decision to dissolve the CMEA.

2

The Political Economy of External Transformation

Ben Slay

The external economic situation in which the PETs find themselves is unfavorable in two important respects. First, their debt burden is relatively heavy by international standards. Second, these countries are burdened by the legacy of traditional Soviet-type economic institutions, which created numerous obstacles to realizing gains from trade through specialization. Putting external economic relations on a sounder footing is thus closely linked to the challenge of undertaking the transition.

The significant internal and external imbalances that plagued these economies during the 1980s imply that institutional transformation must be accompanied by domestic adjustment programs and external liberalization in order to improve creditworthiness and make these countries more attractive sites for foreign investment without which it would be all but impossible to acquire the capital, technology, and knowhow needed to sustain a successful transformation of their economy and society more generally.

As with most aspects of the transition, transforming external economic relations is a thoroughly political task. Examining this political economy

Assistant Professor, Department of Economics, Bates College, and Research Institute, Radio Free Europe/Radio Liberty, Munich. I am grateful to Josef C. Brada and Karoly Okolicsanyi for helpful comments on an earlier version. Any mistakes are, of course, mine.

of transition is, thus, crucial to understanding the dilemmas that external transformation poses for those managing the PETs, and this forms the focus of the present chapter. I shall look more specifically at the political influences on the possible strategies for and outcomes of the liberalization of external trade and capital flows. This involves not only examining the calculus of domestic (and foreign) "winners" and "losers" of the transition, but also the manner in which imperatives about regional security or concerns about national sovereignty constrain the liberalization process.

Specifically, this chapter recalls the essential features of the foreign trade mechanism under planning, its barriers to trade, and the steps that are being taken in various PETs to transform this mechanism into something better able to maximize gains from trade based upon specialization according to comparative advantage. Special attention is devoted to the political economy of the links between external liberalization and macro-economic stabilization, privatization, and industrial policy.

The Traditional Foreign Trade Mechanism

The foreign trade mechanism encompasses both systemic and policy elements. There are two systemic elements. One extends to the *institutional* structures of the Ministry of Foreign Trade, trade and/or central banks, the chamber of commerce (and other organizations that deal with trade), the number and types of foreign trade organizations (FTOs), and enterprises involved in trading activities. The other envelops the instruments used to regulate these enterprises, such as exchange rates and techniques for export promotion. Policy issues pertain to the magnitudes the foreign trade instruments take on. The difference between systemic and policy factors can be illustrated by the exchange rate. The decision to use the exchange rate to link domestic to world prices is a systemic decision. The decision to revalue the exchange rate is a policy decision.

Trade policies traditionally emphasized autarky, import substitution, or CMEA integration over export-promotion strategies. Multiple, fixed exchange rates were employed instead of a unified regime. Differences appeared not only between commercial and tourist rates, but various foreign trade multipliers for different branches of industry often meant a wide variety of *de facto* exchange rates for exporters and importers. As a result, only exchange rates observed in black markets reflected market forces, but these in turn were highly distorted and generally inconsistent with purchasing-power parity. Official exchange rates were typically set to cover the average cost of earning foreign exchange, although that required that less profitable exports be subsidized. Partly for this reason, administrative reforms introduced at various points sought to implant submarginal (devalued) exchange rates that would guarantee the profitability of the bulk of planned exports.

Here I shall primarily be concerned with the mechanism's systemic and policy elements, since they are most easily affected by reforms. However, because of the many interrelationships between foreign trade and the rest of any economy, reforms directed at improving the former's performance have little impact if the rest of the economic mechanism and the behavioral patterns underlying it remain unchanged. The changes described below should, therefore, be regarded as elements of a more general program for transition to market-based economic systems. Other elements of this more general program should include price liberalization, macroeconomic stabilization, privatization, and the construction of legal, financial, regulatory, and social welfare institutions appropriate for a market economy (Blommestein and Marrese 1991).

The cardinal weakness of the traditional foreign trade mechanism lies in the lack of direct links between domestic enterprises and foreign suppliers and customers. This results from the interplay of many systemic and policy factors, such as the desire to isolate the domestic economy from disturbances in world markets (policy); treating foreign trade as a buffer for importing shortage goods, regardless of the costs (policy); the state foreign trade monopoly, which marginalizes the private sector's role in trading activities (systemic); and the lack of horizontal information flows from the international economy to producing enterprises (systemic).

This absence of direct connections between domestic and foreign agents can also be seen in the instruments used in trade planning and management. Enterprise production for export was dictated by the logic of plan fulfillment: Enterprise export targets were derived from macroeconomic calculations of the export volume required to finance the planned quantity of imports and debt servicing, subsequently disaggregated by the central authorities to the enterprise level. Enterprise import demands were transmitted through the relevant intermediating organs (most commonly the official FTOs or else the units under the supervision of the relevant branch ministry) to the Ministry of Foreign Trade, which then aggregated these demands and issued purchasing orders to FTOs. Domestic enterprises had few if any direct contacts with foreign firms, nor were they well-informed about import/export possibilities. Instead, they executed orders issued by the central bureaucracy which, although better informed about trade opportunities than the producing enterprises, did not know how to put this information to best use.

External transformation, therefore, requires breaking the administrative barriers separating production from trade. Interactions between traders and producers must be governed primarily by considerations of flexibility, mutual self-interest, and specialization according to comparative advantage. This implies replacing the traditional mechanism with a more decentralized set of institutions and policies under which producers and traders interact horizontally with one another, as well as with foreign partners, and are influenced primarily by market forces.

On the Political Economy of the Traditional Mechanism

Who benefited from the traditional mechanism? To the extent that a lack of support for economic reform in high places could be viewed as a revelation of the system directors' preferences, the top leadership under planning could be perceived as a key supporter of this system. This presumably reflected the political benefits the leadership derived from close supervision of foreign trade, in the form of direct control over interactions with the outside world, insulation from external shocks, and the like. Moreover, the traditional foreign trade mechanism (excepting in Albania and Yugoslavia) was linked to the role played by the CMEA in tying these economies to the Soviet Union, thus affording the USSR an additional means of control over Eastern Europe.

On the other hand, complaints about unsatisfactory trade performance by leaders of the planned economies are of long-standing. And while some political leaders of the old regime (such as Husák and Zhivkov) may have looked favorably upon close economic ties to Moscow, others (such as Gierek and Kádár) did not. This implies that reformist tendencies at the top were constrained not only by the pre-Gorbachev Soviet leadership, but also by domestic actors who benefited from the *status quo*, including industrial branches and firms that could shield themselves against foreign competition. As Brada (1991) points out, protection from world market forces under the traditional mechanism created lucrative possibilities for rent seeking and corruption. Privileged firms, sectors, and sociopolitical organizations standing behind them, thus, constituted powerful lobbies opposed to any change that threatens their preferential access to imports, foreign exchange, and technology. While firms in the military-industrial and energy/extractive complexes were often the strongest of these lobbies (and in many cases, they are now reinforced by strong workers' organizations), agricultural lobbies exerted important pressures on investment and trade policies in Hungary and Poland during the 1980s.

On the other hand, consumers and firms in some import-sensitive industries who were denied the variety and better product quality that come with a more liberal import regime and import competition suffered. So did firms and branches (especially in the private sector) that were unable to compete in bureaucratic struggles for foreign exchange and imports, but could be winners in a more liberal trading environment. Perhaps the biggest loser was society in general, as potential gains from foreign investment and trade were not realized. To the extent that the traditional mechanism impeded export performance, and thus debt-servicing capacity, foreign creditors may also be classified as losers.

The revolutions since 1989 in the former Soviet bloc can be seen as a case of the losers under the traditional system turning the tables upon the winners (Schill 1991). While noneconomic factors obviously played crucial roles in these revolutions, rampant consumer dissatisfaction with the system's inability to provide western products and living standards and pressure by western creditors to improve debt-servicing performance were also important factors. After the revolutions, however, the questions become: How will the political and economic forces unleashed by the collapse of the traditional mechanism affect the balance between liberalization and protection? and Which elements of liberalization and protection will be adopted by the new economic systems arising from the rubble of Soviet-type socialism? Although the imperative of external liberalization is implicit in the logic of the economic transition, it is not clear whether the political economy of the transition is consistent with these goals.

Breaking with the Traditional Mechanism

Although external transformation is inconceivable without fundamental changes in the domestic economy (including price liberalization, privatization, and macroeconomic stabilization), breaking with the traditional foreign trade mechanism is conceptually separable from the more general tasks of systemic transformation. In particular, external transformation requires changes in overall trade policy, trade liberalization, financial instruments, and currency convertibility.

External transformation implies a change in economic philosophy, a renunciation of autarky and a special form of integration within the framework of the former CMEA area, in favor of emphasizing integration into the international economy largely through vigorous export promotion. While the leadership in some countries (such as Hungary and Poland) realized that this shift was necessary even prior to the introduction of *perestroyka* in the former USSR, the geopolitics of the Warsaw Pact prevented the successful implementation of a fundamentally different philosophy (OECD 1991b, Slay 1992b). The leadership in other countries, such as Bulgaria and Czechoslovakia, continued to pursue traditional external policies until the revolution erupted in late 1989.

International economic integration implies breaking the isolation imposed by the (former) Soviet bloc and establishing or upgrading contacts with multinational organizations. The collapse of the old structures does not mean that changes in external regimes are occurring in an international political vacuum, however. Decisions about membership in multilateral groupings inevitably reflect geopolitical differences, which in turn have implications for political economy in such areas as diplomacy. For Czechoslovakia, Hungary, and Poland eventual full membership in the EC seems both a necessity and a realistic possibility. By contrast, EC membership does not seem realistic for many of the former Soviet republics during the next two decades at least. The pull of the Pacific Rim is likely to be much stronger for the Far Eastern areas of the Russian Republic, while many of the new Caucasian and Central Asian states are looking to China, Iran, and Turkey for new trade ties. In the Central Asian region, this process in February 1992 led to the inclusion of Azerbaijan and the four former Soviet Central Asian republics (not including Kazakhstan) into the Economic Cooperation Organization (ECO)—the so-called Islamic Common Market—founded by Iran, Pakistan, and Turkey in 1963 (Lyon 1992, Wright 1992). Moreover, individual states may realize important benefits by forming new multilateral groupings. Examples of this include the CIS, the Central European triangle (Tökes 1991), and the Central Asian Consultative Council, established by the five Central Asian republics in August 1991 to coordinate economic policies (Brown 1992).

While integration within these groupings is unlikely to elicit injections of much-needed capital, technology, and knowhow, coordination of economic policies, freer trade, and protection against undesirable changes in regional trade levels or patterns, and more bargaining power *vis-à-vis* other international groupings could yield important benefits.

External transformation means that traditional administrative restrictions separating producing and trading activities must be abolished. Producing enterprises must be free to contract with trading and foreign firms as desired, and trading firms should be permitted to expand upstream into production or service activities. Producers must be able to trade directly with foreign firms. The goal is removing barriers to organic, commercial links between the domestic and international economies. In addition to abolishing the state monopoly of foreign trade and payments, this means allowing all firms to reap the benefits—and face the burdens of—international economic integration. This implies that, regardless of whether they are privatized, virtually all FTOs should be run on a profit basis and that import, export, and production licenses to firms from all sectors should be granted virtually on demand.

This condition requires both a significant increase in the autonomy of state-owned enterprises (SOEs) and deregulation of the private sector. One important factor in all this is far-reaching external liberalization, although questions about the extent of this opening and the manner in which it occurs are resolved differently in individual countries. Note that few FTOs have thus far been privatized. Indeed, the recent experience does not bode well for their prospects regardless of ownership form. In Poland, for example, where the private share of import-export activity has expanded significantly to about half of imports in 1991, this growth is due largely to the appearance of new private firms rather than to the privatization of FTOs. The former GDR is an even starker case, where most FTOs will be abolished, rather than privatized (Langenecker 1992).

Since administrative commands are the antithesis of external liberalization, financial instruments, such as exchange rates, tariffs, and export subsidies, must be used to link domestic to world prices and guide enterprise behavior. This calls for a single, unified exchange rate at least for commercial transactions and uniform regulatory treatment for all exporters and importers, with deviations from these principles being the exception, not the rule. It also implies a convertible currency.[1]

---

1. See Brabant 1991d, pp. 66-68 for more on the theory and concepts of convertibility.

Although many capitalist countries that are well-integrated into the international economy do not have completely convertible currencies (Polak 1991, p. 23), increasing the degree of currency convertibility in the post-communist context can be seen as the fiduciary derivative of the previous three conditions. By guaranteeing access to foreign exchange, convertibility provides import competition for domestic monopolies and helps improve the quality and variety of consumer goods and services. It also makes domestic markets and assets more attractive for foreigners, thus improving prospects for foreign investment. Increasing the degree of convertibility means moving towards a domestic market for hard currency, as well as setting equilibrium exchange rates and adopting a macroeconomic policy regime consistent with stability of the exchange rate.

Conceptually, achieving an acceptable level of convertibility seems to be a simple matter of devaluing the currency until the domestic demand for foreign exchange is balanced with its supply. In practice, however, both the demand for and supply of foreign exchange are influenced by macroeconomic policies: Expansionary fiscal and monetary policies increase the demand for imports and foreign exchange as a hedge against inflation, while deflationary policies suppress aggregate demand, reduce the demand for foreign exchange, and force firms to export to survive. The Yugoslav dash towards convertibility in early 1990 shows that maintaining convertibility without an effective macroeconomic stabilization program is almost impossible (Adamović 1991); and developments in Poland in 1990 (Slay 1992b) and Czechoslovakia (Zahradník 1991) in 1991 show that, even in the post-communist context, large trade surpluses can go hand in hand with import liberalization, if the latter is accompanied by deflationary macroeconomic policies. Moreover, increasing convertibility can be facilitated by creating the institutional and legal infrastructure necessary for currency markets to function. The Polish experience in particular shows that, even under state socialism, the introduction of hard-currency bank accounts for households and enterprises, foreign exchange auctions, and hard-currency bank loans can help "grease the skids" of the subsequent transformation of foreign trade (Slay 1992b).[2]

Convertibility can be divided into internal and external convertibility. Different approaches to external transformation place different emphases

---

2. *Editor's note*: This provides more an argument for than against declaring currency convertibility in the conventional sense (Brabant 1991d) for exactly the reasons summarized in chapter 3.

upon establishing one type of convertibility first. Internal convertibility, in the sense of permitting duly authorized agents, but not necessarily private persons, to buy and sell foreign exchange in an essentially unrestricted manner for current transactions, can be established by linking the legalization and/or deregulation of foreign exchange transactions by businesses, households, and banks with restrictive macroeconomic policies and, possibly, the establishment of a currency stabilization fund backed by gold, foreign exchange, or other assets. Such funds can be set up on either a national or multinational basis, the latter of which amounts to some sort of payment facility (Brabant 1991a, d; 1992c). External convertibility is more important for attracting foreign capital, at least once significant capital-account convertibility is achieved. Relatively speaking, external convertibility would seem to be especially important for countries like Russia and Ukraine, whose large internal markets could attract foreign investment and joint ventures, provided that local-currency profits can be repatriated. But the latter condition could also be ensured by other means than capital-account convertibility.

On the other hand, the Polish experience with partially freeing up the market for foreign exchange prior to 1990 also shows that allowing foreign exchange to partially supplant the domestic currency as a means of exchange has its drawbacks. Dollarization can have important economic costs, both in terms of increasing the demand for foreign exchange (thus depreciating the exchange rate of the national currency), reducing the willingness to accept domestic currency as payment for services rendered, and magnifying exchange risk. This is particularly likely if movement towards convertibility is not accompanied by anti-inflationary macroeconomic policies that reduce the demand for foreign exchange by importers and speculators hedging against inflation and devaluation.

On the Political Economy of External Liberalization

Political obstacles faced by those managing systemic change constitute some of the most important aspects of the economic transformation. Privileged winners under the old system are likely to resist the changes associated with the economic transition or, failing that, to seek to adapt them to suit their own purposes. A classic example of the latter tendency is the "privatization of the communist *nomenklatura*" (Levitas and Strzalkowski 1990, Staniszkis 1991, Stark 1990); and the difficulties encountered in attempts at converting the military-industrial complex to civilian production show that the restructuring of heavy industry in the PETs will inevitably be a protracted and painful process.

But it is easier to identify the political obstacles to economic transformation than to determine how they will affect the course of external liberalization. Whereas the heavy-industry lobby may no longer dominate industrial policy as before, it is unclear how trade, investment, and financial policies will be affected by the development of the private sector and, more generally, by the new behavior of interest groups emerging from the economic and political transitions.

The political economy of developing new aggregate trade strategies is somewhat clearer, as is the interplay of geopolitical opportunities and constraints in terms of international economic diplomacy. The promise of EC membership is an important economic opportunity for the Central European countries in terms of expanded access to markets, capital, technology, and aid. EC membership may be these countries' best hope for a sustained recovery from their current recessions. Not surprisingly, the imperative of obtaining EC membership has strongly influenced Czechoslovak, Hungarian, and Polish trade and diplomatic strategies.

National political and security concerns can also act as important constraints on the development of aggregate trade strategies. First, there is the issue of economic sovereignty. The nationalisms that were a driving force behind the collapse of the Soviet empire have predictably spilled over into numerous economic policy areas. Advocates of economic sovereignty often oppose the sale of land and property to foreigners. Significant FDI or trade liberalization that subjects domestic firms to "excessive" competition are also frequent targets of criticism. Economic sovereignty concerns are most apparent in Czechoslovak and Polish fears about German economic influence, although these concerns have not yet prevented the development of trade strategies emphasizing integration with Western Europe—principally Germany.

Second, there are related regional security issues. In the successor Soviet and Yugoslav states, many political élites and much of the body politic seem to prefer economic isolation to significant reforms and economic integration with their neighbors, even at the cost of mutually destructive beggar-thy-neighbor trade policies.[3] Although it may still be

3. *Editor's note*: The same policy, but now oriented to Western Europe, characterizes

possible to cobble together workable trading arrangements in these areas, the trade strategies pursued by the present governments will inevitably be dominated by regional security concerns. This will cast a long shadow over the prospects for successful economic (and perhaps political) transition in the former USSR, Yugoslavia, and perhaps Czechoslovakia. The economic dislocations in the East can also raise difficult questions for Western Europe, such as problems of the dissolution of multi-ethnic (and, in the Soviet case, nuclear) federations on their borders. Moreover, refugees fleeing turmoil in the East can impose heavy economic and political burdens upon Western Europe, as seen, for example, in the successes of right-wing parties during parliamentary elections in France and Germany in early 1992.

If the macropolitical economy of external transformation is relatively clear, the political economy of external liberalization at the level of individual industries and interest groups is much less so. It is exceedingly difficult to predict how new patterns of interest articulation emerging from the economic and political transitions will affect the balance between liberalization and protection. Although the shock of external liberalization hurts many of the winners under the traditional mechanism (such as heavy industrial firms and their workers), the devaluation associated with price liberalization and the introduction of convertibility may be the best hope many of these firms have for survival through increased export competitiveness. While the injection of foreign capital into these firms is undoubtedly necessary, it can bring a stiff price in terms of demands by transnational corporations (TNCs) for tax holidays, subsidies, and reductions in import competition. And although the privatization imperative has fundamentally improved the lot of private firms, the recession, increased import competition, and the end of the cozy symbiosis of private with public firms threatens many of the former with bankruptcy.

It is apparent, however, that nationalism, economic sovereignty, and regional security concerns, as well as demands for restraining imports and capital inflows (in the form of opposition to foreign economic penetration or dominance) are likely to be at the heart of protectionist policies in the PETs. The nexus of these concerns has the potential to unite public- and

---

notably the Central European leadership. In spite of efforts to forge a coalition for establishing a free trade zone (not even a customs union), thus far hardly any progress at all has been booked. In any case, the best that could be hoped for is emulation of what these countries have committed themselves to in their so-called Europe agreements with the EC.

private-sector interest groups hurt by the transition, thus providing a
ready political constituency for anti-western populists. In addition to
encumbering the economic transition, this combination could also cast a
long shadow over political democratization. For Czechoslovakia, Hungary,
Poland, and perhaps the Baltic states, Croatia, and Slovenia, the pull of
the EC should be sufficient to institutionalize relatively liberal external
economic regimes and pluralistic political systems. For the other members
of the former Soviet bloc, however, the lure of Europe may prove too
weak to fend off opposition to liberalization.

Exchange Regimes and Convertibility

A separate set of issues is associated with the political economy of choosing between fixed and floating exchange regimes. For three reasons, fixed-
rate regimes have generally been adopted in the PETs. First, the market
infrastructure (in terms of telecommunications and banking facilities)
necessary to directly link policy decisions and interpretations (and future
expectations) of policy by currency holders to transactions in currency
markets is either underdeveloped or absent. Second, the lack of developed
capital markets in the PETs implies that autonomous capital flows are
small relative to trade and official capital flows. This affords central
bankers in PETs greater control over currency movements than their
western counterparts, a necessary condition for maintaining fixed-rate
regimes. Third, and most importantly, exchange rate policy has generally
been viewed as a key element of macroeconomic stabilization programs.
Fixed exchange rates have served as nominal anchors linking inflation
rates for tradables (and close substitutes) to the lower rates prevailing in
key western trading partners.

On the other hand, the political economy of fixed-rate regimes in the
PETs is not without its problems. First, only in Poland, where consumer
price inflation was reduced from 640 percent in 1989 to 70 percent in 1991,
can the use of fixed-rate regimes in the transition be termed an unequivo-
cal anti-inflationary success.[4] Inflation rates during 1990-1991 generally

---

4. *Editor's note*: Many observers of the Polish scene would disagree with this undifferentiated statement, if only because the exchange rate was fixed and started off at far too low
a parity in early 1990. There has been a wide-ranging controversy, notably among Polish

showed an upward trend in the other economies. Of course, these have been affected by many factors besides exchange rate policy, including price liberalization (introduced in Bulgaria, Czechoslovakia, and Romania in 1991, and the former Soviet republics in 1992); the devaluations that accompanied price liberalization and initial attempts at establishing convertibility; the trade shock linked to the switch from TR to world prices and financing in 1991; and the war in Yugoslavia. Still, since there is no obvious link during 1990-1991 between falling inflation rates and fixed exchange rates, the nominal-anchor argument must be made in a somewhat more sophisticated manner (perhaps by simulating the inflation rates that would have obtained under more flexible exchange rate regimes in order to be completely convincing.

Second, fixed exchange rates leave the domestic economy relatively vulnerable to external shocks. The insulation from shocks emanating from Russia (and perhaps Ukraine) afforded by floating rates could become attractive particularly to the other Eastern countries that have reduced direct controls on trade and introduced their own currencies.

Third, fixed exchange rates create opportunities for damaging exchange-rate arbitrage involving currencies of differing degrees of convertibility. This is seen in the so-called ruble affair in Poland, when Polish firms during 1990-1991 took advantage of the złoty's undervaluation *vis-à-vis* the ruble to exchange billions of rubles for dollars (Długosz 1991, Święcicki 1991).[5] The substantial volume of dollars sucked out of the financial system by these inconsistent cross-rates was a high price to pay for any deliberate attempt to generate a surplus that might be offset against the inherited ruble debt. The policy error could have been mitigated by a more flexible złoty-ruble cross-rate policy.

---

economists, about the wisdom of excessive devaluation and fixed parities in an inflationary environment. For some of the flavors, see chapter 3.

5. *Editor's note*: The mechanism relied on the overvaluation of the TR in official transactions (about TR4.5 per dollar) as compared to the free-market exchange rate (which was much higher). Authorized exporters obtained złoty for their TR earnings which they could exchange for dollars at the official parity of 9,500. The undervaluation of the złoty may have been set in order to generate a substantial TR surplus to offset the sovereign ruble debt with the USSR, but that was never official policy. The latter, in fact, stressed the need, in coordination with the Fund, to drastically curb the TR surplus and not prepay the ruble debt. And that current-account surplus, in the end, has not yet been earmarked against ruble debt in any case.

Fourth, the combination of fixed exchange rates and higher (than Western European) rates of inflation guarantees that PET governments will all too frequently face unpleasant choices among overvalued currencies, devaluations that disorganize import-sensitive industries, and possible backsliding on convertibility and import liberalization. While the PETs are hardly alone in facing this dilemma, the failure of dinar convertibility can be partially traced to the inability of the Marković Government to resolve this conundrum. It is also partly responsible for the slow progress made in external transformation in Bulgaria and Romania.

It is interesting to note that Poland and Hungary both opted for compromise solutions to this question by moving to a crawling peg during the second half of 1991. By guaranteeing depreciation in a more predictable manner, the crawling peg removes some of the uncertainty from exchange rate policy. On the other hand, it injects regular (albeit small) inflationary impulses into the domestic economy, thus maintaining inflationary expectations. Moreover, in the Polish case at least, the crawling peg has not eliminated the need for abrupt corrections in exchange rate policy, as seen in the 12 percent złoty devaluation of February 1992. As of early 1992, it seemed that only Czechoslovakia, by virtue of the convergence of its inflation towards West European rates, has managed to resolve this dilemma.

Fifth, fixed-rate regimes with convertible currencies can raise important economic sovereignty issues. Although protests about Germany's tight monetary policies have traditionally been voiced in London, Paris, and Washington, the day is surely coming when Budapest, Prague (or Bratislava), and Warsaw join the chorus. And it is hard to imagine central bankers in Kiev accepting Russian influence over Ukrainian monetary policy that a fixed rate regime between the *hryvna* and ruble would entail. The same would certainly apply to Croatian and Slovenian attitudes towards fixed rates with the (truncated) Yugoslav dinar.

It may be that the optimal transitional exchange rate regime may be a hybrid, consisting of fixed rates *vis-à-vis* western currencies and more flexible rates *vis-à-vis* other PET currencies.[6] Such a hybrid would provide the anti-inflationary benefits of the nominal anchor with the west, while simultaneously offering some protection against external shocks from the East as well as avoiding a repetition of Poland's ruble affair. Floating

---

6. *Editor's note*: This would seem to be workable only if segregated exchange markets could be maintained. Without them, arbitrage would close the gap.

against currencies of other PETs would also remove the exchange rate distortions inherited from the traditional mechanism, and this would facilitate the rationalization of trade among the former CMEA countries. Ultimately, the exchange rate policy of those PETs seeking full EC membership will presumably need to be determined by the EC's regime, or its post-Maastricht equivalent.

Poland's ruble affair underscores the importance of connections between exchange regimes and different degrees of convertibility. This raises more general questions about the most appropriate strategy for introducing convertibility. Should internal convertibility precede external convertibility, or *vice versa*?

In contrast to international experience, in which the introduction of current-account convertibility for international transactions has generally preceded capital-account convertibility and even internal convertibility, many factors argue for establishing capital-account convertibility first in the PETs. Because current-account convertibility provides households and firms with expanded access to foreign exchange, its introduction requires a relatively larger devaluation, *ceteris paribus*, in order to balance the increased demand for foreign exchange with its supply. Such devaluations can have inflationary consequences and disrupt import-dependent sectors of the economy. By contrast, because capital-account convertibility is directed first and foremost at foreigners, and because the Eastern economies were relatively closed to foreign investment and capital transfers, introducing it is unlikely to entail such a large a shock. Moreover, whereas current-account convertibility encourages increased imports, pushing the balances of trade and payments towards deficit, capital-account convertibility creates incentives for foreign firms to invest directly in the host country or to build new plants (or expand and modernize existing ones) in order to service the domestic market or to produce for export. This inflow of foreign exchange appears as a credit in the capital account and the balance of payments. While foreign exchange reserves must be sufficient (under capital-account convertibility) to finance the repatriation of local-currency profits, these losses of convertible currency are likely to be less than those incurred by importing the products involved under current-account convertibility. This is because the latter requires that foreign exchange be used to cover the costs incurred (by foreign firms) in producing and marketing the imports, as well as the profits the firms make on the imports (which would presumably approximate the profits to be repatriated under a scenario of FDI with capital-account convertibility).

This illustrates the fact that capital-account convertibility can generally promote the inflow of funds, capital, and technology in ways that current-account convertibility cannot. Finally, FDI promoted by external convertibility can inject foreign exchange into the domestic economy by financing the initial capital cost of the investment project (or joint venture) and by generating hard-currency export revenues, some of which stay in the host country.

Despite these theoretical arguments, internal convertibility for current transactions has generally received priority in the transformation strategies of PETs that moved towards more liberal access to foreign exchange. Capital-account convertibility may increase the country's attractiveness for foreign investment, but it does not help to force inflation rates into line with those in world market. Since these benefits are provided by internal convertibility for current transactions, and since price liberalization and macroeconomic stabilization are usually regarded as imperative steps in the transition, the emphasis upon domestic convertibility is not surprising.

In addition to promoting macroeconomic stability and helping to bring domestic prices in line with world prices, internal convertibility for current transactions provides four other important benefits: it promotes the import competition needed to prevent monopolies from abusing market power after price liberalization; it can eradicate the black market for foreign currencies which comprises a significant share of the underground economy; it promotes the development of a domestic market for foreign exchange, which is necessary for the introduction of a freely floating exchange regime; and by allowing individuals to purchase convertible currencies—the gateway to the west and symbol of a normal life—on demand, internal convertibility conveys an important and early benefit of the transformation directly to consumers. Since the experience of 1990-1992 indicates that living standards fall for the vast majority of the population during the first years of the transition, the benefits from having direct access to foreign exchange for households may be valuable indeed.

Once a satisfactory degree of internal convertibility and external balance has been attained, external convertibility can be introduced as well. Poland and Czechoslovakia, which officially introduced internal convertibility in January 1990 and 1991, respectively, had by mid-1991 become able to guarantee the repatriation of profits made via foreign direct and financial investment. In Poland by late 1991, only formal restrictions on the ability of tourists to buy foreign exchange with złoty and lingering foreign uncertainties about the złoty, preventing it from trading widely abroad, stood between the złoty and external, possibly full, convertibility. Czechoslovakia in early 1992 was not far behind. On the other hand, the attempts at introducing internal convertibility in 1991 in Romania, 1990 in Yugoslavia, and 1992 in Russia have been much less successful. The lack of effective macroeconomic stabilization programs was probably the key factor in these cases, although the absence of well-developed institutional prerequisites (such as hard-currency bank accounts and auctions) also played an important role, particularly in Romania.

Only Hungary has thus far emphasized establishing external convertibility, possibly because the reform measures introduced gradually since the late 1950s had (relative to other countries) reduced the importance of the stabilization and liberalization imperatives in Hungary's transition. In large measure, the emphasis on external convertibility also reflects Hungary's attractiveness as a site for foreign investment. Moreover, FDI in Hungary is attractive not because of the relatively small domestic market, but because of the prospects for easy access to Western Europe. This means that foreign firms earn a relatively large share of their sales revenues in hard currency, which in turn may reinforce Hungary's foreign exchange reserves.

Even in Hungary, however, the endeavor to establish external convertibility has been accompanied by far-reaching import liberalization, which has effectively provided Hungarian firms with access to foreign exchange upon demand since 1989. Since this amounts to *de facto* internal convertibility for duly authorized agents, the Hungarian emphasis on working towards external convertibility has not precluded the liberalizing and stabilizing effects of internal convertibility upon domestic producers and traders. In effect, only households are not permitted to purchase foreign exchange on demand. Although the authorities have been unwilling to reverse the latter, presumably because of the inflationary devaluation that would accompany increased household demand for hard currency, the introduction of full internal and external convertibility is now slated for late 1993 (Lynn 1992).

Different answers to the question of sequencing convertibility have varying implications for political economy. Internal convertibility benefits households, the private sector, and other state and cooperative firms that did not enjoy the blessings of the central authorities under the former system. It also favors exporters, who are more likely to be able to sell their export receipts to the highest bidder, if necessary by keeping receipts abroad. On the other hand, households and import-dependent industries are hurt by the shock of the devaluation that comes with internal convertibility. Winners under the traditional system are likely to be two-fold losers, in terms of reductions in preferential access to foreign exchange and imports, and increased import competition. External convertibility benefits foreign firms and investors, as well as the domestic property owners likely to profit from the increased foreign demand for their assets. Firms and sectors that receive foreign capital, knowhow, and technology also benefit. Losers include economic sovereignty advocates and domestic firms crowded out of markets for credit and possibly investment goods by foreign firms with ampler resources.

Moreover, the devaluations necessary to equilibrate demand and supply of foreign exchange can produce equilibrium exchange rates at which domestic assets are "too cheap" for foreigners. According to economic sovereignty advocates, capital-account convertibility under these conditions can lead to the national wealth being sold "for a song." According to this view, protection from harmful capital inflows requires either a slower, more restricted introduction of external convertibility or establishing a regime with dual exchange rates, one for current-account transactions and capital outflows, and another, lower rate (in terms of domestic currency units per dollar) for capital inflows.

Two features of political economy seem to be of primary importance in countries (such as Russia and Ukraine) where this position is being taken. First, macroeconomic stabilization has been less successful in the former Soviet republics than in Central Europe, so that larger devaluations are required to restore external balance and introduce convertibility. Second, because of the nationalisms released by the breakup of the USSR and the inexperience of the successor states with FDI, the body politic tends to view foreign capital as, at best, a decidedly mixed blessing. Since the two largest CIS economies seem likely to adopt dual rate regimes in 1992 and questions about convertibility throughout the former Soviet Union are intertwined with plans for introducing national currencies, other former Soviet republics are likely to follow in the footsteps of Russia and Ukraine. Fears about selling off the national wealth below fair value are, therefore, likely to be a major constraint upon the introduction of external convertibility and unification of exchange regimes in the successor republics. These constraints could be important stumbling blocks to external transformation in the former Soviet region, if and when direct controls on trade are removed. In the long run, introducing a convertible currency with a unified rate would both promote foreign investment and remove the accounting confusion inherent in dual exchange regimes.

Liberalization, Privatization, and Industrial Policy

Important tensions are apparent in the interplay between external transformation and privatization. For example, the combination of external and internal convertibility, import liberalization, and aggressive promotion of FDI may prove unsustainable in the PETs, at least in certain sectors. This can be seen in the negotiations surrounding investment by TNCs in the automobile sector in Czechoslovakia, Hungary, and Poland. As conditions for their investment, large western TNCs (including Fiat, General Motors, Mercedes-Benz, and Suzuki) have been pressuring governments into raising protection, sometimes through tariffs but also through quotas. All have succeeded in obtaining important concessions, albeit at a lower rate of effective protection than they had first asked for. Similar examples in other sectors could be cited. The scale of the tax holidays, debt amortization, and other subsidies demanded by these TNCs may actually make FDI a money-losing proposition for the PETs (Stefański 1992). Thus, the price of saving, for example, Poland's automobile industry may be extending net subsidies to TNCs, temporary (it is hoped) backsliding on import liberalization, and allowing its sizable market to be carved up by three TNCs. Similar observations apply to Czechoslovakia and Hungary.

This raises the question of the extent to which the privatization of SOEs should be subordinated to industrial policy concerns, the latter being understood as the use of trade, credit, and tax policies to promote desirable (and prevent undesirable) structural changes in industries and firms. This is really part of a broader question about the industrial policy most appropriate for the transition. Implicit in the emphasis upon external liberalization is the liberal (in the European sense) economic philosophy which can be reduced to the proposition that "market forces are the best industrial policy." According to this view, industrial policy should largely be subordinated to the imperative of the economic transformation. Emphasis should be placed upon creating the missing institutional infrastructure necessary for a market economy to function properly, rather than picking winners among industrial (or agricultural) enterprises and branches. Market-based industrial policies should promote privatization, provide a clear break with the interventionism of the past, and subject hidebound

SOEs to the bracing winds of international competition. In this way, market forces should play a dominant role in the much-needed restructuring of industry and agriculture. Eastern European liberals thus combine many western economists' suspicions about the state's abilities and motives in making such decisions.

Though Central Europe very quickly introduced a quite open regime in 1990-1991, serious problems with this approach soon surfaced. The most fundamental is that privatization and other reforms have not occurred rapidly enough to create the orderly system of property rights required for the smooth functioning of the market mechanism.[7] Opponents of the liberal industrial policy can, therefore, argue that shortcomings of industrial policy makers pale in comparison to the folly of leaving strategic economic decisions to the invisible hand of a private-enterprise economy that has not yet come into existence.

Second, attempts at accelerating privatization can have important economic costs. In Poland, using fiscal discrimination against SOEs to compensate for tax breaks for private firms has starved the state budget of revenues and helped produce the current budget crisis.

Third, noninterventionist industrial policies can leave domestic producers vulnerable to aggressive or unfair export-promotion strategies practiced by trading partners. Czechoslovak, Hungarian, and Polish farmers, for example, saw import liberalization at home during 1990-1991 result in increased (and heavily subsidized) EC farm imports, while export growth to Western Europe, though considerable, was restrained by the EC's Common Agricultural Policy (CAP). Farm lobbies in PETs can, therefore, claim that western advice to entrust agricultural restructuring to the invisible hand is little more than self-serving propaganda designed to ruin competitors and gain new markets. Similar stories could be told by representatives of the steel, automobile, and textile industries, sectors where import liberalization has thus far been unmatched by corresponding reductions in western protectionism. These problems are aggravated by the disproportionately large damage that EC imports can do to domestic

---

7. *Editor's note*: Property rights' reform and privatization are not necessarily identical. Thus, one could envisage establishing crystal clear property rights under public ownership and privatization without unambiguous property rights, as has been the case in several PETs over the past several years. The key issue if often effective monitoring of property rights and circumventing noxious principal-agent problems than assigning property rights *per se* (for ample details, see Brabant 1992g).

producers, compared to the relatively small impact of growing Eastern exports on EC markets.

Fourth, the emphasis upon market forces penalizes many SOEs as they labor under an inefficient or outdated capital stock, resulting from investment decisions made under the old regime over which current management had no control.

Finally, other than emphasizing the need to remove barriers to labor and capital mobility, market-based industrial policies have little useful to say about the sociopolitical problems of closing down uncompetitive branches of industry. The liberal response implying that much of state industry is doomed no matter what policy makers do, and that profitable activities will eventually be taken over by private producers, be they national or foreign, may be intellectually correct, but is unlikely to sway domestic interest groups.

Not surprisingly, the political consensus for liberal industrial policies weakened in Czechoslovakia, Hungary, and Poland after the initial phase of free-market euphoria. This break is most apparent in Poland, where the Bielecki Government was forced to adopt more interventionist policies during the second half of 1991 and the same is likely to be embraced by the Olszewski Government, if it survives its tug-of-war with the *Sejm*.[8] Guaranteed minimum agricultural prices were promised during the summer of 1991, as were bailouts for the tractor, defense, and aircraft industries during the fall 1991 parliamentary electoral campaign. A new tariff regime, which tripled average tariff levels to 18.1 percent, was introduced in August (Dziewulski 1992), and new restrictions on the production, sale, and import of alcoholic beverages, tobacco, non-ferrous metals, fuels, and intellectual property were issued in December 1991 and March 1992 (Niezgódka-Medvoda 1991). Backsliding on import liberalization was visible in Czechoslovakia and Hungary as well, although on a smaller scale. Much higher tariffs were introduced on a variety of agricultural imports in Czechoslovakia on 1 January 1992 (Kobylka 1992); while import-licensing procedures were tightened in Hungary during 1991 (Okolicsanyi 1992).

Correctly or not, external liberalization is coming to be viewed less as a mechanism for promoting industrial restructuring, and more as something that, if not managed correctly, can do serious damage to the do-

---

8. *Editor's note*: The Olszewski Government in mid-1992 failed as did its short-lived successor.

mestic economy. A similar tendency is visible in official attitudes towards privatization. Policies towards the sale of state property have gone from the hands-off approach visible in the spontaneous privatization processes in Hungary and Poland during 1989-1990 to regimes of much greater state control and direction. This tilt towards more control is apparent not only in the Czechoslovak voucher program (Brada 1992) and Poland's mass privatization program (Slay 1992a), but also in attempts to explicitly manage the nexus between privatization and industrial policies. This is seen in the Polish sectoral privatization program and the Hungarian coordinated privatization programs, both of which were introduced during 1991. These programs attempt to first consider the role of private ownership and foreign capital in selected industries within a more general economic policy context before trying to sell stock (usually to foreigners) in entire branches of industry or agriculture (Marrese 1992, Slay 1992a).

While this trend towards more interventionist industrial policies may have been inevitable in light of the weaknesses of the liberal approach, it does raise a new set of issues. Are industrial policy makers in PETs better at picking winners than their predecessors were? If so, do they possess the financial and analytical wherewithal necessary to conduct the salvage operations that saving even a portion of the state sector in many PETs will require? While the collapse of the traditional system swept away some of the lobbies responsible for the shortcomings of industrial policy under state socialism, it remains to be seen whether interest groups in PETs will produce dramatically superior decisions about industrial and agricultural restructuring. Doubts are raised by the policies adopted towards foreign investment in automobile sectors, as described. Moreover, a tilt towards more interventionist industrial policies could further slow the pace of privatization. For these reasons, it is difficult to be optimistic about interventionist industrial policies in PETs.

Conclusions

Although attempts at introducing more liberal external regimes have been a major feature of programs for transformation in the PETs, the realities of economic nationalism, continued difficulties with macroeconomic stabilization and recession, and problems of privatization and industrial restructuring have made some degree of retreat from external liberalization inevitable. This is most apparent in the reversals suffered by the quite liberal external regimes introduced by Czechoslovakia, Hungary and Poland during 1989-1991.

Attempts at external transformation are unlikely to meet a common fate throughout the PETs, however. The association agreements with the EC, whose trade aspects provisionally came into effect on 1 March 1992, seem likely, within the next 3 to 5 years, to impose relatively uniform and open trade and industrial policies on Czechoslovakia, Hungary, and Poland. This should help institutionalize a relatively open regime for trade within the EC, which is already these countries' largest trading partner. The fate of extra-EC trade will presumably depend upon the outcome of the Uruguay Round, as well as the international political economy that emerges in the relationship between the EC, the nascent North American Free Trade Association, and the Asian-Pacific trading area. Simultaneously, the relative importance of trade with the former Soviet republics and the Balkans is likely to decline. This is the inevitable product of Central Europe's deliberate east-to-west trade reorientation. The long-term economic outlook for Central Europe does seem relatively clear in that it is likely to be directly linked to the fortunes of the EC.

No such clarity is visible for the rest of the East. As of early 1992, the inflationary fires raging throughout the region have yet to be brought under control. This continues to complicate movements towards convertibility and external liberalization, and reduces the benefits associated with this movement. Not surprisingly, many administrative controls over trade and currency movements are still in force in all of the successor states to the Soviet Union and the Balkans. Whereas external reform has been one of the most positive aspects of the transformation in Central Europe, the dismantling of the traditional institutions is proceeding more slowly elsewhere.

In stark contrast to Central Europe, for whom the importance of trade relations with the former Soviet republics has been declining steadily, the importance of interrepublican trade flows among all republics of the former USSR is likely to remain paramount at least over the medium term. Prospects for accession to the EC for Bulgaria, Romania, and some of the former Yugoslav republics, while brighter than for most of the former Soviet republics, still seem much less promising than for Central Europe.

Ultimately, however, the domestic political economy implications are likely to be at least as significant as geopolitical factors in determining the balance struck between liberalization and protection in the PETs. It is unclear how the new interest groups emerging from the economic and political transitions will articulate their views and affect the external transition. Although the shock of external liberalization will hurt many of the winners under the traditional mechanism (such as heavy industrial firms and their workers), the devaluation associated with price liberalization and the introduction of convertibility will also increase their export competitiveness. FDI may be necessary, but the example of the automobile sector shows that it may cost the host economies dearly. And, the recession, increased import competition, and the end of the cozy symbiosis with the state sector threatens many private firms with bankruptcy.

The western literature on the political economy of protectionism in market economies links the degree and type of protectionism to asymmetries in factor ownership (Hillman 1989, 1991), especially ownership of capital. In the PETs, the nature of resource ownership and the attendant system of property rights is currently undergoing a fundamental redefinition. This is true of labor, as well as capital and other forms of property (Slay 1991a). While the successful conclusion of the transition may in many cases ultimately produce patterns of factor ownership similar to those now prevailing in industrial countries, developments occurring along the way may yield some surprising results with unanticipated consequences for political economy.

3

Transition, the World Economy, and Economic Unions

Jozef M. van Brabant

The tumultuous remaking of the eastern part of Europe has been accompanied by a variety of economic and other developments that have surprised the majority of observers. Particularly in the economic arena, many analysts claim to have been caught unaware. Realizing and admitting this, some (Portes 1992a, b; Summers 1992a, b) have recanted to various degrees earlier pronouncements, among others, on the need for speed and comprehensiveness in conceptualizing and implementing the transition without really having to worry much about its sequencing (Portes 1991), and indeed the concrete specification of the transition's agenda, given the starting conditions in the aforementioned PETs. While some of the recent events in the East have surprised nearly all observers, the most negative features of the overhasty remaking of these economies and societies into market-based economic systems with pluralistic political decision making for which the (pre)conditions were not fulfilled, could have been foreseen. The more skeptical observers of the East's unique scene since 1989, while shocked by the sheer magnitude and duration of the slump engendered

---

Principal Economic Affairs Officer of the Department of Economic and Social Development of the United Nations Secretariat in New York. The opinions expressed here are my own and do not necessarily reflect those that may be held by the United Nations in general and its Secretariat in particular.

by the transition, nonetheless had warned against overhastily abandoning old structures without having alternatives in place (Brabant 1990, 1991a, b; UNECE 1990).

Some of the events witnessed over the past three years originated from mistakes made both by policy makers of the PETs and the legion of newly official or self-appointed western advisers, individual as well as institutional, including the mixed chorus that gleefully applauded and fomented the willful destruction of existing institutions, policies, and policy instruments on the assumption that the market would quickly pick up the slack. From the several areas that could thus be identified, lax property rights; excessive and misguided attention to privatization of large SOEs; lack of a functioning banking infrastructure to intermediate between savers and investors, clear accounts, and market new financial instruments; the precipitous destruction of the existing TR price, trade, and payment regimes in the context of the now defunct CMEA; and the lack of attention to maintaining the positive sides of the monetary unions of the Soviet Union and Yugoslavia before their rapid unraveling, deserve to be highlighted. One could easily devote an entire tome to each of these challenging topics, but this is not, of course, within the remit of this chapter's objectives.

Instead, I should like to focus on dismantling the legacies of central planning in the areas of foreign trade and payments. I first point to two major fallacies of opening up these previously highly sheltered economies if some modicum of order is to be maintained. The desirability of having a convertible currency and integrating into the world economy in general and the EC in particular is on the order next. This is followed by a discussion of the likely outcome of the remaking of intragroup relations on economic grounds. Whether it would make economic sense to rescue, at least partly, the erstwhile unions, particularly for the dinar and ruble areas, but even at this stage possibly for the former TR area or major components thereof as well, is subsequently briefly touched upon. Finally, I explore several means available to rectify some of the failures and forestall their being repeated in the successor states, wherever possible with western assistance, indeed western prodding, and perhaps even intrusive supervision. Whether this is done in the context of the current assistance efforts, as examined notably in the chapters by Losoncz and Smolik, or in a broader approach to assisting the East, I discuss in some detail in chapter 5.

Fallacies of Opening Up Eastern Markets

From the very first steps of the transition process, there has been considerable unanimity about the urgency and need of the PETs to open up their economies soonest to international competition, meaning world markets, through some variant of currency convertibility and low protectionism. This recommendation, while laudable in and of itself, suffers nonetheless from ignoring two major weaknesses, namely inelasticity of domestic supply and inability of the PETs to quickly conform—at an affordable adjustment burden—to what is usually called "world market conditions." Inability to shift quickly to world conditions at a sociopolitically acceptable cost was especially important in explaining the calamitous dimension of the destruction of the TR regimes. But it also played a role, albeit not a key one, in the destruction of the dinar and ruble currency regimes as well as in the reluctance on the part of policy makers to come to grips with the fact that moving to conventional trading conditions among the successor states would call for precipitous adjustments that should best be sidestepped.

Adjustments Through Stabilization and Structural Change

There can be no doubt that at the outset of their transitions, the PETs faced domestic and external imbalances, whose elimination required painful adjustments no matter what course the new leaderships would have chosen. These derived in large measure from policy mistakes made under communist-style planning as well as the decreasing suitability of planning for managing a society at some level of economic maturity. In its stead, degenerative administrative planning set in, engendering development crises of various dimensions. I need not delve into the details of what went wrong with the communist-run societies to gain concurrence on several critical facets. Arguably central is that at their inception the PETs' peculiar economic structure is inefficient in terms of delivering goods and services to support steady gains in *per capita* incomes and not very competitive in world markets, while most resources are committed to undertakings that are much too inflexible to permit an expeditious shift towards the competitive production of "new" goods and services.

Especially the inflexibility of the supply side, regardless of the transition policies embraced, should have formed one critical element in the

thinking about the comprehensiveness, speed, and sequencing of the transitions. True, the revolutions in the East careened into contemporary history and admittedly afforded little time for deliberating on how best to shape policies. But these realities themselves do not justify the obduracy of adhering to improvisational policies for as long as the PETs have. Without firm action in the microeconomic sphere, notably production, the transition simply cannot be advanced beyond curbing absorption.

Because of the inherited imbalances, there is no doubt that the PET must embrace soonest demand-management policies to regain some semblance of macroeconomic stability at any activity level and thus sharply cut back effective absorptive capacity. In several PETs, this may in fact amount to a low-level equilibrium trap from which managers of the transition find it very difficult to extricate the economies entrusted to their care. Surely, domestic markets are now better provisioned and the proverbial waiting lines have disappeared; external balance has improved, in many cases through temporarily sharp export gains in new markets; and new economic activities, largely in services, trading, and arbitraging, are mushrooming. But all this is taking place at a comparatively low platform of sustainable levels of economic activity, whence it has proved to be very difficult indeed to veer away because compressed demand can prop up only this level. Without a firm jolt on the supply side, the situation is unlikely to become unstuck any time soon.

To change supply, pro-active policy measures need to ensure not only that existing firms are transformed through privatization, but also that new domestic and foreign capital is invested in the best way circumstances allow. Transition policies in the beginning counted too much on sizable inflows of FDI to revive and restructure supply. This has not materialized for good reasons. FDI, let alone other forms of foreign investment, is understandably leery about moving *en masse* into economically, politically, and socially unstable environments, even with considerable concessions such as tax holidays and protection against competition that may, in fact, be quite dysfunctional to the transition (see chapter 2).

What should reformers do? Clearly, once some measure of macroeconomic stability has been regained policy attention should be widened to the supply side. At any rate, stabilization should not be an end in itself. It should certainly not be an occasion to take advantage of realities and simply "loosen up" as many economic levers as possible without making firm allowances for progressing with structural reform. And the latter is on the whole not a macroeconomic but a very fundamental microeconomic supply problem. Successful transition indeed requires laying rapidly the microeconomic foundations for macroeconomic stability.

The reluctance of the new governments in the PETs, in many cases loudly applauded by those involved in delivering assistance to the East, to take responsibility for the supply side, including making headway with restructuring the large SOEs, is just a "symptom of the broader failure to appreciate the fundamental role of government in a market economy and its even more fundamental role in a transforming economy" (Summers 1992b, p. 61). Whereas there undoubtedly was very wide room to reduce the role of government in the economy, there can be no doubt that there exist many tasks that are necessary for economic health in a market environment, and even more in a transforming situation, that only government can discharge.

My preferred tie-in of stabilization and structural reform is through a more evolutionary transition than the abrupt shock treatment championed by many. The immediate aim should be beheading the party and industrial ministries, including all of their appendages; seeing to it that political rents are simply not transferred to those now favored by the changed political circumstances; and creating a solid environment within which economic agents can operate on their own account. This requires an unambiguous legal infrastructure, hence making effective progress with the institution of the *Rechtsstaat*, and solid macroeconomic policies (at least monetary and fiscal, and in my view also price and incomes policies). That environment must hold for all agents and be enforceable. There is no point, for example, in pursuing fiscal reforms while at the same time authorities are unable—or unwilling—to enforce the rules on new private businesses for fear of discouraging them.

Moving to World Market Conditions and Its Implications

The dissolution of the TR regimes was prompted by the avowed need to obtain world-market conditions in economic relations among the former CMEA members. In the case of the dinar and ruble regimes, it was more a question of whether and how best to redistribute resources among the constituent republics and who was subsidizing whom than moving to conventional market rules *per se* that triggered the fragmentation of the common economic areas. But after dissolution of the union, interrepublican trading rules will move closer to world conditions just the same, and so it is useful to delve somewhat deeper into its meaning.

World conditions in Eastern parlance means essentially four things: transactions of goods and services are negotiated by microeconomic agents on their own account; market-clearing prices of a sort, given that there are really not yet genuine markets in the East, are the terms at which goods and services, as well as production factors, are exchanged; imbalances are settled in convertible currency on a current basis or periodically (in the case of clearing); and the usances of world trading, notably on payment conditions (that is, immediate payment for raw materials and fuels, and 90 to 120 days supplier credit for many manufactured goods), need to be observed rather closely. Instituting these "values" in intragroup trade should, in the end, help bring about greater rationality in the PETs, particularly those bent on liberalizing the domestic economy to allow microeconomic agents room for seeking profitable resource allocation within an overall arena cordoned off by the institutions and rules of the new political and economic frameworks. But the implications of doing without the former regimes and moving to world conditions should be clearly understood, rather than muddled about as it has been, notably in the western advisory assistance to the PETs.

First of all, any switch to some form of market-clearing prices modifies the prevailing terms-of-trade. This will be particularly marked in countries that largely eschewed price reform prior to embarking on transition. In the case of the CMEA, it notably entailed a sharp deterioration for Eastern Europe as exporter of manufactures and a sizable gain for the exporters of fuels and raw materials, particularly the Soviet Union. Within the unions, some republics are bound to benefit not only from the external price adjustment but also from aligning domestic with trade prices. These shifts are the inherent resultant of the upward drift in prices of raw materials, fuels, as well as foodstuffs of all kinds, while, at the same time, prices of manufactures are under downward pressure, especially in the medium run, provided economic activity remains buoyant.

Second, demand and supply schedules change because old and newly autonomous agents begin to act in their own interest. Given greater freedom of choice, they are unlikely to emulate the earlier behavior of ministerial bureaucrats. Under the CMEA's circumstances of around 1990, especially in the short run, the demand of the smaller Eastern countries for shipments from within the area were likely to change more radically than their supply, given that not all countries were reforming at the same pace and there existed considerable asymmetry between the trading patterns of the Soviet Union and the rest of Eastern Europe. In the case of the successor states, however, demand and supply schedules will change too, but not necessarily in response to microeconomic agents taking over from the erstwhile ministerial bureaucrats. At least for now, it is mainly one ministerial bureaucracy succeeding another, rather than the impact of private agents caring about their profit-and-loss account, that has been modifying demand and supply schedules.

Third, because of the absence of the normal institutions that facilitate trade (such as banks, export credit guarantees, insurance companies, rediscounting facilities, and settlement institutions), the precipitate discontinuation of the TR regimes forcefully complicates conducting transactions at world conditions.

Finally, arguably the most important impact of moving away from the old regimes is a rise in the demand for convertible currency, particularly in the trade-dependent countries. The demand for reserves expands for both transaction and precautionary reasons. To finance any emerging imbalances, which are likely to occur with new agents conducting trade, adequate reserves are required. Also the transaction demand for convertible currency grows, basically for three reasons. One is the rule of thumb that it is prudent for a country to hold reserves equivalent to about three months' worth of imports. Another is that private trading and related transactions previously all conducted at special bilateral clearing conditions, or in local currency in the case of the former federations, must be financed. Finally, because of the asymmetry in export structures, the net importers of fuels and raw materials and net exporters of engineering goods must extend supplier credit for most of their net exports of manufactures but pay cash for their net imports of fuels and most raw materials. Even if alternative modes of financing can be explored, the net borrower must, on balance, absorb any borrowing cost differentials. Such stocks of required convertible currency can be built up by running a net current-account surplus now or in the future (if borrowing were feasible). Doing this in the short run would be impossible, given the already excess import demand, and it would be very costly. Borrowing might help, but only if the funds are appropriated for structural change, hence capable of soon generating a current-account surplus.

In sum, the switchover to world conditions was from the beginning destined to exert a profound impact on traditional trade and payment relations. With limited ability to divert exports to other markets, and even then policy makers must reckon with sizable terms-of-trade and export-revenue losses, there was a real danger of a massive collapse of the former intragroup trade without adequate gains being made with outside markets. This has been a highly dysfunctional outcome of the destruction of intra-CMEA relations. The calamity for Eastern Europe could be partly rectified by bolstering exports to the west, on favorable one-off conditions. In the case of Yugoslavia, the impacts of the ruptured dinar zone on some of the successor states (notably Bosnia-Herzegovina and Macedonia) are likely to be much more severe than on others (Croatia and particularly Slovenia). Most pronounced are the repercussions of the unraveling ruble zone for many successor states to the Soviet Union, notably those that are net importers of fuels and raw materials and in the past benefited from implicit subsidy transfers, particularly from Russia.

Although reconfiguring intragroup relations on the basis of economic criteria, including interim measures to facilitate the transition from the *ancien régime* to near-world conditions, should rank high on the policy agenda, it has not so far. This stems basically from political opportunism rather than sound economic calculus. Once the latter consideration gains attention, the twin guideline in policy making should be how best to maintain trade flows while restructuring trade as part and parcel of the gradual shift to market-based decision making, including putting in place the necessary institutions to sustain these relations.

Integrating into the World Economy

The transformation of the trade and payment systems of the PETs has been one of the most widely debated topics of designing comprehensive, speedy, and properly sequenced transition policies. There has been little disagreement about the need of these countries to disengage themselves from the inherited TR trade and payment systems; of course, the TR pricing environment was precipitously abandoned in the course of 1990 and early 1991, when the last use of that "currency" was made. Equally unanimous has been the advice on the need to open up the PETs and expose them to international competition. The latter's relative prices, given a proper exchange rate, usher into the PETs the necessary competitive discipline to credibly transform the rules at which economic agents are henceforth held responsible for their economic performances and contain the potentially adverse behavior of the highly monopolized industrial structure of PETs upon liberalization. There has been little argument about the desire of these countries to integrate quickly into the world economy through a trade regime comprising few nontariff barriers and low, preferably uniform, tariffs. I shall only discuss the core issues.

Trade Liberalization

The case for trade liberalization has been based on incontestable, if highly theoretical, credentials. The discussions have at times given the impression that a liberal trade regime by itself can do wonders for a country's economy, and most economists involved in proffering advice to the East's policy makers have not hidden their conviction that trade liberalization is unambiguously beneficial. It is expected to improve resource allocation in line with social marginal costs and benefits; to facilitate access to more advanced or better-suited technology, inputs, and intermediate goods; to enable an economy better to take advantage of economies of scale and scope; to bolster competition in domestic markets; and to provide progrowth externalities, including by shaking up established transformation activities, thereby creating a favorable "Schumpeterian environment especially conducive to growth" (Dornbusch 1992, p. 74). These benefits accrue in a static environment. Arguably even more important will be the beneficial growth-promoting, hence dynamic, effects of trade liberalization, which should forge a new growth path for the economy as a whole. In spite of these promises in principle, the actual record of trade liberalization is, at best, debatable (Dornbusch 1992a, pp. 73ff.), notwithstanding some undifferentiated claims (Dollar 1992) *a contrario*.

Looking realistically at the issue, the benefits of trade liberalization do not become self-evident at least until the economy being liberalized will have gained an environment conducive to comparatively flexible adjustments to the new demand and supply schedules, that is, an ambient market-oriented environment. Otherwise foreign competition may eliminate domestic production, perhaps inadvertently and inordinately through shifts in demand for "new" goods, without the freed-up resources being redeployed for growth-promoting activities. The outcome may then be a potentially sharp cutback in aggregate economic activity, which cannot but compress sustainable levels of absorption or welfare. Whether this occurs right away after trade liberalization, apart from flexibility on the supply side, will largely be a function of foreign exchange reserves.

Liberalization and the Exchange Rate

The orthodox case for trade liberalization in the PETs has been predicated on relatively low protection with an exchange rate that should help maintain equilibrium in the current account, at least over the medium run. Because the gap between pre-transition and world prices is considerable, no single devaluation can avert palpable adjustments in demand and supply. And because export schedules are unknown it is by no means obvious by how much the home currency should be devalued to enable policy makers to sustain external balance. However, questions of by how much to devalue the home currency and how stable the nominal exchange rate should be thereafter, perhaps to function as a key anchor for the design of transition policies, have arisen.

The answer given to date in the advisory proffered by the most market-oriented adherents has been unambiguous: Choose the nominal exchange rate as anchor once the home currency is sufficiently reduced to compensate for unknown, but anticipated corrective inflation, preferably erring on the side of caution by undervaluing the domestic currency, and then hold it stable for a sufficiently long period of time to impart confidence and credibility to transition policies. This choice has been suggested more by concern about infusing some anchored certainty into an exceedingly volatile socioeconomic and political situation than by solid economic arguments. On the latter ground, the choice is probably wrong as it may unduly lower the exchange rate, particularly if the structural adjustment is of such a nature that target policies are likely to improve matters in a comparatively brief period of time; this may indeed have been one of the reasons why in postwar Western Europe a payments union was preferred over massive devaluations to eliminate the chronic dollar shortage. If so, devaluation debilitates economic activities that, under more normal conditions of the market, would have been able to survive on their own. In addition, most observers have not given sufficient attention to the potentially destabilizing effects of a fluctuating *real* exchange rate because domestic inflation will quickly hollow out the temporary comparative advantage afforded by a marked devaluation of the nominal rate. Yet, an unstable real rate cannot but add to the hazards of revamping the domestic economy paced by an export-led restructuring and growth strategy. This is particularly so since the PETs, given lost CMEA markets and geopolitical realities, are bent on redirecting trade to western, hence, "new" markets. Nonetheless, holding on to a stable nominal exchange rate may be wise political economy provided it does not become a fetish. Unfortunately, there are no unambiguous guidelines to how best to proceed.

Regarding the foreign-exchange regime, there can be no doubt that the perplexing multiplicity of exchange rates under planning must be replaced by a single one or, at best, two (one for duly authorized commercial transactions and another for private trading). Whether the key commercial rate should be fixed or flexible (and how it is to be linked to any other rate) is one of those "either-or" choices that many theoretical economists and unwary policy makers are fond of. In practice, the policy question will be more about what kind of crawling peg should be entertained and at what intervals the exchange rate should be adjusted to avoid imparting adverse credibility effects. The issues at stake are paramount to book progress towards current-account convertibility. Only under those circumstances is there a realistic chance of attracting the kind and volume of FDI that most PETs are hoping to muster if only to confine the costs of the transition and identify a new growth paradigm.

In this connection, currency convertibility is often invoked as a critical aspect in the design of the transition. The latter has become "something of a virility symbol" (Ash 1992, p. 26) for the new policy makers and, arguably even more, for the chorus of outside advisers. I do not wish to dwell at length on this issue here, if only because I have recently had plenty of opportunity to discuss it elsewhere (Brabant 1991a, 1992c). Let me emphasize that the PET leadership should promote fast and far-reaching liberalization of access to foreign exchange. But that may be quite distinct from seeking currency convertibility. There may be circumstances in which it might be advisable to pursue this generalization of the foreign-exchange market over some period of time (months rather than years, of course) by organizing open auctions for increasing amounts of foreign exchange accessible to all duly authorized agents (such as licensed traders), if only to minimize capital flight. Critical in advocating such auctions is the flexibility of the nominal exchange rate for liberalized transactions. By monitoring auctions in such a manner, those managing the transition can obtain a more rounded, informed impression of where the equilibrium exchange rate in the short to medium run may be.

Surely, if all foreign exchange can be appropriated for currency auctions, the authorities may just as well move to a flexible exchange rate for duly authorized agents (capital flight still being forestalled to the extent circumstances permit). However, the experience with flexible exchange rates in recent decades, both in developed and developing countries, has been far from strongly supportive of uncontrolled flexibility. Frequent overshooting has imparted into the economic environment greater uncertainty than is desirable from most points of view. This consideration should apply with full force to the PETs too and strengthen the case for some measure of foreign-exchange control until policy makers can confidently set a reasonable exchange rate and, barring untoward events, maintain it for some period of time (perhaps 6 to 12 months) without being unduly pressured by differential price movements. The authorities must also have in place the institutions and policy instruments necessary to manage the exchange regime, preferably according to a crawling peg or an otherwise adjustable rate.

Trade Liberalization and Protectionism

The nature of protection in the PET has chiefly been seen as based on a fairly low and uniform *ad valorem* tariff. But this chorus of endorsements has been challenged by the case made, notably by Ronald I. McKinnon (1991a, b) and John Williamson (1991a, b), for substantial transitional protection. They suggest that very early on in the transition all barriers to trade be converted into explicit *ad valorem* tariffs structured into perhaps half a dozen cascading categories. Moreover, such protection should remain rather high, possibly by maintaining for now the level that was earlier implicit in the bewildering variety of trade-inhibiting institutions and instruments under planning, assuming such could be assessed with any precision. Furthermore, they argue that the PET should commit itself in a precise time schedule to reduce these tariffs and eventually narrow their dispersion. The policy objective would be to forestall the collapse of large segments of industry (especially the so-called "value-subtracting" or "negative value-added" enterprises) early in the transition.

I sympathize with the recommendation to translate as many quotas and related nontariff barriers to straight *ad valorem* tariffs. Whereas some protection of existing economic structures could usefully be entertained under precisely defined conditions, I deem it counterproductive to erect formidable trade barriers for the PETs. Certainly, this would permit policy makers to gradually alter output structures, hence, avoid sudden dislocations of existing production with all attendant consequences. But it would also inhibit competition and the desirable transfer of relative prices for traded goods. Furthermore, in view of the weak central actors in the PETs, credibility for the phasing-out of customs duties would be low.

Rather than aggravate price distortions and introduce levies that may be hard to repeal later on according to a set schedule, if only for want of credibility, the PETs could resort to temporary income transfers. This would permit sectors potentially threatened by bankruptcy to operate below real cost, yet the government would not have to support full unemployment claims. Such a policy choice could also enable valuable assets to survive the rigors of the transition, provided they will be profitable once this comprehensive policy of change is well advanced. There is, of course, little hope that PET policy makers can neatly separate the potentially profitable firms most deserving of subsidies from others that in any case have to be fundamentally restructured or eliminated. But some guidance can be taken from those able to cover their variable costs under changing circumstances.

As an important footnote, one must, of course, acknowledge that any government commitment to the phasing out of a subsidy scheme is likely to be viewed with apprehension, especially at a time of fiscal stringency. This would be particularly so if matters were left completely up to the newly installed, rather inexperienced governments of the PETs. However, as argued in the last section, a comprehensive effort should be made to assist the PETs in a number of respects. And the authority of this international assistance should lend credence to the ability of government decision makers to phase out the subsidy scheme fairly and on a timely basis.

Future Linkages and Supporting Policy

Opinions about the desirable path of disengaging from the erstwhile unions that were either not politically desired or not truly based on economic factors have ranged disturbingly from an advocacy of maintaining the union (for example, Slay 1991b) to its most rapid destruction (for example, Gros 1991). The latter point of view derives essentially from presumptions that in the long run—essentially the equilibrium position in a comparative statics perspective—most of the component economies would do better by seceding from the union than from committing themselves to not very credible gradualism. The former position essentially argues that the costs of disengagement are so large that it would be sheer folly to seek rapid dissolution. Although both positions are suspect, I would ally myself more readily with the one advocating some gradual dissolving of the union than to the other that propounds shock therapy, evidently relying on the tacit assumption that "market-based" adaptations will emerge quickly, hence, that the short-term cost of complete destruction will be inferior to that of any gradual solution.

Even if such a quick, moderately costly transition were feasible, I am suspicious of arguments that propound to be able to forecast the desirable trading and integration patterns of economies that are being—or should be—radically revamped. For one thing, I find it almost ludicrous to entertain seriously any eventuality that the PETs must return to their trading patterns of the 1920s, either before the Great Depression for Eastern Europe (Bofinger and Gros 1992, Collins and Rodrik 1991), including the Baltics and, of course, Albania and Yugoslavia; or before the institutionalization of administrative planning in the Soviet Union (Bofinger and Gros 1992, Vavilov and Vyugin 1992). Even the presumption that the trade orientation registered at that time was in any sense an equilibrium is suspect, if only because of the enormous adjustment difficulties encountered after World War I and the very substantial trade barriers (not necessarily of the tariff kind) erected by the successors to the empires swept away with that war. There simply is no reason to presume that the industrialization and related structural change of the past half century have been all for naught, hence, that these countries would be well advised to return to their spuriously imputed prewar equilibrium. Similarly suspect are forecasts based on gravity equations constructed for presumptively comparable market economies (Bofinger and Gros 1992; Rosati 1991, 1992; Vavilov and Vyugin 1992) for a number of technical, measurement, and conceptual reasons that I cannot examine here in any detail (Brabant 1992d, e). It strains the imagination to read policy advice into the results obtained from interpolating aggregate values for the successor states of the Soviet Union into simple equations estimated for most developed market economies.

Renewal of Intragroup Cooperation on Economic Grounds

Prior to the collapse of the Soviet Union, relations among its constituent republics devolved more from administrative convenience—and often political imperatives—than any economic rationale. In other words, trade and payment relations between, say, then Byelorussia and Ukraine were no different from relations between, say, firm *A* in Leningrad and firm *B* in Moscow. All transactions in principle devolved from planning decisions or negotiated contracts at rather inflexible prices with the clearing of transactions ensured through the technical apparatus of the monobanking system, backed up by agreed-upon plan priorities, including automatic credits from the banking system. That system had been crumbling for some time prior to the formal collapse of the union as sovereignty claims were being staked out and delivery obligations against ruble accounting were being flouted. But just like the TR regime continued beyond the gradual interruption of contract discipline presumed in bilateral trade and payments agreements (BTPAs), beginning on a more than trivial scale in 1988, the ruble zone and the unionwide technical clearing of settlements were kept intact until the dissolution of Gosbank; some formal substitute was created by Russia in early 1992 (Yasiliev 1992) and subsequently endorsed at the Tashkent meeting of the CIS on 14-15 May 1992. But it is unclear whether this was ever meant to function. Credit limits were still to be negotiated (*Financial Times*, 14 May 1992, p. 12). Inasmuch as they were the key hindrance to putting the scheme in place, it should not be surprising that Russia has since been taking unilateral action by which ruble payments from other republics are accepted only if that republic has deposits in the central bank of Russia or if Russian firm owe that republic for deliveries in rubles.

The situation was similar for Yugoslavia, although it was much less a centralized than a hypertrophied decentralized nation without a firm helm and a tattered consensus on how interrepublican economic relations should be dealt with. Key was interrepublican and interenterprise credit without having in place either a firm overall monetary policy or effective bankruptcy enforcement for SOEs.

Matters among the CMEA member countries were slightly different from those within the ruble and dinar zones proper. For one thing, regardless of aspirations of some key players in the CMEA tug-of-war and the integration framework agreed to, there never was a unified economic space in the CMEA. The essence of the TR regimes was: market separation through the state monopoly of foreign trade and payments adhered to by each country according to its own rules; artificial trade prices; rather rigid equalization among domestic, TR, and east-west prices and trade decision making within each country; and comprehensive interstate BTPAs "with a few absurd but, in principle, necessary rules: one had to have prices to exchange goods [and] an exchange rate to settle [these transactions]" (Lavigne 1991, p. 6). For that reason, TR prices and exchange rates were almost purely invented. In any case, these artificial magnitudes were only remotely linked, if that, to world prices, relative scarcities in the area, or the voluntaristic domestic price policies.

Given the above environment, it is easy to understand that CMEA trade flows did not emanate from genuine natural or strategically elaborated comparative advantages, though they probably became more rationally structured over time than the flows among the various constituent Soviet republics; but rationality was not a distinct feature of interrepublican trade in Yugoslavia either. Goods were traded at prices that reflected neither domestic costs, however factored, nor real scarcities in the region or in world markets, and these prices were as a rule not directly passed on to domestic agents in any case. Eastern markets were captive. In the CMEA context this was especially so for goods built within the context of intergovernmental specialization agreements and jointly financed investment projects. The former were mainly in support of machine building and manufacturing more generally. The latter were principally designed to shore up the buoyant exchange of fuels and raw materials, mostly from the Soviet Union, for manufactured products, chiefly from the smaller countries. Similar market reservation prevailed in the former USSR and Yugoslavia, though there interrepublican trade was not negotiated at the intergovernmental level. Rather, it was set through interministerial negotiations in the USSR and mostly interenterprise negotiations in Yugoslavia. And, of course, there were no visible domestic payment problems within these federations, as distinct from the CMEA. Interrepublican imbalances on trade account, which themselves already introduced a variety of subsidies and taxes, were offset through various planned or administratively accommodated income transfers.

The resulting patterns of trade were on the whole in support of maintaining economies that were by design without competition from within and sheltered against external competition; that engaged in widespread redistribution of incomes throughout their own economy, but were reluctant to do likewise on a regional level, even among like-minded partners; and that had their economic priorities set by the political and bureaucratic powers in place, rather than through a framework from within which economic decision makers could formulate their own strategies and pursue their own profit motives.

Whatever the considerable defects of the TR trade, payment, and pricing regimes—and they were very substantial indeed!—they did support more or less buoyant trade for many decades, even though disequilibrium prices entailed chronic imbalances that plans and plan coordination sought to alleviate with less than full determination; likewise for trade and payment flows in the former Soviet Union and Yugoslavia. These systems began to totter—and, in the end, faltered abysmally—when one major component (such as the Soviet Union in the CMEA) ran into unanticipated adjustment problems that could not be smoothed in any lasting way short of undertaking radical economic transformation that would permit scarce resources to be allocated on the basis of more explicit rationality criteria, including a redirection of trade flows. If the latter is pursued for other than economic reasons, it can only aggravate matters at least for partner economies.

This characterization in a nutshell suggests that the economic space of the dinar or ruble functioned in a much more integrated, if bureaucratically planned, or politicized way than was the case for the TR's economic space. Nonetheless, gains emanated from these unions. In addition, there were forgone gains, meaning opportunities that were not exploited because the decision-making apparatus, at given resources and goals, did not elicit such behavior. With somewhat different resource constraints but much altered development goals, the emerging policy instruments anchored to mediated exchange based on economic advantage is bound to separate past trade flows into several components, including those temporarily warranted on economic grounds, and to identify new trade gains (resulting from more fully exploiting existing comparative advantages, notably for consumer goods and foodstuffs, and new comparative advantages called for by the restructuring of output profiles as a result of transition). That, after all, provides the *economic* rationale for the orderly disengagement of traditional economic relations.

Economic Interdependence and Defunct Economic Unions

Managing unions consisting of several sovereign republics or states in a single currency zone, whether for all transactions as for the dinar and ruble or only trading transactions as for the TR, necessarily raises issues that are familiar from the literature about optimum currency areas. In the TR area, these are confined to external payment problems. In the dinar and ruble zones, however, they in addition revolve around meeting the realistic preconditions for harmonizing macroeconomic policies among the various republics and how this could have been ensured without there being any supranational authority in place or that would even be acceptable in principle. Even so, these problems resemble in many respects key obstacles that confronted the Eastern European PETs when they decided to open up their economies to foreign competition in preference to modifying in an orderly manner the intricate CMEA linkages based on the TR mechanisms.

This is not a facetious way of downgrading the convulsions that have gripped the East. Rather, the common thread that unites the erstwhile TR and the emerging "national" trade and payment problems in the East have to do with the inability of these countries to switch quickly to world-market conditions, as examined earlier, if some semblance of normality in trade and economic activity is to be maintained. Of course, a suitably massive exchange-rate devaluation eventually engenders some equilibrium. But the impoverishment of the country, because of the structures that will thus be destroyed as well as the sheer depreciation of purchasing power in international terms, might be so severe that it is hard to envision how solid sociopolitical support for such a policy could be mustered, except by default.

Being skeptical about the alleged forecasts of the directions in which trading patterns of PETs will necessarily evolve is one thing. Another is to suggest an alternative that would inspire greater confidence. I for one strongly believe this can be done for countries that have been intricately interlaced for so long and whose "natural proclivity" in terms of both geographical proximity and economic complementarity argues in favor of relatively buoyant intragroup trade, provided it can be accommodated. Under prevailing conditions, this may require policy intervention to enable intragroup trade to be restructured in some orderly environment even if in the end the sustainable equilibrium level of intragroup trade were to become negligible. To do so, the basics of optimum currency or economic regimes need to be recalled (Grubel 1973, Mundell 1973). Here I can do so only in a very rudimentary way (but see Brabant 1992f) by contrasting the essence of the ideal theory with the emerging disarray in the former coherent zones, specifically with reference to what appears to be required to shift from a common to a ruptured union, while the leaderships of the successor states can nonetheless cope with *de facto* separate reforms.

There is little point in looking for a neat economic rationale to explain the formation of either the Soviet or Yugoslav federation, or the CMEA for that matter. None of them ever explicitly aspired to reaping the economic gains available within an optimum currency area or regional association. Yet, there would be little point in advocating some return to these states without invoking an economic logic to such an advocacy. Not that economics by itself can persuade sovereign states—or those aspiring to that status—to engage in constructive collaborative undertakings. But it may lead to credible economic tradeoffs for policy makers.

The case for rescuing the trading and currency zones, though the specifics in each case differ, depends on the gains available from moving towards an increasingly better managed union. An economic union with a single currency, provided there is a common policy not only in monetary but also in fiscal affairs, may yield significant economic gains. But these do not necessarily accrue to all, let alone equitably, components of the union. There is, therefore, a case to be made for agreeing on redistributing some of these gains, for example, through regional policies (Eichengreen 1990, Grubel 1973, Mundell 1973). This rationale is, of course, very different from any advocacy of recreating the CMEA mechanisms, say, within a confederated post-Soviet Union as László Csaba (1991) has argued. Doing so for any group of PETs cannot be a desirable option and it should not be invoked as a means to deride proposals for temporary payment mechanisms (see Bofinger and Gros 1992; Brabant 1991a, b; Dornbusch 1992b; Gros 1992; Havrylyshyn 1992a, b; Havrylyshyn and Williamson 1991).

The common formula is that gains of scale and organization can be reaped from having an area with a single currency or multiple currencies that are rigidly and (in the expectational sense) permanently linked through credible exchange rates, but that may periodically be adjusted in tandem to other currencies. The commitment to a permanently fixed exchange rate requires that aggregate monetary and fiscal policies be harmonized so as to maintain long-run equilibrium in the current account and to arrange lending facilities to enable members to stabilize the exchange rate in spite of short-run disequilibria. With a single currency, there is, of course, no need to harmonize policies in order to maintain the overall current account. But regional imbalances, including in employment patterns, must be corrected whenever factor mobility is less than perfect. For that, fiscal policy must be attuned to take over the function that otherwise an exchange rate might play in the adjustment process

(Grubel 1973, p. 101). But even that might not suffice, and it will then be necessary to integrate labor markets (Balassa 1973).

In any effort to restructure, it will be necessary to identify resources, desirable output targets, need for import substitution or export promotion, and other parameters to address systematically the core issues at hand if some modicum of order in the transition is to be preserved. It would be all the more important to follow a similar path if some comprehensive recovery program for the East could realistically be conceived and credibly enacted. It would involve the systematic destruction of specialization patterns in the CMEA that are not economically justified and the identification of areas in which the PETs can be expected to maintain—and gain—a comparative advantage over the near to medium term; the same holds for the narrower dinar and ruble zones, although there domestic specialization occurred, of course, for other reasons. The instruments through which these modifications should preferably be brought about must themselves be solidly anchored to market indicators, but conceived within an overall program of bold adjustments in economic structures and institutions. If only for that reason, they deserve outside financial and other support.

Seen in that light, the payment constraints encountered within the "former national zones" resemble very much the problems that the Eastern European PETs faced soon after their political revolutions. But the adjustment problems of the successor states to the Soviet Union in particular may be even more severe, owing to the fact that production structures in place were chosen through administrative, military, and political priorities, only the scantiest of attention being paid to economic scarcities. The Yugoslav case falls somewhere in-between.

Whatever consensus on restructuring may be gained, it will be necessary to pursue comparatively liberal policies and make as much room as possible for autonomous economic agents to exploit opportunities for profitable trade. For that to work well, policy makers must rectify prevailing domestic and external imbalances and see to it that the new ones bound to arise are kept manageable. To avoid aggravating external imbalances as a result of sheer economic disarray, I deem it very important for these countries to explore joint efforts to avert a total collapse of intragroup relations, whose sociopolitical and economic costs widely exceed the unavoidable. Economically warranted trade should be shored up and new trade opportunities fostered. The rationale of comparative advantage or strategic trade decisions should be self-evident here. But its desirability derives also from the need to impart credibility to incisive transformation blueprints and to elicit vital foreign support that will not simply dissipate under impact of the more slippery aspects of weakly anchored policies.

Correcting Errors and Western Assistance

In pondering what can be done to enhance intragroup cooperation of PETs, it is important to be crystal clear about the complexity of the broad panoply of factors impinging on the transitions, including the mutual reinforcements of simultaneously pursuing deflationary policies and shunning intragroup trade. I cannot discuss all factors here (but see Brabant 1990, 1991a). In addition to recalling the effect on the demand for convertible currency examined earlier, it is useful to bear in mind three critical features of the transition. First, because of the sharp devaluation of the exchange rate in nearly all PETs (Hungary being an exception to some degree), effective import demand at world prices gets curtailed; the same applies to export revenue in the short run because of inability to switch markets and the reciprocal compression in intragroup relations. In addition, the undervaluation of the currency destroys otherwise viable activities because of sharply risen import costs and affords domestic monopolies a sizable protective cushion, thereby blunting the expected benefits of external competition. Furthermore, the policy stance taken by the new decision makers has, in effect, discouraged trade with the former, including "domestic," partners by economic (such as tariffs, quotas and other nontariff barriers) and often indeed other means (such as health-inspection regulations, exchange-rate manipulations, barter and bilateral arrangements down to the enterprise level, political invective, and out-right export denial). Mostly one-sided demand-management stabilization measures have sharply compressed import demand and raised export supply, temporarily more with the west. On balance, real effective protection against former partners has risen sharply while that against the west has been relaxed.

Second, the transitions have invariably proceeded with considerable chaos whose amplitude has been reinforced through the propulsion of instability from within the group of former trading or constituent partners. This has been notably the case for the former Soviet Union, given its pivotal role in supplying Eastern Europe with fuels and raw materials and purchasing the latter's custom-made manufactures; the impact on the successor states is bound to be even more pronounced given the extreme specialization and concentration pursued there. All this is exerting a multiplier effect, guaranteeing a downward spiral for some time. But the initial phase of the transition is probably the worst time for this imported depression to manifest itself.

Lastly, political obstacles have inhibited agreement on successor trade and payment regimes. The inability to embrace world-market conditions and the utter unwillingness to revive some intragroup cooperation have measurably exacerbated the impact of the disintegration of the former zones. Also, the startling lack of imagination on the part of otherwise well-intentioned western donors and assistance agencies has sharply understated the depth and breadth of interdependence among the old and new PETs. The assistance policies formulated under the circumstances have, at best, been poorly designed, as explained in more details in chapter 5. They certainly have not effectively supported the structural changes required before the PETs can hope to regain positive growth and carve out for themselves a sustainable niche in world markets.

These aspects of the disarray suggest that, while some contraction of trade would have been unavoidable, a not negligible part of the collapse can be attributed to chaotic overshooting. This outcome could have been averted without necessarily crimping the ability of the PETs to explore other markets, provided effective successor cooperation mechanisms had been installed. Not only would they have slowed down the contraction of intragroup trade, they would also have bolstered the opportunities for trade creation, as detailed elsewhere (Brabant 1990, 1991a).

How best to come to grips with the broken-down regimes has been the topic of considerable debate among scholars and policy makers. No foreign impulse by itself can revive these economies. Such must necessarily emanate from domestic supply-side policies. Countries can do so in isolation or they can try to cushion the blows through cooperation. Just like the intermediate solution to restructure the former CMEA trade envisaged the creation of a payments union as part and parcel of a broader effort at transforming these countries with international support (Brabant 1990, 1991a), I am still convinced that a collaborative effort among the successor states, and perhaps other PETs, may succeed faster and at a smaller cost than the courses that are now being explored for implementation in the near-term.

Of course, there are other solutions than a payments union that can in principle be entertained. In the end, all focus in one way or another on how to relax the payment constraint. I do not want to repeat the pros of such a solution nor to rebut the myriad of objections that have been launched (Brabant 1991a). Some have, of course, been well taken. But they are incidental in the sense that whatever the international community may wish to launch for these countries short of imposing world conditions is bound to be discriminatory. My scheme for a payments union forms in fact a small component of a much more comprehensive and bold international effort to buttress the legitimate aspirations of the PETs while averting dysfunctional repercussions of the remaking of the East on other parts of the global economy. That is to say, the agency managing the basics (not the technical settlements) of the payments union would have to be fully embedded in this cooperative reconstruction of the East.

Rather than exploring this option, the approach now widely advocated by the international community has been to provide more general financial and other support for the transitions, while not meddling in domestic economic policy making beyond ensuring that policy targets agreed upon in programs with the Fund are somewhat adhered to. This approach is being promoted in mantra-style fashion in blatant disregard of the experiences of the past three years or so. It is unlikely to work for the successor states of the Soviet Union (see Brabant 1992a, b, f), if only because policies are not in place that would stabilize the economies, hence create the conditions under which affordable convertibility could be attempted. Furthermore, it is uncertain what exchange rate should be supported and how. And there simply is not the commitment on the part of donor countries to sustain sufficiently large and flexible stabilization funds to permit credible experimentation.

In the absence of adequate foreign-exchange reserves to weather the initial adversities of the transition and given that a rapid transition to currency convertibility (dinar, ruble, or new republican ones) is rather implausible, the only alternative would seem to be a cutback in aggregate demand to levels that will permit a sustainable foreign-exchange situation. That compression may be very marked indeed, certainly much larger than experienced thus far in Central Europe and than ultimately required as present economic activity is squeezed out by the enormous devaluation either for lack of demand, owing to the sharp contraction in real incomes and monetary wealth, or for inability to afford the sharply risen cost of necessary imported inputs.

If the above assessments are valid, the only feasible solution short of disastrous deflation is the earmarking of some funds for a facility that would ensure current payments within broadly agreed-upon guidelines under external supervision. The latter would be required, in the narrow sense, to reconcile payment requirements with available funding and, in the broad sense, to ensure that foreign-trade adjustment policies are conceived as much as possible within the overall framework of transitional policy making.

I have elsewhere argued *ad nauseam* the case for such a facility for all PETs committed to broad market-oriented reforms (as summed up in Brabant 1991a). Now that several ex-Soviet republics are in principle committed to a similar purpose, I deem it even more important to erect such a facility. Not only would it facilitate payments, it would also impart a decisive impulse to breaking as quickly as feasible with the inherited consequences of administrative regulation of trade. Instead of this being conducted at the union level, it now consists of bilateral pairs of republics with their respective authorities engaging in all kinds of agreements, barter, and other ways of interfering in trade decisions of decentralized economic units (including SOEs). Of course, the facility for the successor states to the Soviet Union should be accessible on a voluntary basis to all other PETs.

As emphasized earlier, I see this approach not in isolation and I do not expect wonders from having a payment facility. That could conceivably only arise from having it as one important component of a broader assistance effort. The latter could be mounted not only by the international community, such as the Group of Twenty-four (G-24) and the IEOs, as explained in chapter 5. Perhaps even more important is gaining an understanding on the part of the PETs that cooperative policies are the preferred means towards rendering the transition less painful and accelerating it. Indeed, the PETs need all the self-help that can possibly be mustered to maximize the usefulness of western assistance, however delivered. To avoid artificially obstructing intragroup trade, yet persuade policy makers there to take some risk, should form one component of such a cooperative strategy in which the international community at large fully participates. Reinforcing mutual commercial ties would be very helpful in shoring up the rebuilding of trade in conjunction with industrial restructuring. Not only would it support the reform trends from within, such a way of proceeding would also transfer western assistance in a form that would least interfere with the emerging economic incentives for microeconomic actors. Finally, it would stave off either the pressure on western markets to accommodate significant trade diversion or the contraction in levels of domestic economic activity in the PETs during the restructuring process because of built-in supply rigidities in the PETs that are legacies of planning under communism and, in a number of cases, of the way in which the development process in the eastern part of Europe progressed prior to World War II.

Conclusions

One thing is the desirability of invigorating intragroup trade among the PETs. Another is how best to accomplish it. To do so through all kinds of *ad hoc* arrangements hammered out in a near vacuum, hence unenforceable, since 1990 cannot but hamper proper decisions on restructuring these economies. Enterprise barter is less desirable than enterprise bilateralism, which itself is less desirable than intergovernmental bilateralism, and that in turn is certainly inferior to solutions feasible within a multilateral environment. This is particularly so when it becomes crucial to prop up intermediation, given the pivotal role of having microeconomic agents, private or otherwise, decide on how best to allocate their resources at their own risk under the emerging market conditions. Whereas a fully multilateralized environment (such as completely free trade) is not attainable in the short run, there are opportunities for underpinning better solutions than the bilateralism that many advocate. This is especially true in the case of the former Soviet republics, where republican bureaucracies have substituted themselves for the erstwhile federal bureaucracy (Havrylyshyn 1992a), with little change in the behavior of these government agencies in line with the *desired*, as distinct from the *prevailing*, heavily distorted economic realities, at least for now.

Now that the remaking of the successor states to the USSR is a burning issue on the international policy agenda, I deem it even more important than when the TR regimes were being deliberately ruptured to put in place a temporary mechanism that can help sustain viable levels of trade and alter those trade patterns that, once the adjustment phase will near completion, will no longer be economically warranted. The answer of the international community has been to bet on stabilizing the ruble and maintaining the ruble regime so that trade among the former Soviet republics can be maintained at a reasonable level. This effort is misguided, as was the one that succeeded in rapidly obliterating the infrastructure for TR-based economic relations.

Much less thought has been given to the dinar regime, although also there a structural reform will need to be undertaken. But this will most likely be much easier and smoother than either the TR or ruble regimes, once the hostilities in the former Yugoslavia will have been concluded, and economic relations among the republics can be rebuilt from their presently artifically compressed levels.

4

Post-CMEA Trade and Payments Arrangements in the East

Harriet Matejka

There are three approaches to the reorganization of trade and payments in the East following the dissolution of the CMEA. The first, which is associated with the IMF, advocates immediate, nondiscriminatory liberalization and a measure of currency convertibility. The second, explored by the United Nations, focuses on discriminatory, and perhaps provisional, union of the PETs. The third is the discriminatory practice of the West European integration groups, that is the EC and EFTA, which are extending their area of free trade to the eastern half of the continent. The first approach is open to the criticism that, in the absence of a policy apparatus enabling the authorities to maintain internal equilibrium, convertibility is likely to be short-lived, and to absorb much of the financial assistance made available by the international community in the meantime. The second runs up against the resistance of the proposed partners both at the political, but also at the purely practical, level for all are economies in transition; many are newly independent states to boot. The third is unlikely to encompass all PETs.

In this chapter, I discuss economic union among Eastern economies. First I describe the breakdown of trade and payments among them since

Associate Professor at the Institut Universitaire de Hautes Etudes Internationales, Geneva, Switzerland.

1988. Then I list the integration areas that either exist or are being proposed in the East, and the reasons given for the creation of unions among these countries. Considering these arguments critically, I find next that Eastern unions are not feasible under present circumstances because of the lack of appropriate institutions, and are ill-designed to fulfill the short-term objectives for which they are frequently advocated. I argue that the west should give priority to the creation of viable market systems in the PETs and, in the short run, sustain their mutual trade through international financing. I conclude with a summary of the main findings.

Trade and Payments in 1988-1992

The trade and payments of the countries in the East have undergone four major disruptions since 1988. The first was the disappearance of the GDR, the second was the disintegration of the CMEA, the third the disruption of orderly relations in vast areas of the East, and the fourth the collapse of production. The disappearance of the GDR began with the economic unification of Germany in June 1990 and was completed by the entry into force of the Unification Treaty in October 1990. The first measure removed the GDR, which accounted for some 15 percent of the trade among the European CMEA members, from the Council's trade and payment arrangements.

The disappearance of the CMEA began with a major reorganization. This was the shift from bilateral clearing in TRs at CMEA prices,[1] to convertible currency settlements at world prices in trade between member countries. It was decided in January 1990, ostensibly introduced on 1 January 1991, and succeeded in June 1991 by the decision to dissolve the Council.

The political and economic disintegration of vast areas of the East has been manifold. As the USSR, to begin with, fragmented from the end of 1988 onwards, war erupted at several points, notably between Armenia and Azerbaijan, within Georgia and Moldova. Certain republics, notably Belarus', Russia, and Ukraine, concluded trade agreements of their own

---

1. The TR was introduced as an accounting unit among CMEA members in 1964. The CMEA price formula was formally introduced in 1958, and established world prices, averaged and fixed for a period of years, as the basis for intra-CMEA trade.

with foreign partners.[2] The Moscow *coup* of August 1991 led to the independence of the Baltic states in September, the creation of the CIS by Belarus', Russia, and Ukraine on 8 December, which the other remaining republics, save Georgia, joined, and then the formal dissolution of the USSR on 26 December 1991. To the south, in Yugoslavia, civil war, which began in June 1991, led to the breakaway and then the recognition of the independence of Slovenia, Croatia and Bosnia-Herzegovina in 1992. From 1989 onwards, new customs frontiers as well as trade barriers thus began to appear in the East. In Central Europe, the separation of the Czech lands and Slovakia was announced in June 1992.

Plummeting production throughout the East was the fourth factor of disruption. This was due in part to the three sources of dislocation just described but, essentially and independently, to the transition from plan to market and to the rigorous stabilization policies, which were frequently introduced to accompany it. In 1991 alone, falls in national production reached 26 percent, unemployment reached 12 percent, and there were spectacular reductions in investment attaining 50 percent (UNECE 1992). Before the end of 1991, the scale of the collapse in the East prompted the United Nations Economic Commission for Europe (UNECE) to compare it with the depression of the 1930s (UNECE 1991b, p. 5).

The chaos produced by this succession of shocks meant that, while trade flows denominated in TRs all but disappeared in 1991,[3] payment restrictions, which had characterized central planning, persisted or were quickly resorted to. Although the convertible currency settlements decided upon by the CMEA were formally introduced and should have multilateralized the intragroup payments in the East, their bilateral agreements often provided for interenterprise compensation. Their exchanges with their chief Eastern partner, namely the USSR and subsequently Russia, continued in certain cases to be constrained within bilateral clearing or even barter agreements.[4] The absence of reserves of the newly independent republics of the former USSR, with the exception of Russia, meant that their mutual exchanges, or those of their local authorities, took place

---

2. The Russian Federation, Belarus', and Ukraine signed agreements with Czechoslovakia in March, April and July 1991, respectively.

3. The percentage of ruble-denominated trade fell to 8-10 percent of intra-CMEA trade in the first half of 1991 (UNECE 1992, p. 85).

4. Czechoslovakia concluded a bilateral clearing agreement with Russia for 1992 and a sum of $3.3 billion, one of the purposes of which was the settlement of the Soviet ruble debt towards Czechoslovakia.

on a barter basis, as did some of their trade with the rest of the world.
Thus payment arrangements over this period probably increased rather
than reduced the barriers to trade among the Eastern countries.

The outcome of this sum of forces was the breakdown of intra-CMEA
trade as shown in table 4.1. The fall over the three years 1989-1991 was
spectacular in the case of Bulgaria, and especially steep for the group of
Eastern European countries whose intragroup trade dropped by half in
nominal terms as compared to 1988. Yugoslav trade, which is not included
in the table and for which no complete records exist for 1991, showed no
decrease until then except for exports to Eastern Europe which fell in
1990.

It is to foster the recovery of trade, and to arrest the further fragmentation of exchange and payments, in the East that payments unions, free
trade areas, customs unions, and economic unions have frequently been
advocated for the countries that embark on market-oriented economic
restructuring. All promote transactions between members in preference to
those with nonmembers, payments unions doing so *inter alia* by providing
credit to part-finance deficits between member countries, and free trade
areas, customs unions, and economic unions doing so by abolishing trade
barriers between them. Both types of schemes thus foster integration or
economic union,[5] and it is one or other of these two terms that will be
used in what follows to denote preferential arrangements in general, as
well as the processes they induce.

New Arrangements

The dissolution of the CMEA has paved the way for a major reorientation
of the East's trade towards the developed west, particularly on the export
side, and for the inclusion of the Eastern countries into new organizations. Two poles of attraction have drawn the former members of the
CMEA, and later the former republics of the USSR, towards them. The
first has been Western Europe, and more particularly the EC. The second

---

5. In the general, as opposed to the institutional, sense in which an economic union is
defined as the complete merging of previously separate economies into a common market,
and the transfer of their sovereignty in all matters of economic policy to a common union
authority.

Country	1989	1990	1991	1989	1990	1991
	Exports			Imports		
Bulgaria						
Total	-12.0	-21.3	-34.2	-9.9	-23.8	-51.5
Eastern Europe	-16.6	-38.6	-58.3	-21.3	-28.2	-61.5
Soviet Union	-8.2	-31.0	-24.3	-15.8	-21.7	-39.9
Czechoslovakia						
Total	-3.2	-10.5	1.6	-3.4	0.3	-15.6
Eastern Europe	-6.6	-33.1	19.0	-4.1	-11.5	-46.7
Soviet Union	-13.8	-25.8	-10.1	-9.0	-26.7	41.8
Hungary						
Total	-3.3	-1.3	7.1	-5.4	-2.7	32.8
Eastern Europe	-9.7	-31.4	-21.2	-13.4	-16.9	5.4
Soviet Union	-11.9	-20.7	-29.1	-16.7	-15.9	6.9
Poland						
Total	0.6	24.7	-18.5	-0.4	-2.5	24.3
Eastern Europe	-3.3	-2.1	-52.2	-9.1	-39.4	-11.2
Soviet Union	-5.4	4.6	-60.6	-13.9	6.7	-31.6
Romania						
Total	-10.0	-43.4	-7.1	8.8	18.1	-17.6
Eastern Europe	-14.9	-56.9	-8.8	-8.1	-1.8	-28.7
Soviet Union	-11.1	-37.3	30.7	2.0	-18.7	-8.8
Eastern Europe						
Total	-4.5	-5.2	-9.6	-2.7	-2.6	-0.2
Eastern Europe	-8.4	-26.5	-25.7	-9.8	-20.8	-28.3
Soviet Union	-9.8	-19.2	-31.9	-12.0	-14.9	-8.3

Table 4.1: Eastern Europe and the Soviet Union: Growth of Trade, 1989-1991

(in percentages)

Source: all data are drawn from the common data base kept at UNECE which is based on national statistical publications, direct communications from national statistical offices, and (for 1991) in part on trade partner data. Both export and import values are expressed f.o.b., except for Hungarian imports which are shown c.i.f. in the national returns. Growth rates are calculated on values expressed in dollars. Trade with the East in the years prior to 1991 was valued in an adjusted dollar measure reflecting consistent ruble/dollar crossrates. All trade values for 1991 were converted to dollars at the appropriate national conversion coefficient (usually the commercial rate quoted by national banks). The partner country grouping follows the practice until recently prevalent in the national statistical sources. The former GDR is included in the data for 1989-1990, but not in those for 1991 and in comparisons between 1990 and 1991.

has been Turkey and Iran in competition, vying with each other to extend their spheres of influence.

By mid-1992, the Community had ratified trade and cooperation agreements, that is "first generation" agreements, with the former CMEA members, and had signed such agreements with Albania, Estonia, Latvia, and Lithuania. It had signed "second generation" agreements,[6] that is association or Europe agreements, with Czechoslovakia, Hungary, and Poland on 16 December 1991, the trade provisions of which entered into force on a provisional basis on 1 March 1992. It was negotiating Europe agreements with Bulgaria and Romania. It was also preparing agreements somewhere between the first and second generation with four of the successor states of the Soviet Union, namely Belarus', Kazakhstan, Russia, and Ukraine. The Community, in other words, was drawing the East into its orbit, establishing close ties with the northern republics of the former USSR and preparing eventually to extend the area of four freedoms to Bulgaria, Czechoslovakia, Hungary, Poland, and Romania. Nor did it exclude the conclusion in the future of further Europe agreements with the other countries benefiting from first-generation agreements. Meanwhile, in March 1992 EFTA concluded, and began to implement, an agreement on free trade in industrial products with Czechoslovakia, and it was negotiating similar agreements with Bulgaria, Hungary, Poland, and Romania.

Mention should further be made of two European cooperation arrangements. The first, the Central European Initiative, has as its purpose political, economic, and environmental cooperation. Having succeeded the *Hexagonale*, which was established as the Adria-Alps initiative by Austria, Italy, Hungary, and Yugoslavia in 1989, as well as Bavaria at the first meeting, and was joined by Czechoslovakia and later Poland, it admitted Croatia and Slovenia as observers in March 1992. The second, the Baltic Council, bringing together Denmark, Estonia, Finland, Germany, Latvia, Lithuania, Norway, Poland, Russia, and Sweden, was launched in March 1992 to promote economic and cultural cooperation.[7]

---

6. *Editor's note*: the terminology is not standardized. Some commentators refer to simple trade agreements as first-generation agreements and to trade and cooperation agreements as second-generation agreements. If so, the Europe agreements should be termed "third-generation" agreements. The new agreements under negotiation with the successor states are called "partnership agreements," situated somewhere between the first- and second-generation agreements.

7. *Editor's note*: these initiatives do not appear to have made much progress since they were first launched.

On the former USSR's southern flank, Turkey and Iran were active in organizing areas with the republics of the Caucasus and Central Asia. In 1990, Turkey launched the idea of a Black Sea Cooperation Area which led to the signature of the Istanbul Declaration on 25 June 1992, by eleven countries in the region, namely Albania, Armenia, Azerbaijan, Bulgaria, Georgia, Greece, Moldova, Romania, Russia, Turkey itself, and Ukraine. These agreed to promote free trade and the free movement of capital, and to cooperate in the fields of transport, industry, tourism, communication, agriculture, mining, energy, medicine, and the environment. Iran responded to the Turkish initiative by reactivating the ECO, the successor to Regional Cooperation for Development (RCD) created by Iran, Pakistan, and Turkey in 1963, and obtaining the accession of the muslim republics of the ex-USSR in February 1992, with the exception of Kazakhstan, which remains an observer. The expanded ECO agreed on a tariff reduction of 10 percent as a first step towards the elimination of all tariffs, export subsidies, and nontariff barriers. At the same time, but separately, Iran proposed a Caspian economic area to bring together five countries, namely Azerbaijan, Iran, Kazakhstan, Russia, and Turkmenistan.

Overt conflict between member countries, the rivalry between Turkey and Iran, and the economic and political upheavals occurring in the republics of the former USSR mean that effective integration, as distinct from declamatory commitments, is a thing of the far future in the three areas just described. Nonetheless, their actual or proposed existence is encouraging the creation of new trade channels and is opening the economies of the former Soviet republics of the Caucasus and Central Asia, in particular, to their southern neighbors.

Between these two major forces, the first of which has so far achieved most in drawing the East into its economic area, various integration schemes and payments unions between Eastern economies have been proposed and, in certain cases, negotiated, although none so far has entered into force. A number include countries already belonging to the areas just examined.

Immediately after the Eastern European revolutions, the Central European Payments Union (CEPU) among Czechoslovakia, Hungary, and Poland was put forward,[8] and initially conceived of as extending to other

---

8. The literature is considerable (including UNECE 1990, pp. 147-50; Brabant 1990, 1991 a, d; and Bofinger 1991), and growing. Thus, the European Bank for Reconstruction and Development (EBRD) convened a conference on the subject in London in March 1992.

countries, including the USSR, in due course. Some of these proposals were linked to the proposal for a Central European Economic Union (Brabant 1991a, UNECE 1990, pp. 118-19), an idea which, in the less ambitious form of a free trade area, was taken up by the Visegrád three, namely Czechoslovakia, Hungary, and Poland.[9] Poland and Ukraine discussed a possible extension of this scheme to include the latter. A common market (UNECE 1991b, p. 86) but also a customs union was urged on the Baltic states which, finding these too complex, negotiated towards the conclusion of a free trade area. The CIS agreed on the preservation of a single economic space anchored to the ruble,[10] and in March 1992, Kazakhstan, Kyrgyzstan, Russia, Tajikistan, and Uzbekistan concluded an agreement on the creation of a customs union, and Armenia, Belarus', and Moldova subscribed to some of its articles. A payments union for the CIS, which would unite the republics introducing new currencies to those retaining the ruble, has also been widely discussed (Brabant 1992f, Havrylyshyn and Williamson 1991; UNECE 1992, pp. 134-35).

The reasons given for advocating economic union in the East are many. The CEPU, but also a payments union among members of the CIS, have been justified as a means of sustaining trade but also of achieving convertibility (Brabant 1991a; IMF 1992, pp. 19-20; UNECE 1990, pp. 147-50). Free trade areas, customs unions, and economic unions have been urged on the East because they would be trade creating, help restructure without being exposed to world markets while reaping economies of scale, as an aid to transition, as a means of integration into the wider Europe and the world (UNECE 1990, pp. 118-19) or, quite simply, because membership of a wider area is advantageous (UNECE 1991, p. 86). More generally, the creation of integration areas among Eastern economies is being justified, in the first instance, to avoid trade destruction, but also to

---

9. The first meeting of the presidents of Poland and Czechoslovakia, and the prime minister of Hungary, took place in February 1991 at Visegrád, near Budapest, to establish trilateral collaboration in the fields of security, the economy, and other areas.

10. The preservation of a single economic space and currency area are among the objectives of the Economic Pact made at Minsk (IMF 1992, pp. 29-33) by the leaders of Belarus', Russia and Ukraine on 8 December 1991. But the later "Agreement on Regulation of Trade and Economic Relations between the States of the Commenwealth of Independent States in 1992," concluded in February 1992, is, with the exception of one article on the creation of a Customs Council to elaborate and execute a common customs policy, devoted essentially to the conditions for ensuring supplies within the framework of bilateral interrepublican agreements.

facilitate a coordinated approach to the establishment of market-based economic systems and, ultimately, to integrate the PETs into the world economy.

The inspiration behind the payments union proposals has been the European Payments Union (EPU), which was instrumental in restoring the convertibility of the Western European currencies in 1959. But the arguments in favor of other forms of preferential areas in the East show the influence of the discussion of integration for developing countries in the 1960s and, no doubt, also owe much to the recent conversion of the United States to integration and to the emulation that has seized the world following the EC's decision to introduce a single market in 1993.[11]

Union

What is remarkable about the preceding list of reasons for economic union in the East is the scant attention it pays to the conclusions of integration analysis, its disregard for the notion of first-best intervention, and its assumptions that the Eastern economies have the institutions enabling them to establish and operate preferential arrangements. For, as a moment's thought makes plain, the schemes described are neither feasible at the moment, nor necessarily welfare-enhancing and their other aims either cannot be achieved by, or do not necessarily follow, the creation of preferential arrangements and may, in the latter case, be attained more economically by other means.

The administrative prerequisites of integration can be considered to start with. For as economic union merges markets previously separated by state intervention, it presupposes their endowment with an administrative framework. Thus free trade areas, customs unions, common markets, and economic unions, all of which are arrangements for free trade among a limited number of countries, presuppose that, prior to their creation, members each have a clearly delineated customs territory, a customs administration, and a tariff within an overall system of trade regulation. A payments union, in turn, which is an arrangement enabling countries with inconvertible currencies to progress from the bilateral to the multilateral clearing of their mutual payments, presupposes that, prior to the

---

11. The regionalism of the 1980s is acutely described in Bhagwati 1992, pp. 11-16.

union's establishment, each member has its own currency, monetary authority, and foreign exchange regime. These statements may seem trivial until one remembers that the prerequisites cited are generally not satisfied by the successor states of the former Soviet Union and, perhaps to a lesser extent, by some of Yugoslavia's.[12]

Beyond that, integration requires the market. A payments union, which works on the principle of the short-term, collective financing of a proportion of the deficits of the members' payments, and the correction of imbalances by the debtor countries using devaluations or expenditure-reducing policies, requires the market for these measures to be effective. The deficit country's resort to devaluation demands both that the market operate, so that domestic demand and supply responds to the increase in the price of foreign exchange, and that a macroeconomic policy apparatus be in place and work within the market, so that the policy authorities maintain internal balance while the external disequilibrium is being corrected. The authorities' resort to expenditure-reducing policies, on the other hand, requires their operation within the market to restore external balance.

Preference and free trade areas, customs unions, common markets, and economic unions, in turn, cannot be established if the mutual tariff concessions granted among the members are made inoperative by price controls, state orders, obligations under bilateral balancing agreements, the automatic subsidization of loss-making operations, and other measures of direct state intervention that paralyze the market. Nor will a single market be created if the authorities do not have an apparatus of policies with which to maintain aggregate equilibrium within their respective markets and so avoid the restoration of trade barriers for balance-of-payments purposes (Meade 1955). Moreover, the implementation of an integration agreement will be impossible to monitor if the partners' economies are so highly centralized that their governments issue directives directly to producers and traders (Matejka 1990, pp. 143-7).

While these considerations show why integration is not feasible between newly independent states or between economies starting on their transition from central planning to the market, they may seem not to

---

12. *Editor's note*: It is useful to distinguish between the management of currencies, to which the author is referring, and the accommodation of imbalances, regardless of currency (Brabant 1992f). Even in a fully integrated ruble zone with separate monetary authorities or with one monetary authority unwilling to extend credit, a payments union might still work.

apply to Czechoslovakia, Hungary, and Poland. For these have concluded Europe agreements with the EC, are already implementing their trade provisions, and thus appear to have proceeded with their transition sufficiently to integrate their economies into the Community. But this is to draw the wrong conclusion for three reasons.

First, the Europe agreements, as is the case for the EFTA arrangement with Czechoslovakia, are asymmetric: They provide for the EC's dismantling of its trade barriers before the Eastern partners dismantle theirs, and they additionally allow the three countries to raise trade barriers temporarily if this is required for restructuring. During the ten years of transition foreseen by each agreement, therefore, the Eastern partners are not required to integrate their markets with the EC's and receive a transfer of resources from the Community, which lifts its barriers first. Second, an important part of the agreements is devoted to the forms and conditions under which the EC is to provide economic, cultural, and financial assistance to Czechoslovakia, Hungary, and Poland. In other words, the agreements are as much, if not more, a framework for the EC's aid and assistance to start with, and turn into an instrument of integration only once transition has been achieved. Third, there is increasing evidence that the three countries are having difficulties in establishing their customs administrations[13] and that the creation of an integration area between them would, for this reason alone, be premature. What is increasingly clear, however, is that they will dismantle their mutual barriers to trade at the same time as they dismantle their barriers on imports from the EC, thus moving the frontiers of the EC's area of four freedoms eastward once their transition is completed. In sum, the entry into force of the Europe agreements constitutes no evidence that the Central European economies can effectively integrate with the EC during transition.

Feasibility apart, there is the question, second, of the gains to be reaped from integration. For economic theory does not teach that membership of a wider area is advantageous. It states, on the contrary, that as integration describes a reallocation of resources that takes the economy from one second-best situation, characterized by nondiscriminatory tariffs, to another, characterized by geographically discriminatory tariffs, there may be a net gain or a net loss as a consequence of union. There are, it is

---

13. In Poland, the release of customs-based trade statistics was delayed through early June 1992, owing to gross inaccuracies and errors in the control and verification of customs documents (PlanEcon 1992, p. 3).

true, probabilities of gain under certain initial conditions but these, by definition, do not amount to certainties. Only an examination of the actual circumstances of integration in a particular case makes it possible to determine whether or not resource allocation will in fact improve as a result of it.

But to undertake such a calculation in the PETs is premature. For, although the prices fixed for essentially political reasons under central planning have been, or are being swept away by price liberalization, the major disequilibria erupting throughout the East mean that relative prices are changing rapidly and extensively. To take the present pattern of prices as the starting point for a calculation of the production and consumption effects of a preferential arrangement would thus be to run the risk of taking the wrong decision as the price system was disrupted by a subsequent shock. To put it differently, trade creation and diversion cannot be assessed until the PETs have stabilized.

Theory does predict that the growth, as opposed to the allocation, effects of integration, will be positive, however. But they too have to be calculated on the basis of relative prices, and thus await the emergence of a stable system of prices as transition proceeds, before they can be included into the overall estimate of gain or loss. In sum, integration among Eastern economies cannot be justified by the necessary gain that would ensue, and the calculation of the outcome of any actual proposal cannot be undertaken while the Eastern economies are in the first stages of transition.

There remain the other reasons for union in the East. Transition and marketization may be dealt with briefly. For the previous discussion has shown that integration requires the accomplishment of these two processes, and not the other way around.

Convertibility, next, may be achieved by means of a payments union, as the EPU proved. But it may equally well be attained by the liberalization of a country's exchange regime under the aegis of the IMF to meet the conditions of Article VIII of the Funds' Charter.[14] A group of countries whose mutal payments constitute a high share of their total payments will be able to achieve convertibility by lifting exchange controls within a payments union, so that this type of scheme could be proposed

---

14. Countries subscribing to Article VIII undertake to allow the unrestricted sale and purchase of their currency against other currencies at a single exchange rate for current transactions (for details, see Brabant 1991a).

to the republics of the CIS, for instance, once they complete their transition. But the same will not be true of a group of countries which, like Czechoslovakia, Hungary, and Poland, settle only a very small share of their total. A payments union will liberalize only their mutual payments and would be better replaced by the nondiscriminatory liberalization of the countries' individual exchange regimes.

Nor would this union, obviously, serve to sustain trade, which is another justification for integration in the East. Moreover, although this is not generally stressed, integration need not increase the volume of trade between member countries (Vanek 1965, pp. 213-14). Integration, finally, will be virtually powerless to sustain trade, if the cause of trade reduction is not the segmentation of markets through trade intervention, but major income changes due to production plunges and the fracturing of institutional frameworks, as is occurring at present in the East. In such cases, practical, but also first-best considerations, suggest subsidization which, in the very short run, can take the form of financing the export of excess supply in one country to meet excess demand in another, as the Community has done to shift agricultural production from Eastern Europe to the former Soviet Union. In the medium term, it can take the form of the financing of payment deficits on a multilateral basis by the international organizations, the G-24, and the EC.

As for the argument that an economic union will enable countries to reap economies of scale while restructuring in a protected environment, it may be true, but is not necessarily so; integration among Estonia, Latvia, and Lithuania appears unlikely to produce this result, for instance. A country implementing a policy of restructuring which, while using a tariff, relies on nondiscriminatory export promotion will have the world market to sell to,[15] and may reap greater scale economies still.

Finally, at any given time, union among the Eastern economies will not promote integration into the EC or the world economy if it is trade diverting. And, dynamically, the path leading from a small integration area to a large union, or from integration to nondiscriminatory free trade on a world scale, is unknown (Bhagwati 1992).

In sum, economic union is not a magic wand. There are things that it cannot do, such as marketize nonmarket economies. There are many things that it may do, but need not, such as raise welfare, raise trade,

---

15. *Editor's note*: Provided the Eastern countries will be allowed to broach world markets on the basis of their competitive strength.

achieve convertibility, and ensure the reaping of economies of scale in the course of restructuring. In addition, among the things that it may do, there are those that can also be achieved on a nondiscriminatory basis. These include the raising of welfare through trade liberalization, convertibility, and benefiting from scale economies as a result of restructuring. Integration should thus be considered as one among a number of alternative policies whose costs and benefits should be carefully calculated.

Rather than wish a multitude of integration projects on the East during transition, when anyway they are unworkable, the west should thus give priority, in both its technical and financial assistance, to the building of viable market economies in the region. Once this has been achieved, the Eastern economies will be in a position to integrate if they find this beneficial.

In the meantime, however, there is the danger that they will develop individually and, given the shocks to which they are exposed, do so behind high protectionist and stringent payment barriers. This may be avoided, however, by drawing them into the world trade and payment system. Their membership of the IMF and IBRD, on the one hand, will not only provide them with advice and assistance in establishing their payment regimes, but will also encourage them to liberalize their payments. For the majority of Eastern countries which are not contracting parties to the GATT,[16] on the other, it appears necessary to introduce a provisional form of contract for the duration of the transition, which would enable these countries to benefit from technical assistance in establishing their trade regimes, and particularly their tariffs, would subject them to GATT procedures devised to maintain tolerable protection levels, and prepare them for full accession to the General Agreement. Where trade is concerned, this would seem to be one of the most urgent tasks for the west to undertake at the moment (see chapter 5).

Conclusions

This chapter has analyzed the breakdown of trade and payments between Eastern economies, has identified the organizations that are filling the

16. Aside from Yugoslavia, the only Eastern countries that are contracting parties are Czechoslovakia, Hungary, Poland, and Romania.

void left by the dissolution of the CMEA, and has focused on the payments unions and trading areas proposed for PETs. I contend that the creation of preferential arrangements between them is premature, because the necessary administrative prerequisites and market institutions are lacking in the PETs. Moreover, as integration cannot achieve some of the objectives it is advocated for, and may, but need not, achieve others, I argue that the west should give priority to the creation of viable market systems in the East, rather than to immediate integration there. Its action should include the financing necessary to sustain the mutual trade of the Eastern economies in the short run. Once these economies have successfully completed their transition, they will be equipped to choose economic union, or not, as one of several, alternative policies to attain a given target.

The threat of the Eastern economies pursuing highly protectionist trade and restrictive payment policies is best avoided by integrating them into the world trade and payment system. This would include their membership of the IMF and the IBRD, giving them access to advice and technical assistance and encouraging them to liberalize payments, and the negotiation of a special, transition status within the GATT, which would ensure their obtaining technical assistance in establishing their customs administrations and tariffs, and their being held to the implementation of tolerable tariff levels.

Integration agreements, if they are concluded at all, should be of the asymmetric variety in which the partners of the PETs dismantle their trade barriers first, leaving the Eastern countries to do so when they can effectively execute their undertaking, that is upon completing their systemic transformation.

5

The New East in Multilateral Economic Organizations

Jozef M. van Brabant

With the resolve henceforth to move steadily towards market-based economic decision making, all PETs have committed themselves to reduce significantly, albeit to varying degrees, obstacles of long standing to external commerce and other forms of interaction abroad. Old barriers have been replaced with more conventional institutions and commercial instruments, as noted earlier in chapter 3.

The broad objectives of installing market-based economic decision making in the PETs embody opportunities and challenges to the global community. There are at least four reasons for this. One derives from the fact that, under communism, key countries shunned the international organizations in place and derided the international regimes that they were designed to serve. From this emanates a challenge of how best to usher the PETs into the existing regimes and how to adapt the latter to this expanded membership. Immediately related to this is that the transitions are being assisted by national, regional, and international organizations, and that key facets of these efforts are being entrusted especially to

Principal Economic Affairs Officer of the Department of Economic and Social Development of the United Nations Secretariat in New York. The opinions expressed here are my own and do not necessarily reflect those that may be held by the United Nations in general and its Secretariat in particular.

the Fund. Because the organizations in place have been based on the principle of universality, one may inquire how the IEOs can cope with one group of countries that exhibit problems for which the supposedly universal solutions and approaches may not be the most suitable. Finally, although these IEOs were created after World War II and have undergone several transformations over the years, central questions have arisen as regards their relevance to contemporary and prospective global economic problems, some of which have a direct bearing on the PETs.

This chapter proposes some answers to these important questions. The flow of the argument is as follows. I first discuss the key obstacles in associating the planned economies with the postwar IEOs and their underlying regimes. Next I give a brief inventory of which PET belongs where at this stage at both the global and the regional levels. Then I touch upon the problem of how existing institutions with their established frameworks can deal with a group of members that apparently exhibit unique problems. In a fifth part, I consider potential incompatibilities between the missions assigned to the specialized organizations and the unique tasks that they have recently received in assisting the PETs. After presenting a brief overview of the global challenges and opportunities that, thus far, have not been sufficiently addressed, not even conceptually, the chapter concludes with a plea for moving towards a different route in assisting the PETs.

The Planned Economies and the Multilateral Frameworks

The global economic framework envisaged during and immediately after World War II exhibited a paradox of sorts (see Brabant 1991c, pp. 25ff.). One ambition of key negotiators revolved around the establishment of a free, liberal economic order, in spite of the adverse experiences of the interwar period; the appalling disarray caused by the war especially in Europe; and the magnitude of the adjustment problems that were anticipated to emerge with the launching of efforts to restore buoyant economic activity once hostilities ceased. But at the same time the initial impetus to the Anglo-American plans for postwar global economic organization was inspired by a reconsideration of the role of the state in economic matters. The paradox may be resolved by reconciling the ambition to reestablish a free trading world with the recognition at the time of the inevitability of an ascending role of the state in national and international economic management, given the perceived shortcomings of market-driven economic adjustments, for example, as experienced during the interwar period.

The major objective, especially of U.S. planners, for the postwar economic order was to provide for a world within which competitive market forces could operate with minimal state interference. This core philosophy was predicated on the belief that in the longer run market forces yield optimum results for all, provided the enabling environment is available. Yet the eventual role of the state in domestic and international economic management figured prominently in the deliberations about the specific tasks of trading, financial, and monetary institutions yet to be created. This commitment to multilateralism and free trade, among others, was part of a broader concern among policy makers about how best to ensure steady growth and full employment through national and international state regulation.

Aside from efforts to prepare for the postwar economic order as a matter of overall foreign policy, the chief participants in the debates had more limited, practical as well as pragmatic, objectives. Resource mobilization in support of the war effort had distorted the production and price structures of every country, and without some guidance inflationary pressures were bound to erupt and create havoc as soon as price and exchange controls would be lifted. Loath to curtail markets through deflationary policies, central decision makers were eager to devise plans that would permit countries to foster near-full employment, if necessary by availing themselves of exchange controls for balance-of-payments purposes. Such restraints on the flow of trade were, however, to be gradually, but with determination, removed as proper commercial policy would be at the heart of the postwar economic system. Proper in this sense referred to the basic U.S. precepts on reciprocity in reducing tariff barriers and in removing nearly all nontariff barriers or translating them into *ad valorem* duties in a nondiscriminatory fashion. In this, financial arrangements undertaken as a means to buttress profitable commerce—that is, the current-account management through proper exchange rate policies, convertibility for current transactions, and trade liberalization—were to support the overriding macroeconomic goal of high employment and rapid economic reconstruction of the war-devastated economies, particularly on the European continent.

In these deliberations, little attention was paid to how planned economies could fit in.[1] For one thing, the only planned economy was the Soviet Union, with a minor aside on Mongolia. Some of the negotiators were certainly hoping that the wartime alliance could be resumed in peacetime and would, in some form, lead to the liberalization of the Soviet economy as well. On the whole, little attention was reserved for the special problems of the planned economies, in spite of their mushrooming number, also because of the outbreak of the Cold War and the general feeling that the global organizations were, in fact, there to serve the interests of market-based economies.

For these and other reasons the planned economies shunned the postwar organizations and remained most critical of their institutional and behavioral features. The latter were felt to have been put in place chiefly for the benefit of a select few developed countries, which were allegedly seeking dominance through currency hegemony or by insisting upon a unilaterally favorable distribution of voting power in the management of these organizations that ran counter to the respect for greater equity in international life, on which socialist ideology insisted as a matter of principle. This stance reflected chiefly the various organizational obstacles that particularly the Soviet Union had objected to during the Bretton Woods negotiations.

Apart from politics and ideology, including the belief that a deep capitalist recession was imminent in the late 1940s, bringing the planned economies into the global economic framework was bound to encounter serious technical problems. One sequence of factors derived from the emergence of the Soviet bloc and the creation of the CMEA under the USSR's aegis. The latter exercised hegemony in various forms that, even from a purely technical point of view, would have been hard to accommodate, let alone to condone, in the global organizations. The creation of the CMEA also led to the innovation of a sequence of trade, pricing, and payments arrangements that sought not only to insulate the socialist from the capitalist world, but also to protect each of the planned economies against unplanned interferences with its economic policies from the outside.

Perhaps a much more crucial reason for the lack of interest in participating in the global organizations was economic: The cost of membership

---

1. The same applied to the developing countries, but that topic I cannot explore here (see Brabant 1991c).

far-outweighed its potential benefit (Assetto 1988, p. 65). Indeed, these IEOs then had little to offer to economies that had adopted comprehensive physical planning, adhered to strict commodity and currency inconvertibility, practiced rigid bilateralism, and operated with exchange rates that were not real prices and served no substantive function. Also, given the rapidly deteriorating east-west environment, the planned economies decided that it was not in their best interest to provide extensive economic intelligence to the IEOs that would inevitably be widely disseminated. Furthermore, they had no reason to subject their exchange regime and broader macroeconomic policies to Fund surveillance. Finally, though it was attractive to gain access to finance from the World Bank, this was obtainable only through Fund membership for which the price to pay was probably deemed to be excessive.

The technical incompatibility between the IEOs as constituted and the way the planned economies were designed to be managed can usefully be illustrated by contrasting the latter's goals with the Fund's principal purposes. The Fund's initial aim was to mobilize its resources for the stabilization of agreed-upon exchange rates with the objective of gradually eliminating exchange controls for current (in the first instance, the key current-account) transactions, promoting multilateralism, liberalizing capital flows, and similar developments whose positive functions in resource allocation are predicated on the existence of real markets. The comparatively small volume of trade of the planned economies and the fact that the bulk of it was, in any case, conducted under reciprocal BTPAs left little room indeed for stabilization. This feature became very much stronger as traditional central planning was implanted throughout Eastern Europe by the end of the 1940s and commercial relations with market economies were being forcibly curtailed. Further, the particular development strategy chosen by planned economies and the supporting planning institutions and associated policy instruments called for deliberately minimizing the role of money and external finance in fostering rapid industrialization. Not only that, these countries severely curtailed their economic interaction with external markets, they deliberately curbed the potential benefit that could be derived from balance-of-payments financing or from external financial assistance for structural change that might undermine their "socialist sovereignty," and chose to veil their national and regional development efforts in great secrecy.

In other words, the planned economies stayed away from the IEOs for a host of political, ideological, managerial, and other, more metaeconomic reasons. But even if these obstacles could have been resolved or assuaged, as they were in some cases, key features of the planning systems, even when modified over time, would have made these countries ill-suited to play a constructive role in these near-universal organs.

But one encounters a dilemma here: If centrally set plans are implemented on schedule, the planned economy has no reason to subject its exchange regime and broader macroeconomic policies to surveillance by IEOs. Yet, what the planned economies try in principle to accomplish through planning is exactly identical to what surveillance, such as by the Fund, is trying to achieve through induced macroeconomic policy mixes tied to external financing.

Indeed, although a different format for surveilling policies in planned economies may have been required, some of the principal objectives of the Fund coincided eerily with those held by the Eastern countries, and any accommodating institutional frameworks should have been quite acceptable to the latter. For example, the Fund gave a paramount role to fixed exchange rates in the medium to long term whose par value would be changed only upon fundamental disequilibria. This basic mission blended in rather well with the goals of economic stability sought by the planned economies. Barring untoward circumstances, fundamental disequilibrium could be avoided through central planning in a comparatively brief period of time, perhaps within the five-year planning compass. These countries could, therefore, have been expected to be interested in maintaining a fixed exchange rate regime. Furthermore, some being gold producers, they would have had an intrinsic interest in managing the price of gold or in policies leading up to the determination of the price of the precious metal.

Perhaps the major exception to the Fund's regime would have been the currency inconvertibility that the Eastern countries maintained, largely as a byproduct of the high priority accorded to domestic policy autonomy; but I would not argue (see Brabant 1987, pp. 357-84; 1989, pp. 304-5) that currency inconvertibility in and of itself was an immanent feature of these countries (as argued in Diebold 1979, Holzman 1987). True, only constrained convertibility for nonresidents and a limited form of commodity convertibility for tourist transactions, with restrictions suitably modified to avert conflict with Fund obligations, could have functionally emerged. And such arrangements might have been quite palatable to the Fund, particularly because currency convertibility in its true form[2] was not being enforced upon other Fund members. The most important potential dilemmas would have stemmed from the role of the dollar—a national currency—as anchor of the global monetary system, intrusive surveillance and stabilization measures prescribed without heeding the specific features of planning, and free external convertibility. But with some good will, even these obstacles could have been circumnavigated. Similar remarks can be made with respect to the GATT and the World Bank (see Brabant 1991c).

Unfortunately, the key industrial countries that were instrumental in the creation of the IEOs were on the whole patronizing towards the economic problems faced by planned economies and offered them conditions of membership that were humiliating in a number of respects. There never was a real understanding of the particular and sometimes peculiar problems posed by the economic and institutional characteristics of planned economies. These included multiple exchange rates as a necessary reflection of the tiered domestic price systems; currency and commodity inconvertibility because of the planned allocation of resources; BTPAs, particularly in intragroup relations, to facilitate trade planning; and pervasive exchange controls to help insulate domestic from foreign markets and the CMEA region from east-west relations, and thus to protect the considerable amount of policy autonomy sought by decision makers. Note that this distinctiveness of the planning framework should not be exaggerated for multiple exchange rates, artificially set administrative prices, multiple domestic and external pricing regimes, trade controls, a sizable state sector, and other features associated with planned economic administration are by no means the exclusive preserve of planning. That is to say, at least during the first decade or so, when the rules of the international regimes were, at best, incompletely adhered to even by the key members, the planned economies were asked to abide by principles and to commit themselves to policies that the bulk of the actual members did not heed themselves.

---

2. Recall that at war's end, Sweden, Switzerland, and the United States were the sole Fund members with a truly convertible currency for most current transactions. Much the same could be argued for the GATT, whose lofty principles of reciprocity, transparency, nondiscrimination, and safeguards were hardly assiduously enforced. In any case, also these could have been rendered compatible with the planning framework if serious efforts to that effect had been mustered (see Brabant 1991c).

In spite of the variety of obstacles that inhibit participation in IEOs, notably the Washington financial institutions, several Eastern countries joined or sought to join them, from about the mid-1950s on,[3] well before the economic disarray of the 1980s led to systemic changes. One may well ask why these countries did seek membership, usually without seriously bargaining about specific accommodations, in spite of the peculiarities of state trading and CMEA bilateralism, not to mention the organizational, political, and ideological hindrances. For one thing, this evolution testified to the flexibility of the IEOs in persuading some countries to join and keep others out. True, by the time the Fund was asked to come to grips with the macroeconomic problems of planned economies in the 1980s, it had slightly expanded its arsenal of policy tools particularly in the direction of making positive efforts to alleviate the burden of adjustment by restructuring supply to some degree.

This paradoxical situation can be resolved only through a dual assessment. One involves a balanced evaluation of the advantages and drawbacks of participation in IEOs with particular reference to the experience of the planned economies. The other requires that one should be fully cognizant of the major difference between many economies with less than integrated markets and planned economies: In the latter, policy makers exert considerable central control over demand and especially supply, including their external relations. This may lead to friction over who really conducts adjustment efforts, which may help explain the at times stormy relations between the IEOs, notably the Fund, and particularly Hungary, Poland, Romania, and the former Yugoslavia after they joined (Robinson, Tyson, and Woods 1988), unless the policy packages were first formulated in the country itself (Assetto 1988).[4] Unless such policies were firmly embedded in the planning environment of the targeted socialist country, of course, the adjustment program tended to be watered down. Also, conditionality conditions that were not fully predicated on the country-designed adjustment program tended to entail serious political conflict, including over the issue of reform and structural adjustment.

---

3. Recall that Czechoslovakia, Poland, and Yugoslavia (as well as China and Cuba) were charter members of the IMF and IBRD; Poland was not in the GATT, however. Czechoslovakia withdrew from the IMF-IBRD in 1954, after Poland had done so already in 1950.

4. Incidentally, the same applies to Cambodia, China, Cuba, Laos, and Vietnam, quite apart from the problems that are typical for market-based developing countries.

The planned economies joined or sought to join the IEOs not because they needed to be taught adjustment, resource mobilization, or trade policies, but because they deemed it to their advantage to be within the international regimes in place. At the least, this offers greater certainty to public as well as private partners, and indeed access to finance through the Washington institutions and to trade gains in the context of the GATT. In this connection, it is not expenditure reduction and switching that are in doubt. Rather, it is the methods used to accomplish those tasks, both technically and politically, that differ measurably for countries that by and large adhere to substantial nonmarket methods of policy formulation and implementation. Of course, the questions of policy autonomy and the ways in which international surveillance can be exercised in planned economies should not be disregarded.

Membership of the PETs in International Organizations

The economic liberalization currently pursued by the PETs will eventually fuse these economies much more profoundly into the global economy than this has been the case throughout the postwar period. This will occur through various channels. One will be the conventional exchange of trade and services, and through the mobility of production factors, notably capital flows into these countries. Another will be much more encompassing, normal participation in the IEOs and in the management and organization of the world community more generally. Because of the disappearance of the CMEA and the emerging rapprochement of the PETs notably with the EC, the opening up of these economies will inevitably entail institutional adjustments and policy reorientation in the regional organizations, particularly Europe's.

Regularization of the PETs' positions in IEOs has been on the policy agenda of the new leaderships from the transition's very inception. For those countries that were members, this new attitude towards organized economic affairs has led to strengthening their cooperation and participation as full, equal members. Others have sought regular, and active, membership in the IEOs. These include the successor states of the Soviet Union and Yugoslavia, all of which are now in the process of joining the organizations or have already done so.

Thus, all countries of Eastern Europe and the Baltic states are now members of the IMF and the World Bank; the other successor states of the Soviet Union have joined recently. However, ratification procedures, including raising the convertible currency share of membership quotas, of course, take some time so that normal operational membership may be attained only in the near term; for example, Russia did so only in July 1992, even though it joined in April 1992. Note that in some cases developed countries have advanced the required funds to enable the PET to obtain a standby loan equivalent to or higher than the required membership deposit in convertible currency. Thus, Switzerland advanced such funds from its assistance budget for the East to several successor states of the Soviet Union bent on joining the "Swiss voting group" in both the IMF and the World Bank. And to accommodate all these new clients, the number of Executive Directors with their constituencies has been raised from 22 to 24, the two new ones being allocated to Russia and Switzerland (with its group).

The status of the successor states of Yugoslavia and indeed rump Yugoslavia (that is, Serbia and Montenegro) in international organizations is still unclear, but Slovenia has requested full accession to the GATT and Bosnia-Herzegovina, Croatia, and Slovenia to the IMF and World Bank. Slovenia's request to GATT invoked the accession of Bangladesh, after its secession from Pakistan, as precedent. However, the GATT Council has since decided that Slovenia must follow regular accession procedures. A Working Party to that effect has already been established.[5] This will in all likelihood set precedents for other countries bent on seeking full contracting party status. Some of the successor states (including Bosnia-Herzegovina, Croatia, and Slovenia) will have to formally accede to the IEOs. They can be expected to do so in due course.

Except Albania and Bulgaria, all Eastern countries minus the former Soviet Union and its successors, are Contracting Parties to the General Agreement, hence participate actively in GATT.[6] Negotiations about Bulgaria's full accession, which was first requested in 1986, have received a new impetus. Countries that during their planning period held a less

---

5. See GATT document C/M/258 of 4 August 1992, pp. 4-5.

6. It should be recalled that Czechoslovakia is a charter Contracting Party in the GATT, but its status changed, in fact, after the communist *coup d'état* of February 1948, when it began to be treated as a "state-trading country," just like other planned economies. Czechoslovakia's relations in the GATT remained in this legal limbo until recently (Brabant 1991c).

than equivalent full status in the GATT (such as Czechoslovakia, Hungary, Poland, and Romania) have by now regularized their status or are in the process of renegotiating it.

The former Soviet Union acquired observer status in early 1990 and, prior to its disintegration, was eager to join the GATT as a full Contracting Party. Armenia, Estonia, Latvia, Lithuania, Moldova, Turkmenistan, and Ukraine submitted their requests beginning with June 1992 and most soon thereafter obtained observership, as did Albania. This quick action was made possible because the GATT Council meeting of 19 June 1992 decided to extend the rules agreed upon in May 1990, when the Soviet Union's request for observership was being considered, to the successor states as well as Albania.[7] This should permit all republics that request observership to obtain it very swiftly indeed. In any case, most have already been receiving assistance from the GATT in preparing their requests for observership.[8]

One may well inquire into the rationale for this sudden rush into the IEOs and what the PETs expect from such membership. The most obvious answer, pertinent to the current efforts, is, of course, that international assistance has been predicated on these countries joining the Fund in the first instance, and by implication the other IEOs. But this does not explain why some countries already in the 1950s began to explore membership or, for that matter, what other benefits the PETs may expect to derive.

In pondering the benefits and drawbacks, it is useful to distinguish conceptually between two discourses. One encompasses the present and future gains and losses that may directly ensue from belonging to a specific regime in the strict sense, other than the extraordinary assistance currently being extended. The other is the recognition that there are corresponding, if asymmetric, advantages and drawbacks of profiling a country's position on issues, irrespective of its specific place in the regime under review, thus forestalling the emergence of arrangements that narrow the arena for fruitful interaction.

For the larger PETs, the more general advantages of being within the system, rather than outside it, probably outweigh the specific gains that they can reap from joining. Once within the system, particularly the larger PETs could help shape the global institutions and their policies.

---

7. See GATT document C/M/257 of 10 July 1992, p. 3.

8. "GATT sets a special training course to guide reforming countries" (*Press communiqué* GATT/1541 of 25 May 1992).

Because of the position of some PETs, such as China and Russia, as world powers or their aspirations to obtaining such a status in due course, being absent from the near-global institutions prevents them from discharging their actual and perceived responsibilities as sovereign states in an inter-dependent world. But one should acknowledge that such participation in the global dialogue is not something on which the leadership of the PETs has been bent, at least for now. More on this issue later.

There are, of course, also drawbacks chiefly in the political domain. For better or worse, the IEOs may be seen as potentially meddling in the internal affairs of PETs. To be sure, this affords a particular negotiating posture, including in domestic squabbles over reform, and it may conceivably materialize. This is likely to be especially touchy during ongoing debates on the depth, breadth, and pace of economic transition. Even highly technical reform proposals have political overtones and social implications that will probably be contested, as a reform cannot simply be a zero-sum game. Political tangles are also felt once the reform enjoys firm consensus and is being put in place. Because some IEOs, especially the Fund, deal essentially with government bureaucracies, they cannot avoid having to walk a highly sensitive tightrope. But with a bit of good will and recognition of realities, these obstacles should not be blown out of proportion, as they have on occasion in some PETs. I shall return to these questions shortly.

Economic Cooperation in Europe and Remaking the East

Because actual cooperation to date between eastern and western Europe is discussed more fully in other chapters in this volume, here I focus only on key perspectives of regional economic organization and how it may affect the management of the global economy.

From the very beginning, the PETs have sought a formal rapprochement with the EC and EFTA. In the case of the Baltic states, Eastern European countries, some of the other successor states of the Soviet Union, and Yugoslavia and now its successor states, the ambition has been full EC membership in a not too distant future. The EC has resisted making any firm pledge of accelerated membership negotiations for its own reasons and offered instead to work out so-called Europe agreements, which give the Eastern countries a special association status.

The agreements reached to date involve notably the establishment of differential trade liberalization for most manufactures. That is to say, the EC will gradually remove its import duties on these products, usually over a five-year period, beginning in 1992. The Eastern signatory will have to reciprocate usually over a similar period of time, but with the introduction of the tariff cutbacks being delayed to the second half of the 1990s. This means that the Eastern signatory will gain a relative competitive edge over EC producers and also over outside competitors that do not benefit from a similar preferential status. Czechoslovakia,[9] Hungary, and Poland have already obtained this status. They have been working out a similar instrument with the EFTA members, but only the one with Czechoslovakia has been completed[10]; those with Hungary and Poland have apparently run into serious snags, owing mainly to disagreements on liberalizing trade in agricultural products, which is, in fact, outside the EFTA's traditional mandate, though it has been partially assigned that task in the case of the negotiations with the PETs. Negotiations between the EC and some of the other PETs, notably Bulgaria, are under way. The ongoing efforts to establish free-trade ties between EFTA and the Baltic states, Bulgaria, and Romania are expected to be concluded by the end of 1992.

The beneficial economic nature of these agreements, as distinct from the political and psychological gains they may impart, should not be exaggerated, however. Indeed, "sensitive" products, including agriculture and fisheries, but also certain manufactures, are being dealt with separately in annexes to the Europe agreements.[11] Although the EC has bound itself in principle to relax its import restrictions on these products over time as well, and this is a firm commitment in the case of iron and steel products, for example, in other cases the commitment is more in the nature of a hedged promise than a firm resolution to provide room for these products from the East in EC markets.

---

9. With the breakup of the republic in early 1993, and if a customs union can be maintained between the Czech and the Slovak republics, the essence of the agreement with the EC will apply to both successors in equal measure. Otherwise, the pact will have to be renegotiated.

10. For some detail, see GATT document C/M/258 of 4 August 1992, pp. 31-32. Sweden has signed a free trade agreement with the three Baltic states about which some details are also available in C/M/258, pp. 32-33.

11. The complete Europe agreements have been released in *Official Journal of the European Communities*, Vol. 35 (1992), Nos. L114, L115, and L116 (30 April 1992).

Improved access to developed-country markets, in the first instance in Western Europe, is pivotal to successful transformation, particularly for the smaller Eastern countries. It is the most crucial form of assistance that developed nations can extend to the Eastern economies. Lowering tariff barriers and removing some quantitative restrictions are certainly useful policy measures. However, for a number of key products, market access, including in the EC and EFTA, is still being regulated through quantitative means, although there is likely to be much less rigidity over the medium term. Now, it so happens that these sensitive products (including agriculture and fisheries, textiles and clothing, steel products, footwear, and some chemicals) account for a substantial share of the exports of the Eastern countries to the EC[12] and happen to be, at least for now, the products in which the East has an apparent comparative advantage and could quickly raise its sustainable export volume.[13]

For some of the successor states of the Soviet Union it may be unrealistic even to aspire to a special association status with either the EC or EFTA, and so these countries have negotiated, or are in the process of negotiating, special so-called partnership agreements on trade and cooperation, particularly with the EC. Agreements[14] on trade and commercial and economic cooperation were signed on 11 May 1992 with Albania and the three Baltic states. The latter three were essentially an acknowledgement that the old EC-USSR agreement was no longer applicable. All four allow for the eventual negotiation of Europe association agreements "when conditions will have been met."

---

12. In 1990, the combined export shares of sensitive product categories (defined as agricultural products, textile and clothing, and iron and steel products), as distinct from products that face specific import constraints, to western markets as a whole still amounted to 32 percent for Czechoslovakia, 41 percent for Hungary, and 37 percent for Poland, after a rapid expansion in exports of other goods in 1988-1990 (see UNECE 1992, pp. 79-81). The shares in exports to the EC are higher than these magnitudes. In some cases, notably in iron and steel, the Central European countries were close to exhausting the ceiling of the quotas arranged under voluntary export-restraint (VER) agreements.

13. Data compilations for 1991 are unfortunately still too incomplete to permit full coverage. In the case of Poland, for example, export volume in 1991 increased only for metallurgical products (by 18.4 per cent) and agricultural products (by 25.6 per cent); and the smallest drop (2.9 per cent) in total export volume was recorded for processed foods (*Handel zagraniczny, styczeń-grudzień 1991, dane ostateczne* [Warsaw, Główny Urząd Statystyczny, March 1992], p. 23). Most of these goods were sold in Western European markets, particularly the EC.

14. These are the so-called "first" or "second-generation" agreements, as distinct from the Europe agreements, which are third-generation agreements, as explained in chapter 4.

These various arrangements may entail some diversion of trade in favor of Eastern partners, chiefly in the form of new exports to Western European markets, as a result of both special discriminatory arrangements and increased competition in EC markets. The direct effect thereof on industrial countries is likely to remain confined, given the small scale of Eastern exports of manufactures and agricultural products. Even for developing countries as a group, the larger presence of Eastern countries in western markets is not likely to engender any substantial loss in competitiveness. Neither is there evidence of competition in labor markets. The migration flows that have thus far materialized have been chiefly on account of tourism, now that individuals from the East can readily travel abroad; commercial and diplomatic or quasi diplomatic ties; and to the exchange of students, scholars, and technicians. Certainly, some professionals have found occupations in western countries but their numbers have remained insignificant. In fact, free movement of people is one of the "four freedoms" that will now be settled in negotiations between the EC and the Eastern signatories of the Europe agreements sometime in the future. For now, however, it forms part and parcel of the annex protocols to the agreements.

Although the formal rearrangements in the EC and EFTA have been minor in scope, the overall framework for east-west cooperation, particularly on the European continent, has undergone fundamental changes, not only because of the events in the eastern part of Europe and their repercussions, but also because of autonomous changes in attitudes towards European integration in the western part of Europe, notably the conclusion of the single market by 1993, and the interlinkages between events in the eastern and western parts of Europe. All this has been exerting negative as well as positive effects on the rest of the world in general and economic relations in particular, and will continue to do so in a changing mix that on balance, with solid recovery in the East, should become increasingly more positive as time progresses. But this vast topic of inquiry is really beyond the reach of this chapter.

The Tasks of the Transitions and the International Framework

Whereas the prospects for economic recovery in some PETs are improving at this stage, the early signs of a mild upturn in the pace of economic activity, notably of some Central European countries, or a slowing down of the contraction, notably in some of the Balkan countries, should be treated cautiously. They may be harbingers of steadier improvements in the distant offing. But these potential gains are not likely to materialize in the next year or so. Constraints on external payments in nearly all PETs and continuing difficulties with controlling inflation in most suggest that these countries will on the whole continue their protracted austerity, holding absorption to comparatively low levels, for some time to come.

Elsewhere, however, and this includes most of the successor states of the Soviet Union, as well as Albania and some of the successor Yugoslav states, the problems ahead are much more daunting. The prospect for the near term is for a further sharp contraction in levels of economic activity and political uncertainty about crucial markers of the societal reform programs. Until such a basic consensus on transformation can be found and sustained, credible economic stabilization can be enforced, and decisive measures put in train to begin with the restructuring of these, in some respects footloose, economies, a sharp reversal in their economic fortunes is unlikely to crystallize.

The transitions as they have been charted to date exhibit major differences in scope, depth, and range. Even so, the time frame of even the most modest blueprint on desirable transition policies is now widely recognized to stretch far into the future, its duration ranging from one to several decades. This is much longer than had erroneously been assumed at the time the revolutions broke out by those advocates of the market framework who thought that markets would emerge spontaneously, and all necessary adjustments would take their cue from there. Furthermore, the transitions are likely to lasts much longer for most of the successor states of the Soviet Union than, say, for the Central European countries. While many arduous tasks still lie ahead, the latter countries have nonetheless already undertaken important steps in the direction of macroeconomic stabilization and some key initiatives that will in time result in significant structural change.

But much remains to be done before any of these economies will be able to embark on a solid path of self-sustainable economic growth. *A fortiori*, the tasks ahead in those countries where the transition policies remain a subject of acute sociopolitical debate, such as in many of the successor states of the Soviet Union, are even more daunting. It would be unrealistic to expect that these complicated matters will be resolved quickly or that the transition processes of these countries can be completed any time sooner than now appears to be the case for, say, the Central European countries.

It is in the interest of the global community to condense the length of this period of adversity, certainly now that realities have amply negated the simplistic assumptions on built-in stabilizers and automatic adjustments, by accelerating the transition through proper policies that are motivated by the need to identify a new, sustainable growth path in the PETs at the earliest opportunity. Although the agenda for the transition was complex from the very beginning, that confronting the international community at this stage, when fundamental issues of the purposes of the transformation remain unsettled in all too many countries, is utterly daunting. Yes, the tasks ahead are frighteningly complex. Yet, all PETs deserve considerable attention, in my view, certainly more than they have received thus far.

One reason is that a reversal of economic fortunes in the East, hence a resumption of growth, albeit from a much lowered base, will stabilize the sociopolitical situation in the PETs and, by extension, on the European continent as a whole. Also, a solid economic recovery in the East will impart a positive growth impulse to the world economy as a whole, opening up opportunities for trade and payments based on standard criteria of competition in global markets. It is, therefore, of paramount importance that available assistance resources be targeted in the proper way, and in as much harmony as possible with the agreed-upon transformation policies. Finally, the PETs that are in all but name developing countries, such as Albania; Macedonia; and the Caucasian and Central Asian successor states of the Soviet Union, deserve international assistance on the same grounds as those underpinning the traditional rationale for development assistance.

As detailed notably in the chapters by Losoncz and Smolik, the response of the international community to the adversities in the East has been substantial. Not only have many countries pledged aid, they have also found it necessary to resort to two focal aid coordination organs—the Fund and the Commission of the EC, with the former being the key to unlocking the assistance pledged chiefly by the latter. And the EC Commission is not only acting on behalf of its membership but also on behalf of the so-called G-24, essentially the membership of the Organisation for Economic Co-operation and Development (OECD).

The key question that arises here is whether these coordinating organs can deliver efficiently on the mandates they have been entrusted with. Let me start with the Fund, whose role in the world economy and possible benefits for PETs are not the subject proper of this chapter. Nonetheless, owing to the Fund's central role in getting the assistance process under way and to assess how well it can perform this task, it is instructive to recall key features of why, in the past, the relationship between planned economies and the Fund, and to some degree also the World Bank, was at times beset by serious conflicts; and why the Eastern countries remained on the sidelines of the policy debates in GATT. The latter is easiest to explain because in GATT all planned economies were *de facto* treated as state-trading countries, thus subjected to special rules that were either formally enacted (as in the cases of Poland and Romania) or that followed from the invocation of specific provisions for those (notably Hungary and the former Yugoslavia) that were ostensibly admitted or formally treated (as Czechoslovakia) as regular contracting parties.

Conflicts with the financial institutions may have had various origins, some of which were cited in the first section. As far as technical matters are concerned, however, friction occasionally arose because the standard adjustment policies recommended by the multilateral financial institutions did not blend well with administrative planning, although *in se* the task of adjustment under planning or market conditions is identical: Expenditure reduction and switching must be accomplished to eliminate deficits on external account. But the Fund's stylized policy on surveillance or conditionality, both heavily rooted in the assumption that functioning markets exist, clashed with the planning environment favored by the Eastern countries.

A few stylized aspects of adjustment policies typically embraced by market economies under Fund conditionality may facilitate understanding of what Fund-type adjustment policies are all about and the problems that may arise during the transition. The common adjustment measures of Fund and Bank policies focus on austerity so as to cut demand through shifts in policy stances, changes in instruments, and perhaps modifications in economic institutions that are intended to promote indirect or market incentive mechanisms, as noted, epitomized by the slogan "getting the prices right." A typical adjustment program consists of a combination of measures aimed at improving the current account through stabilization policies and efficiency through target adjustments in domestic production, distribution, and foreign trade as a tradeoff for obtaining some financing. The conditionality involved consists of the preconditions for adjustment, the fulfillment of quantitative and qualitative policy targets upon which further disbursement of the loans agreed upon in the adjustment package is conditioned, and actions that governments commit themselves to undertake, although these are not normally accompanied with sanctions for noncompliance. These policy actions are primarily concerned with demand management, although over the past decade or so both the Fund and the Bank have increasingly turned also to stimulating supply.

The above suggests that there is normally a tie-in between additional loans, usually derived from estimating the putative "resource gap," assuming that recommended adjustment measures will be realized, and the recommended adjustment measures. Participants in the negotiations normally select a quantum target as well as a time sequence for improving the current account. The decision on the amount by which the current account needs to be corrected over a given period of time is a function of the volume and timing of the inflow of official and private capital. Because it is constrained by conditions in international capital markets, the Fund does not have complete discretion in choosing the depth and speed of a country's adjustment, of course. But it can nevertheless exert considerable leverage over the concrete terms at which commercial banks may be willing to keep lending, especially when the potential beneficiary is heavily indebted or faces problems with orderly debt servicing.

In the case of the PETs, however, the Fund's assumptions are much more contentious. Not only can the Fund, at best, finance a comparatively small share of the identified gap. That gap itself is subject to much uncertainty given the uncharted course of the transition. And it is simplistic to assume that once a program with a PET is in place, the pledged western economic, technical, and financial assistance will be forthcoming and at a suitable point in time.

The second step in an adjustment program revolves around issues pertaining to domestic macroeconomic balance, especially in fiscal and monetary affairs, and economic stabilization. Domestic demand needs to be set at a long-term sustainable level without aggravating imbalances and inflation. If prices are not moving flexibly in response to shifts in demand and supply, inflationary pressures tend to be disguised or repressed. But they leave an imprint on the economy just the same. Stabilization as a rule requires a cut in total absorption so that real expenditure shrinks. Austerity usually has a disproportionate impact on investment, which by lowering the growth of capital reduces the capacity to produce over time. These measures need not depress levels of economic activity. Recent experience has nonetheless demonstrated that Fund-mandated adjustment programs entail a contraction of economic activity, in some cases counteracting the improvement in economic efficiency that the adjustment program was intended to bring about.[15]

Adjustment programs such as those enacted in the 1980s under the aegis of the Fund and the Bank rely overwhelmingly on policy instruments that are appropriate in a setting with integrated markets and that have their largest impact on aggregate demand. However, in an environment where there are serious rigidities in markets or where markets are not fully free by policy design or legacies of past developments, output losses may result that far exceed any efficiency gains from better resource allocation. In some cases, the mandated curbing of demand may be so counterproductive, for lack of any automatic or induced response on the supply side, that the PET may sink into a low-level equilibrium trap. The real tradeoff between adjustment and growth that exists in many economies that have undergone Fund-mandated adjustment would tend to be magnified in the case of the PETs. This potential outcome should be fully heeded in conceptualizing the adjustment programs if constructive balance-of-payments assistance is to be earmarked for the PETs.

Because PETs hope to move towards market status as quickly as possible, prospectively the previous conflict with standard policies of the Fund and Bank will presumably become much less pronounced. At any rate, these countries will seek to avoid problems to the degree that macroeconomic surveillance and outside policy advice remain compatible with overall domestic socioeconomic precepts. But the conflict among static efficiency and sustainable growth is bound to arise in the PETs too. If only for that reason, a program for adjusting to external or domestic pressures in the PETs and monitoring its performance must necessarily be phrased differently from the way in which stabilization has traditionally been accomplished in either market or planned economies. There are two fundamental reasons for this. One refers to the pervasive legacies of central planning, the sort of specific policy and systemic antecedents of these economies under planning that are readily ignored, yet must be

---

15. This conflict between economic efficiency and the need to improve the current account may stem from policy "overkill," rather optimistic assumptions of the potential for expenditure switching to narrow the gap between revenues and payments, bottlenecks in case of import cuts cannot be made up from domestic sources, and disproportionate compression of investment activity (see Brabant 1991c).

clearly understood and factored into the policy deliberations and the package of measures ultimately agreed upon. The other recognizes that, in part because of these legacies, macroeconomic management must include active intervention on the supply side to sensitize economic agents into undertaking the structural changes required to install the rudiments of the coveted markets. For the near future, adjustment even in the PET will require a much more varied policy regimen and institutional setting than envisioned in orthodox policies, such as those largely adhered to by the Fund (Brabant 1990, 1991a). I shall return to this issue later in the chapter.

Assigning Overall Coordination Tasks

It is by now fairly clear that steering the transition is a much more daunting task than simply enacting a standard demand-management stabilization package. If only for that reason, efforts to introduce far-reaching structural changes in the Eastern economies deserve comprehensive international assistance, obviously within the ambit of the resources that can realistically be mustered. However, that assistance itself needs to be managed in a way best suited to imparting positive effects to the transitions, while containing any negative repercussions for other countries. In particular, in addition to meeting emergency humanitarian needs, the assistance should be viewed largely as a catalyst, both in lending credibility to the transformation processes in PETs and in laying the groundwork for mobilizing private initiative, including FDI.

Part of the assistance to the transitions will emerge in tandem with the more active merger of these countries into the international community, while ensuring that global affairs are managed in the interest of all parts of the world economy. Until these countries can begin to play such a full-fledged constructive role, it will be in the interest of the international community to provide assistance. In my view this is not now the case. It is not because of the organs chosen for delivering assistance as well as the way in which the conceptualization and delivery of assistance have progressed so far.

As mentioned, the Fund is *the* critical actor in getting aid under way, with the EC being the coordinating body for the G-24 donors in the case of Eastern Europe and the looser "Washington Conference[16]" format for assistance to the CIS states and Georgia. Virtually all western assistance, other than that rendered for emergency and humanitarian reasons, has been made contingent on the potential beneficiary PET reaching an agreement with the Fund. This holds even with respect to disbursements of funds in support of various kinds of technical assistance for the transition, not just providing stabilization loans or more general support for external payments. For countries not yet in the Fund, such as the Yugoslav successor states at this stage, assistance efforts are conditioned on the country seeking accession. This involves, among other instances of synchronization, coming to a working arrangement with the exploratory Fund mission that normally advises changes in trade and payment practices, recommends the Fund quota assessed in special drawing rights (SDRs) to the Board of Executive Directors, and may smooth the way to the signing of the first standby agreement with the Fund. In any case, in the course of these exploratory exchanges of views on macroeconomic policies, as well as considerations about the underlying efficiency of the microeconomic sphere, there is ample scope to pass Fund precepts on to local decision makers.

I realize that the above charges are loaded ones. If only for that reason they deserve a tightly reasoned justification, for which this chapter, unfortunately, does not provide adequate space. Let me here simply assert that the tasks of the transition are too complex to be entrusted to any firmly entrenched multilateral organ. I shall return to this in the last section. As regards my concerns about the IMF's involvement, they stem largely from the specialized nature of that organization in contrast to the far-reaching, unprecedented changes in the PETs that must be fully factored into assistance packages. For one thing, the IMF's credo runs fundamentally counter to managing operational, tailored-made assistance programs. With all due respect for the professionalism of the Fund's rightly respected

---

16. So-called because the disintegration of the union in late 1991 led to the U.S. initiative to call a conference in Washington, DC, 22-23 January 1992, on conceptualizing and streamlining assistance to the successor states (other than the Baltics) among the principal international and regional agencies, and donor countries involved. Since then a second meeting was held in Lisbon (23-24 May 1992) and a third in Tokyo (29-30 October 1992). The latter signaled a shift from discussing assistance in five segments (food, medicine, energy, shelter, and technical assistance) to country lending. Aside from the EC, Japan, the United States, and the principal multilateral agencies, some 47 countries took part in the first meeting, most as observers; their number in Tokyo reached 70 countries and 19 multilateral organizations.

staff, the nature of the transition is uncharted territory for everyone involved. The tasks ahead require considerable imagination on how to reactivate supply, something that Fund surveillance has not been very good at. The Fund certainly does not have ample experience in assisting reforms of former planned economies and whatever knowledge has been accumulated, to the extent it is still relevant to the PET, it has not been very encouraging (Assetto 1988, Dembinski and Morisset 1991).

The risk of imposing Fund orthodoxy upon a delicately balanced, if not outrightly precarious, domestic sociopolitical situation virtually without precedent does not seem advisable, given the unprecedented problems faced by the PETs. Moreover, because it is a universal organization, it is intrinsically difficult for it to function along guidelines that are special for one group of countries. The recent political brouhaha over whether it should now extend loans to Russia or not is illustrative of the point. As a technical organ entrusted with ensuring that current accounts are manageable, it should not, of course, lend to Russia at this stage. However, political expediency at the moment is such that the IMF is being forced to renege on its own norms for judging packages in support of economic stabilization. This is not a healthy situation for the global economy.

In the same vein, I would argue that it was a serious error of judgment to entrust the coordination of the efforts by the G-24 to the Commission of the EC at a time that this organ was already overloaded with its own agenda, including the completion of the single market; moving towards a unified currency (the ecu); and looking beyond all that to social and political union. Also, the Commission has attempted, admittedly not very successfully, to strengthen its hands as a mover in foreign policy in launching its program of assisting the PETs. Moreover, the Commission even less than the Fund had any comparative advantage at all in coming to grips with the *problématique* of the transition, let alone in coordinating the efforts of its own members and outsiders as concerns the delivery of assistance to the East. The assistance package must consist of far more than simply keeping record of who is giving what to whom at which particular point in time or than of mounting mission after mission ostensibly to find the facts that should enable the Commission to aim at the kind of efficient delivery of assistance.

In launching this criticism, I do not, of course, wish to disparage the generosity of the many donor countries, given their own tight economic situation, or the earnest attempts of the Commission's staff to perform under unprecedented circumstances. Neither do I wish to deny, for that

matter, that some benefits from all these efforts have devolved to the
transitions. Aside from humanitarian and foodstuff aid, however, the
benefits have been overwhelmingly in the form of rents accruing to the
select few with connections rather than crystallizing into catalysts for
what the PETs would seem to require to move towards democracy and,
given the topic here, especially the creation of market-based economic
systems.

Global Opportunities and Challenges

The emerging new framework for east-west economic cooperation offers
opportunities for revamping management styles within the context of
existing economic, financial, monetary, and trade regimes, now with the
full participation of the Eastern countries. But other measures are required
to ensure that the interests of other countries will be heeded. This is
especially important because, in spite of the commitment to additionality
(that is, resources will not be diverted away from traditional developing
countries) and on the whole nondiscrimination against the south, there
simply cannot be any guarantee that this stance can be indefinitely maintained, particularly since it is clear that the East will need support over
the long haul and on a much larger scale than had originally been envisaged.

With the opening up of the PETs and their more active participation in
all forms of international economic relations, management of the global
economy should—and could—be adjusted with a view to coming effectively to grips in a more coherent and consistent manner with the salient
economic problems that confront the global community on the basis of
broadly agreed-upon development priorities. For now, however, far-
reaching concertation of policies remains a distant goal. The new international realities might also create a sufficiently ambient atmosphere for
reconfiguring key aspects of the global economic framework so as to
attune its institutional foundations better to ongoing and prospective
policy concerns. Other countries too stand to benefit from such a better
focusing and concertation at the global level. But this outcome can materialize only in a longer perspective, if only because the tasks of converting
the East into market economies are immense. As the course of the transitions to date has shown, deeply rooted structural problems can be re-

solved only over time and with considerable commitment and societal forbearance. It will also lay claim to vast outside assistance, financial as well as other, to alleviate the adjustment burden and anchor the emerging markets more firmly and in an acceptable time frame. It is especially important that more open, liberal trade policies be pursued. If only for that reason, it is vital that the multilateral trading system be restored and continuously improved, including by bringing the Uruguay Round soon to a successful conclusion.

Improved coordination of international economic and other assistance to the East and additional efforts to attune such assistance better to the requirements of the transitions are important tasks ahead to mitigate the possibly adverse impacts of the changes brought about by the new environment for east-west cooperation. More effective international assistance can speed up the transformation processes in the East and expedite the moment when positive growth can be resumed, thereby beginning to generate the expected gains from the transformation of the eastern part of Europe for partner countries, including developing countries. Concurrently, increased availability and greater transparency of information, including regarding the newly built international linkages, should measurably facilitate the international monitoring process, particularly the identification of new economic opportunities.

It is a remarkable paradox that the global economic framework envisaged at Bretton Woods can now perhaps be implemented, but it would hardly be very relevant to the problems that confront the world in the 1990s and beyond. Thus, all efforts to introduce special arrangements for the former planned economies in the context of the GATT are now superfluous. The real motivation underlying these efforts (see Brabant 1991c) has not, of course, been overhauled by events. Once the PETs succeed in implanting viable markets in the broad sense, their role in the trade system will be very similar to that of market economies at a medium level of development. Until that stage can be reached, however, it would be useful to seek some accommodation for the trade-related aspects of the transition. This would be especially pertinent for delineating the characteristics of the transition to trade and foreign-exchange liberalization that has not so far been factored into scenarios of how countries can mesh themselves harmoniously into the global economy, as discussed earlier.

The salient problems of the former planned economies in the Washington financial institutions were essentially confined to two. One was the issue of currency convertibility and how best to manage adjustment with external financial support. Once the transition will be well under way and economic agents will begin to adapt their behavior, the PETs will need to manage their economies through market institutions and instruments. Until then, however, they face stiff foreign-exchange constraints that must be weathered in part through their relationship with the Fund and the World Bank. Rather than rely primarily on demand-driven adjustment programs, the proper menu of policies that PETs could profitably explore must include a component that fosters structural change through positive supply actions. This could be done by modifying standard adjustment programs or by setting up special arrangements for the PETs, such as a discriminatory payments facility. But it is doubtful whether these institution will wish to modify their "proven" menus (Corbo 1990).

Much the same type of comment would appear applicable to the World Bank's agenda, whose shift away from project financing to structural adjustment programs has entailed a particular development philosophy. That rests primarily on a pronounced advocacy of private enterprise, market-type economic activity, with a strong tilt towards dismantling institutions; policy instruments; macroeconomic policies; and behavioral guidelines that are perceived to hinder market-inspired entrepreneurial activity, whether of domestic or foreign origin. This recipe has been enacted also in the PETs, with disastrous consequences to date. It would seem hopeless to anticipate behavior on the part of economic agents conforming to market criteria when markets do not exist, or they can be expected to perform very poorly, at least for the foreseeable future, and economic agents are bewildered by what the market is all about.

As regards relations on the European continent, once the PETs reach a firm democratic base for decision making and transform their economies so that they can be steered primarily through market-based decisions, there is no reason for these countries to be treated any differently from other credible applicants for accession to the EC, for funding from the European financial institutions, or from participation in the emerging monetary institutions and the all-European monetary regime. But that stage evidently depends critically on the PETs' resolving, mainly on their own strengths, the wide range and depth of transition difficulties.

Whereas these challenges must in the first instance be met by the PETs themselves, the multilateral agencies could help out by adapting their mainstream *modi operandi* and precepts to the immediate and evolving tasks at hand. Because this is not likely to be easy, one might be inclined to contemplate in earnest the possibility of replacing the existing institutions. Newly conceived entities would in principle be in a better position from the start to accommodate countries whose economic conditions, systemic or otherwise, diverge from the context of the mainstream developed economies. However, such can be seriously entertained only if there is ample ground to assume that the international community would be prepared to adopt a set of principles for such regimes that differ from those in place.

In the light of the international debate during the past two decades or so, there would presently appear to be little chance of obtaining a broad consensus among key actors in the global economy on the basic framework of cooperation and its underlying principles and conditions in alternative regimes and institutions. As a result, accommodation for countries and economic models that fit incompletely into the existing regimes and their underlying multilateral economic institutions will have to be sought from within, rather than from outside, the various organs in place.

An honest attempt to usher the PETs more fully into the existing international regimes will, therefore, need a transition phase. Insiders would be assured that some measures will be taken by new applicants and countries that previously could not fully adhere to the agreed discipline to harmonize their systems with those of the regimes in place and the major actors therein. At the same time, such transitional accession would enable the PETs to access some of the benefits of the regime. In this way, the international community could avoid deliberately or by neglect undermining support for the ongoing reform process in PETs. It would also provide some assurance that the transition processes stay on the course of harmonizing the economic features of PETs that now inhibit fuller participation in the international economy. Because this is largely uncharted territory, a successful conclusion of the deliberations will by necessity depend on creative, imaginative proposals being formulated by all parties involved, that is, the PETs themselves, the multilateral organizations, as well as the insiders.

Towards a New Assistance Approach

Here I wish to explain the challenge I mounted in an earlier section, namely that in view of the complexity of the transition it would seem justified to adopt a more comprehensive approach in which each of the existing IEOs and even some regional ones would have its particular role to play (for instance, the IMF in current-account stabilization measures, the World Bank in lending for structural purposes, some institution to oversee the evolution of the trade regimes of the PETs, some institution that seeks to usher the Eastern countries into the "European" fold and is willing to mobilize resources to achieve that end, and some payments institution to manage temporary derogations from the accepted global regimes). If these various efforts could be coordinated by an organ specially created to deal with the particular issues besetting the transition from communism and central planning to democracy and market-based decision making, which would not require the renegotiation of existing regimes *ab ovo*, I feel that the overall cost of the transition, both for the PETs and other states as well as multilateral organizations, would be smaller than what is now coming to the fore.

Such an organ would have three vital tasks that an existing specialized agency, such as the Fund or the EC Commission, would find it difficult to accomplish. It would have to ascertain what the transition is all about and whether there is a reasonable sociopolitical consensus that plans can be carried out. Second, it would have to ascertain to what extent these programmatic policies hinge on obtaining external resources, financial and otherwise, and whether potential donors can muster sufficient support, including among their electorate, to mobilize these means. And most important, the coordinating body would have to ensure that whatever resources are appropriated will be mobilized in the most effective way, as measured by the degree to which the resources are fully blended in with the envisaged transition agenda, and indeed help speed up its implementation and extend its remit.

The actual management of the policies underlying such an approach should, in my view, be entrusted to a fairly small group of skilled macroeconomists and financial diplomats who act on the authority of some outside organization. And the latter will necessarily have to be the major funder or coordinator of the resources that will be mobilized in donor countries to the benefit of the transition. My preference would be for the EC on the grounds that the remaking of Europe is, after all, a supreme European task. Note that I am manifestly not advocating that the EC or its Commission itself get involved in the formulation and implementation of transition policies.

Regardless of what avenue the PETs choose, a major structural shift in the postwar global economic framework is bound to ensue. Although one cannot expect governments to lose sight of politics, a dispassionate analysis of the feasible and desirable should take cognizance of the fact that the newly emerging democracies cannot quickly be brought into the "liberal" economic, social, and political frameworks of Western Europe. Whereas moving resolutely toward a united Europe based on democratic principles may be a highly desirable medium to long-run objective, for the time being the Eastern countries are not ready to assume fully the responsibilities associated with playing their "rightful" role in the concert of nations and the western partners are not quite willing to absorb the adjustment costs required to accommodate the East overnight.

I have also argued the case *for* providing substantial western assistance to the transitions in the East, but of a fundamentally different character than what has thus far been mooted. It would call for a much more involved, comprehensive approach to managing global economic interdependence in general and how best the PETs can be brought into that regime in a constructive manner. This would require fuller commitment to jointly shape the transitions on the basis of domestically innovated programs. Gaining current-account convertibility in old as well as new PETs should then form but one element of a much more demanding transformation agenda.

The principal elements of this agenda should consist, on the one hand, of economic stabilization, whose best modalities may or may not be identical to those that have recently been applied. But structural transformation in the broad sense should form an integral part of the policy concerns leading up to the formulation of a stabilization agenda. It would include privatization in the sense of removing the political organs from micromanaging these economies; commercializing public enterprises; seeing to the rapid development of the financial infrastructure, starting with agencies to collect and channel savings; the firm establishment of property rights, notably seeing to it that public property rights are carefully monitored; and many other aspects of remaking the East.

In such a broader tackling of the issues at hand, a coherent and well-defined program of assistance could play a critical role in improving security and confidence on the part of economic agents in general, including, of course, consumers, and seeing to it that proper adjustments are introduced when the original planks are no longer realistic for one reason or another. It would be critical if all this could be poured into a second recovery program for Europe, as suggested in some quarters (see UNECE 1991b, 1992). This could provide the psychological atmosphere required to give an elan to the transition policies under way, all of which are increasingly suffering in one way or another from fatigue, disappointment, and impatience.

Unlike most participants in the debates on remaking Europe, who have written off regional economic cooperation, I have tried elsewhere (notably Brabant 1990, 1991a) to offer cogent arguments why this may well turn out to be a costly and unnecessary policy error. More than casual thought should, therefore, be allocated to the proper forms in which such trade could best be accommodated and what needs to be done to allow these countries to work out such a more productive relationship with the world economy. The repercussions of remaking Eastern Europe and, in the end, the European economy are many. Some point in the direction of the need to reformulate the postwar global economic framework in more than one respect. Especially critical is how the PETs fit into it and how their position could prospectively be enhanced through reforms of the financial, monetary, or trade regimes singly or in combination.

Regardless of the institutional and conceptual frameworks for assistance that one may envisage, it bears to recall that successful transformation hinges critically on the ability of the Eastern countries to penetrate world markets on a competitive basis. That depends in part on the economic restructuring under way in the East. But it is also a function of the degree to which world markets remain open to market-based competitive forces. Much remains to be done in this respect. Some efforts have been made to relax restrictions on a discriminatory basis, including by the EC and EFTA. It would be even more important to seize the opportunity provided by the historic turnaround in the East to restore and reinforce basic elements of a multilateral trading world.

Conclusions

One of the greatest challenges facing the global community at this juncture is the management of economic, political, and security changes taking place throughout the East. Remaking global relations in line with conditions that prevail today and are likely to emerge in the years to come is not just a task for diplomatists. Neither is it something that can be entrusted only to one or a few key industrial powers. Certainly, hegemons may play a pivotal role in this process. Without proper adaptations of international regimes and their associated institutions, however, it is difficult to envision how a more harmonious world could be constructed by making hay of the historic chance emanating from the Eastern European revolutions. This is particularly so in Europe. With the prospect of establishing pluralistic societies anchored to market-based decision making throughout the East, the divide in Europe could be closed over time. Eventual fusion of countries into all-European cooperation requires several actions that would quickly change the landscape of the PETs.

In this context, one can pose the question of whether the potential impacts on east-west trade, payments, economic cooperation, and integration plans should be dealt with in a comprehensive framework, of which rendering east-west assistance should be one principal component. Or would it be more productive to let markets take care of most of the east-west repercussions if only to minimize interference with the incipient reorganization of the economies in Eastern Europe? There is something to be said for either position. I would favor the first one on the ground that the greatest support for the PETs should be mustered from the means at hand. These include domestic resources, the potential for fruitful commercial interaction, as well as external economic assistance.

What needs to be stressed at this stage, in my view, is the concentration of national, regional, and international efforts on rebuilding a method of conducting international relations, including finance, trade, and payments, that would function as easily and successfully as the one that was slowly regained in Western Europe after World War II. In the broad sense, the PETs' daunting transition agenda and the fact that the transition will last a long time indeed would seem to require some far-reaching reform of the global economic framework and its main institutional pillars. This cannot be achieved quickly, certainly not within any reasonable time frame for moving forward with democracy and laying, anchoring, and cementing in "market institutions" in the East. And because the tasks ahead in PETs now are vastly more complex than simply managing the current account, it would be useful to appoint a purely temporary *ad hoc* managing organ that would formulate, help implement, and monitor cooperation about suitable adjustment policies, the gestation of market economies, and the desirable speed of this process.

6

Official Western Assistance for the Transition of the East

Joseph E. Smolik

When the leaders of the seven largest industrialized countries (G-7) took the decision in July 1989 to entrust the EC with the coordination of western assistance for economic transformation in the east, only Hungary and Poland qualified for support. During the next year, in the wake of the political changes throughout eastern Europe, assistance from the G-24 was formally extended to Albania, Bulgaria, Czechoslovakia, Romania, and Yugoslavia; and after the declaration of their independence, to Estonia, Latvia, and Lithuania (in October 1991). All of these countries have joined or applied for membership in the international financial institutions, as detailed in chapter 5.

With the breakup of the Soviet Union and the emergence of the CIS as policy-making entities, the number of countries embarking on the transformation of their economic systems and requiring external assistance has doubled again. (For the sake of brevity, in what follows, whenever the CIS is used as a shorthand for the successor states of the Soviet Union, other than the Baltic states, Georgia is conceptually included as well, even though it does not form part of the formal arrangement.) In terms of population size, and perhaps the magnitude and range of the problems to

Economic Affairs Officer, United Nations Economic Commission for Europe, Geneva, Switzerland. The views expressed here are not necessarily those of the United Nations.

be tackled, the increase in demand for support is considerably larger. These developments pose unprecedented challenges—and opportunities—for these countries individually and in their group context, but also for the international community's marshaling of resources for assistance, organization, and vision.

In this chapter, I first examine the diverse approaches to western assistance and the various goals being pursued. Next I quantify the volume of assistance earmarked for the East other than the former Soviet Union, which I deal with next. In the fourth section, I examine the various kinds of financial assistance from the west. A brief evaluation of the western assistance effort to date concludes the chapter.

Approaches to and Objectives of Providing Aid

From the very inception of the cited international initiative, there has been broad agreement on the ultimate goals. Foreign assistance is to help the PETs develop democratic political systems, create market-based economies, and reintegrate themselves into the world economy. Humanitarian aid may be necessary to foster the transition process in its early stages. In addition, the western community also has national security interests in seeing the PETs achieve political stability, an acceptable level of living, and a sharp reversal in environmental degradation in these countries. In the longer term, the East constitutes a potentially huge market for western goods and, in certain cases, a source of raw materials.

Achieving the above-mentioned goals is an unprecedented task requiring, among other things, the re-creation of legal and institutional frameworks essential for the efficient functioning of markets, for regaining economic stabilization, for fostering structural change on a broad scale, and, in the end, for establishing the prerequisites for sustained economic growth. The private sector has been assigned a key role by the new Eastern governments and western donors. This is reflected, for example, in the statutes of the EBRD.

In the light of the difficult financial situation faced by the eastern countries during the early stages of transition, external support has been indispensable. It has been advanced in the form of improved access to western markets (see UNECE 1992), wide-ranging technical assistance, and various types of financial support provided by the G-24, the international financial institutions, and, in some cases, the foreign private sector. In the longer term, however, economic growth is to be derived chiefly on the basis of these countries' own resources and foreign private capital. But in developing the public infrastructure a continuing role is seen for the development banks. In general, western governments and also the international financial institutions have tended to view their financial contributions as exceptional and temporary.

Foreign capital is seen as instrumental for easing balance-of-payments constraints and bringing in managerial and marketing skills and new technology. To this end the transition economies have enacted legislation permitting foreign investment, launched privatization programs, and negotiated a network of investment protection and double-taxation agreements with the rest of the world. Many western governments have granted investment guarantees to cover the operations of their enterprises in the PETs and have given the East greater market access with a view to increasing the attractiveness of the PETs to private capital. The EBRD and the International Finance Corporation (IFC) in particular are designed to act as catalysts for FDI.

Virtually all aspects of the transition to market-based economic systems require additional capital resources, in many cases from abroad. The major elements of the transition process (see UNECE 1991a, chapter 4) require substantial injections of technical assistance (see UNECE 1990, chapter 1) and finance. Among the many tasks that could be singled out, I detail below some of the most pressing ones. The first five are key to introducing coherent transition policies. Whereas the others do not strictly form part and parcel of the transition process, they are legacies of the former sociopolitical systems that must be removed as quickly as possible.

Perhaps foremost is the required financial and technical assistance to re-create the institutions of the market. These range from having a constitutional infrastructure to the nitty-gritty of facilitating intermediation between demand for and supply of all kinds of goods and services, perhaps most notably banking services.

Second, substantial technical assistance is needed to upgrade human capital. Even though the educational and skill levels of manpower in the PETs are generally high, there is a widespread need to develop the skills necessary to thrive in a market environment.

Third, all kinds of assistance will be needed to bolster economic restructuring and thus shift the product mix towards goods that can be globally marketed on a competitive basis. An essential requirement thereof is that inputs and technology in production be used more efficiently. Such improvements are to be achieved, among others, through privatization; FDI; and creating a modern business infrastructure, including banking systems, telecommunications, and transportation. Major restructuring in the areas of taxation and expenditure systems is also essential.

Fourth, economic stabilization and balance-of-payments support are required to eliminate inherited economic imbalances and implement fundamental reforms (such as freeing domestic prices, introducing new trade and payment systems, and setting a realistic exchange rate). Such policy changes may widen external imbalances and, hence, need to be backed by foreign reserves, which are low throughout the PETs, and/or by making stabilization funds available. Greater imports of inputs and trade deficits may be necessary to maintain the production levels required to generate sufficient buoyancy for structural change.

Fifth, an inevitable concomitant of structural change and stabilization will be unemployment and closure of unprofitable enterprises. Externally designed and funded social safety nets (including for the retraining of manpower) may be advisable since such expenditures tend to exacerbate domestic budget deficits.

Sixth, because most PETs have to cope with heavy debt burdens, debt servicing complicates the transition in at least two ways. To pay interest and amortize the debt, the country must run an external surplus, which runs counter to the financial needs of most PETs. Also, paying interest on sovereign debt has implications for domestic budgets precisely at a time that stabilization policy requires the limitation of fiscal deficits.

Seventh, experience has shown that many PETs embarking on their transition lack reserves of food and medicines, a situation that in some cases has been aggravated by the emergence of civic strife. The dismantling or spontaneous disintegration of centralized distribution and production networks during the transition may also require temporary shipments of goods, most important foodstuffs, and technical assistance. Furthermore, the PETs must build up a capacity to be able to adjust to external shocks. For most PETs, the demise of the CMEA trading system and the Gulf War entailed losses of exports and terms of trade, leading to large *ex ante* financing gaps that only western financial institutions could offset.

Ninth, once economies are stabilized and markets begin to function, attention will necessarily shift to rekindling economic growth and improving levels of living. Because much of the capital stock is obsolete, it must be replaced in order to obtain productivity gains and export growth.

Tenth, several PETs are afflicted by extensive environmental damage, due in particular to technologies based on low-grade coal. In certain cases, urgent action is required, for example, to deal with the nuclear contamination of CIS lands by the Chernobyl' power plant. New investments are necessary to improve the security of energy supply, curtail reliance on low-grade coal, and, perhaps most urgently, to replace or modify potentially dangerous nuclear plants.

Finally, the principal demands for the East's disproportionately large defense products have collapsed. Conversion of these facilities to civilian production is essential to stem the growth of unemployment and reduce pressures on these countries to seek new markets, and indeed to make best use of limited domestic resources.

This brief discussion suggests that the costs associated with transition will be enormous. Domestic resources will have to play the major role, but much of the technology and knowhow will have to be imported from the West. The EBRD recently estimated (Jacques Attali in *Financial Times*, 14 April 1992) the assistance required by the East at some ecu4 trillion (some $5 trillion at $1.25 per ecu) to help ensure the region's balance-of-payments requirements, finance the privatization of viable enterprises, boost export industries, convert the defense industry, and improve safety standards at nuclear power stations.

Official financial assistance to the PETs became unavoidable, given the reluctance of private capital to move into these countries at this early stage of the transition. Prior to or in the early stages of transformation, all Eastern countries experienced financial difficulties of various severity. By mid-1989, Poland had been forced to reschedule its debt several times and was seeking some reduction of principal. Although Hungary continued to retain access to international capital markets, it was uncertain whether it would fully service its heavy obligations. Bulgaria's debt had been rising rapidly under the former regime, and the country was forced to declare a moratorium on the servicing of its bank debt in March 1990. At the same time, western suppliers experienced major delays in repayment from Soviet enterprises, which was a harbinger for the Soviet request for rescheduling in 1991. All PETs suffered a loss of confidence by private creditors in the wake of the revolutions and, during 1990, from the increasingly bleak prospects created by the Gulf War. In consequence, all experienced a large outflow of private capital and a depletion of their foreign currency reserves (UNECE 1992). As the successor states of the Soviet Union embark on transition they have virtually no financial resources of their own and they too will require access to official financial flows.

Support for the PETs Other Than CIS Members

With the rising number of recipient countries, the effective coordination of official assistance programs, all drawing upon very limited resources, had become an increasingly challenging and pressing issue even prior to the convulsions in the former Soviet Union; the successor states are now pressing for even more western assistance. Efficient allocation of this assistance is desirable not only in its own right, but because it raises the chances for a successful transition to stable democratic and market systems, reduces the large social costs, and shortens the duration of the transition.

Entrusted to the EC at the G-7 summit held in Paris in July 1989, the coordination role now involves, on the donor side, the G-24, the international financial institutions (EBRD, IMF, and the World Bank Group),[1] the European Investment Bank (EIB), and the European Coal and Steel Community (ECSC). On the recipient side, it includes the seven Eastern European countries, treating Yugoslavia as one for the time being, and the three Baltic states.

G-24 assistance has been organized primarily along bilateral lines. Individual G-24 countries have developed programs in cooperation with the PETs, but not all donors have such commitments in all potential recipients. In addition to the individual efforts of the EC members, the EC has organized and funded its own program entitled PHARE (*Pologne/Hongrie: assistance à la restructuration économique*). In its role as coordinator, a key responsibility of the EC Commission is to ensure that the offers of assistance made by the individual donor countries are complementary and also that there is no overlap with PHARE projects. This requires oversight of numerous, often small (amounting to only tens or hundreds of thousands of dollars) and very narrowly defined project proposals, and match-

---

1. This includes the World Bank (the International Bank for Reconstruction and Development [IBRD] and the International Development Association [IDA]), the IFC, the Multilateral Investment Guarantee Agency (MIGA), and the International Center for the Settlement of Investment Disputes (ICSID).

ing them up with the specific requirements of recipients (EC 1990). Efforts are made to identify "gaps" in the provisioning of assistance.

To facilitate coordination, the EC makes available, among other information, an inventory of PHARE projects (EC 1992a)[2] and acts as a clearing house for the information provided by the G-24 countries regarding their programs. The process of coordination is both helped and complicated by direct contacts between donor and recipient countries. On the one hand, this assists the recipient countries to screen out duplicate offers and allows them some choice between similar proposals. On the other hand, since aid packages are agreed bilaterally, negotiations can severely test the limited resources of the recipient countries. Some of those responsible for the coordination of aid in the recipient countries have noted that they have had to undertake simultaneous negotiations with several donor countries on the specific contents of individual aid packages. Recipients have had to define their priorities and match them with specific offers of assistance. However, achieving the desired mix of aid projects has been complicated by the tendency of donors to offer very similar types of aid (such as advice on privatization and business-school training), often to the exclusion of other urgently needed assistance. EC aid coordinators are now present in all Eastern countries of operation to facilitate on the spot coordination.

Donor countries too may find it challenging to achieve effective internal coordination, interact with the EC Commission and the recipient country, and assess the progress of their aid programs. The coordinating ministry's responsibility may extend over numerous national governmental bodies, each often pursuing its own agenda.[3] Typically these bodies deal directly with their counterparts or other interlocutors in the recipient countries. In some donor countries, aid programs have been initiated at both the federal and regional level (for example, the German *Länder* have set up their own aid programs for certain Eastern countries).

---

2. This compendium provides key information on PHARE projects by country of operation (title of program, sector, EC monetary contribution, description, and other features).

3. In many G-24 countries, new administrative structures have been created to deal with assistance to the East. They are separate from those administering long-running aid programs for developing countries. The rationale for this is both political and economic. On the one hand, donor countries have tried to avoid charges that the new programs were being created at the expense of the existing ones. On the other hand, the needs of the countries in transition have been perceived as differing from those of developing countries.

Within the recipient countries, existing ministries have been assigned or new agencies formed to evaluate requirements for assistance and coordinate inflows. Implementation of these functions has often proved difficult because recipients lack experience in dealing with donors as well as in the more general aspects of managing aid programs. Not surprisingly, internal coordination has sometimes proved inadequate and new solutions have had to be tried, as in Czechoslovakia. In certain countries, the responsibility for coordinating assistance may be split between the federal and republican governments.

The EBRD, EIB, and IBRD have started up operations in all PETs. Current activities involve economic infrastructure projects, the restructuring of industrial sectors, and tackling environmental problems. In general, their strategies are focused on telecommunications, energy, transport, agriculture, and the agro-industrial sectors. In a number of cases, these institutions have coordinated their efforts through the cofinancing of projects.[4] In some cases, this simply follows from the statutes of these organizations. Thus, within the framework of an appropriate financing plan, EIB by its statutes is able to provide loans up to 50 percent of the cost of a project.[5] The statutory global limitation on the EBRD's financing of the state sector may constrain its financial contributions to individual projects and encourage cofinancing activities. Not more than 40 percent of the amount of the EBRD's total committed loans, guarantees, and equity investment can be provided to the state sector.

Equity investments by the EBRD and IFC in Eastern firms, particularly in Czechoslovakia and Hungary, have been rising and their participation has been welcomed by foreign investors in view of the prevailing high degree of uncertainty.

The EBRD and EIB have used global loans as a means to provide long-term finance for small-scale projects. Under these schemes the development banks make available finance through an intermediating financial institution, operating on a national or regional basis, which on-lends the funds in a number of subordinate loans for selected small- and medium-sized projects agreed by the Banks. EIB sub-loans under its global loan

---

4. For example, the World Bank and the EBRD are both providing loans for a district heating project in Poland. These two banks and the EIB have cofinanced a telecommunications project in Hungary.

5. It is also a fairly flexible source of finance. It indeed played an important role in the establishment of EBRD by providing appropriate assistance during its startup phase (see EIB 1991).

facility are intended to promote investment projects with a total cost not exceeding ecu15-20 million (EIB 1991).

In the area of restructuring, the EC Commission has coordinated PHARE activities that focus on economic restructuring with the programs of the international financial institutions. In 1990, when the programs for Hungary and Poland were just getting under way, the EC cofinanced preparatory studies for sectoral projects (with the IBRD and the EIB) and several technical assistance programs (with the IFC and the IBRD).[6] Subsequently, the EC funded numerous preparatory studies of infrastructure projects throughout the PETs. Project finance for these is to be provided by the development banks.

Triangular operations in food and medical products aim at specifically involving certain PETs in regional solutions to problems of emergency assistance. The activities now planned are to help the PETs maintain a part of their traditional trading pattern with the USSR through the provision of external finance by the EC. This has been undertaken as an alternative to shipments of food from western stocks, which would only have further excluded Eastern Europe from the ex-Soviet market. With convertible-currency settlements having overtaken the TR regimes, the ex-Soviet states can no longer pay for agricultural goods traditionally purchased from other PETs and the latter cannot afford or are reluctant to extend credits.[7] In earlier triangular operations, Hungary exported food to Albania and Poland. The possibility of meeting Romania's recent request for food through triangular operations has been considered by EC ministers.

Provision and coordination of macroeconomic financial assistance for the East excluding the Soviet Union have been the responsibility of the EC, the G-24, and the international financial institutions. In this process, the IMF has worked with the recipient countries to design programs for stabilization and comprehensive economic reform. Together the two define the domestic policy environment within which the various internationally backed projects and programs can function. Disbursement of

---

6. For example, in 1990 the EC and the IBRD financed studies evaluating SOEs in Poland with a view to preparing them for restructuring. The EC also funded technical assistance and training for the financial sector in Hungary and Yugoslavia (EC 1991b).

7. Of the ecu0.5 billion credit granted by the EC to the ex-Soviet Union (subsequently the loan was earmarked exclusively for Russia), one fourth is to be allocated to triangular operations. The remainder is to finance food shipments from EC supplies (*Europe*, 16 January 1992).

macroeconomic finance contributed by the G-24 is conditional upon the recipient country's meeting performance criteria agreed with the IMF.

By the end of 1991, two kinds of macroeconomic supports for the PETs were in place. At the end of 1989, the G-24 assembled a $1 billion currency stabilization fund requested by Poland (discussed below). A larger, and more complex, initiative involved financing in support of new stabilization programs, reform of trade and payment regimes (including the introduction of a unified exchange rate[8] and internal convertibility), and large ($4 billion) prospective payments imbalances expected to emanate from existing and new external shocks. Funding from the IMF for standby and oil facilities (see UNECE 1991b for details), the World Bank (structural adjustment loans, and project and sector financing), and the G-24 (exceptional complementary funding)[9] was arranged to meet the anticipated requirements.

This operation met with mixed success. Commitments for the full amounts requested by Czechoslovakia ($1 billion) and Hungary ($0.5 billion) were obtained without difficulty. However, the pledges required to cover the entire financing gaps of Bulgaria ($0.8 billion) and Romania ($1 billion) could not be secured, the shortfall in each case amounting to $0.2-0.3 billion, even though in both cases "there was broad agreement among members of the G-24 that the basic prerequisites for the granting of assistance" had been met (EC 1991a). Indirectly, the failure to meet the initial targets contributed to subsequent delays in disbursing committed funds. Under conditions initially set by the European Parliament, the release of EC funds (up to half of each country loan) was to be authorized only when other G-24 countries pledged the full remaining portion. But the EC subsequently relaxed its position when it became clear that the targets for Bulgaria and Romania would not be met and that the

---

8. *Editor's note*: Poland in early 1990 went on a dual exchange rate. A unified one applicable to all duly authorized commercial transactions, which was held stable until mid-1991 and managed by the central bank. Another one, in principle floating within a narrow band of 10 percent around the central commercial rate, remains applicable to private transactions.

9. In addition to multilateral financing, the determination of the level of G-24 complementary financing takes account of any bilateral official grants and credits, including export credits, debt-restructuring agreements with both official and private creditors, and expected flows from the private sector. The evaluation of requests for G-24 balance-of-payments assistance takes place at the level of the "Brussels Network" and is coordinated with the appropriate multilateral institutions. Implementation of G-24 assistance is coordinated by a monitoring group of Financial Counsellors (EC 1991a).

adjustment programs in question were threatened by the delays. Even when donor governments had pledged funds, there were cases where the process of signing contracts and appropriating funds proved slow. In at least two cases the Bank for International Settlement (BIS)[10] played an important role in providing bridging loans to Romania in anticipation of disbursements of IMF and EC commitments (BIS 1991).

These delays were not critical for Czechoslovakia and Hungary. Both enjoyed a boom in imports from the west but still posted small current-account surpluses instead of the projected deficits. But the buildup of reserves was slower than foreseen. However, shortfalls of financing had serious repercussions for Bulgaria and Romania. Since exports were falling and imports were squeezed, thus exacerbating the decline in domestic output, the financial constraint resulted in sharper external adjustment than had been planned with the IMF and presumably in unnecessary losses in economic and social welfare. The experience of Albania appears to be similar. In 1991, the country was engaged in the preparation of an IMF-approved stabilization program. Hence, only emergency aid and limited bilateral loans were available from the G-24. Overall, these outcomes suggest that the present system of cooperation cannot always be relied upon to make funds for balance-of-payments purposes available on a timely basis.

Aside from the question of coordination, problems typically associated with donor-driven assistance in other areas of the world have been reported by the PETs too. For example, donors often focus on, indeed compete for, highly visible projects. While these may be indispensable for a successful transition, less prestigious, but equally essential, projects tend to be overlooked. Also, offers of tied aid have been sufficiently prevalent for the G-24 to make recommendations on the matter.[11] Such issues are always difficult for decision makers in the recipient countries to deal with. In the East, however, the problem is exacerbated by the lack of experience in managing foreign assistance.

---

10. The BIS has been entrusted with the coordination of technical assistance extended by the central banks of the Group of Ten (G-10) and Austria to the Eastern countries. In this respect it has cooperated with the international financial institutions, particularly with the IMF (BIS 1991).

11. At the November 1991 G-24 meeting, ministers drew attention to the "desirability of untying assistance flows, in accordance with the rules recognized by the OECD, in order to provide enhanced opportunities for the economic reform process" (EC, *Press Release*, IP (91) 994).

Given the broad scope and complexity of the overall assistance effort, it is not surprising that some aspects of coordination have been found wanting and that recommendations for its improvement are being made, including that "more effective international support is required to assist countries in carrying through their reforms. This will require more rapid disbursement of resources by the G-24 and the international financial institutions, increased information sharing among donors to avoid duplication of effort, closer cooperation between the international financial institutions and the G-24, and the taking of further steps to increase trade in accordance with the GATT" (EC, *Press Release*, IP (91) 994). But closer coordination of assistance may be difficult to achieve. For various reasons, some G-24 governments and international institutions prefer to run their programs independently, even though this may result in parallel, perhaps competing, efforts. National interests may partly explain the paucity of information on certain programs. Moreover, the overall level of resources allocated to cooperation, including human resources, may be inadequate (EC 1991b).

Support for the Former Soviet Union

The organization of foreign assistance for the Soviet Union and its successor states, except the Baltics, has evolved somewhat differently from that for other PETs. International assistance has been extended chiefly on a bilateral basis, without a coordinating structure comparable to the EC and G-24 arrangements. In early 1990, with the emergence of the first signs of external financial difficulties, the international community pledged loan guarantees and trade credits worth over $20 billion. These were generally restricted to specific purposes, arranged bilaterally, and, in contrast to the conditionality attached to similar credits for other PETs, not formally linked to fundamental economic reform commitments. However, donors did strongly encourage the Soviet authorities to put a credible reform program in place.

A large share of this financial assistance was designated for the purchase of food. Responding to growing Soviet needs, the EC and the United States allocated some $3 billion in food credits and grants in late 1990. Subsequently, a package amounting to some $7.5 billion was assembled under the auspices of the G-7 (including commitments made the previous year), with the EC, Japan, and the United States pledging equal amounts. Separately, Germany launched major relief initiatives, including significant private participation. In the emergency efforts undertaken during the winter of 1991-1992, some donor countries provided transportation to the CIS states and distributed the food locally to selected groups. The EC program involves selling donated food, chiefly in Moscow and St. Petersburg, which have been hit particularly hard by the breakdown of the centralized distribution system. This policy aims at bringing prices down without discouraging the entry of new suppliers into the market. Revenues raised through sales are treated as counterpart funds earmarked to support the needy. In addition, the Soviet Union has received increasing amounts of technical assistance from bilateral and multilateral sources.[12] In general, the immediate aim is to help the country mobilize its own resources to solve problems in the areas of management, financial services, energy, transport, and foodstuff distribution. But longer-term structural issues are also being addressed.

Against the background of a worsening domestic supply situation and the multiplication of western aid initiatives, the United States called an international conference (the so-called International Conference on Humanitarian Assistance to the former USSR) to improve coordination and plan new initiatives. It was held in Washington, 22-23 January 1992, with the participation of 47 countries and international organizations, including the G-24. Five working groups were set up (technical assistance, energy, medical assistance, shelter, and food assistance). Each group identified the key problems in its area, established working plans for future action, including consultations with CIS authorities, and agreed on how to set priorities. A common thread running through the plans is the application of market solutions and external assistance to strengthen emerging markets. The EC hosted a followup conference in Lisbon in May 1992 to examine the progress of the working groups and a third meeting was held in Tokyo in October 1992 (see chapter 5). Currently the conference is the only formal structure for coordinating bilateral assistance to the CIS.

The success of these microeconomic measures hinges on the solution of macroeconomic problems. The large imbalances currently plaguing the

---

12. The EC allocated ecu0.4 billion for technical assistance to the ex-Soviet Union in 1991 and a further ecu0.5 billion for 1992. The EBRD has established a program of technical assistance, which has been extended to the successor states while the World Bank allocated $30 million following the formalization of the country's associate membership.

CIS need to be corrected and confidence in the ruble restored if the new decentralized distribution systems are to function properly. This implies the revival of interrepublican trade links, supported by a functioning payment system.

Acting on behalf of official creditors, the G-7 has undertaken to resolve certain questions stemming from the ex-Soviet Union's financial crisis. In October 1991, the group was instrumental in persuading most of the republics to accept responsibility for collectively servicing the union's debt. Although this agreement appears to have broken down since then, its signing was significant for two other reasons. G-7 governments made new credit guarantees to individual republics conditional upon their adherence to the accord. And it set the stage for the formal rescheduling of the ex-Soviet Union's outstanding official (Paris Club) and commercial (London Club) bank obligations in January 1992.

Several issues pertaining to the servicing of the ex-Soviet debt have led western authorities to freeze certain credit lines (some originally arranged in 1990). The latter actions were prompted by the political upheavals in mid-1991 and the absence of credible interlocutors. The facilities were reactivated only in early 1992. Second, Ukraine's decision to service its share of ex-Soviet obligations (16.37 percent) independently has disqualified it from new loans. A third problem encountered by western lenders has been the reluctance of the financial authorities of Russia to guarantee new loans. This stance is reported to have delayed agreement with the EC on an ecu1.25 billion ($1.6 billion) credit (among others), which was pledged at the EC summit in Rome in December 1990 and earmarked for purchases of food and medicine.

Unlike the other PETs, the Soviet Union never was a member of the Bretton Woods organizations and thus was not entitled to draw upon their considerable resources. In 1990, the Soviet authorities cooperated with several international organizations to prepare a study on the Soviet economy (Joint 1990) undertaken at the behest of the G-7 summit in Houston in July 1990. A special association status in the IMF was granted in October 1991. This entitled the Soviet Union to technical assistance, but not credits. More recently, the IMF has been very active in collecting the information required to design economic reforms and stabilization packages for the successor states.

Early in 1992, many observers argued for the admission of the successor states to the IMF and the creation of large-scale assistance packages at the earliest possible date. Given the poor financial position of the successor states, the timing and commitment of adequate macroeconomic resources may be crucial. The rapid decline in domestic output continues and inflation remains a major problem. In such a situation, the announcement effect of a credible stabilization and financing package could be very powerful, demonstrating the commitment of the international community and instilling some confidence in the national currency. This in turn might slow capital flight[13] and enable the CIS states to rely more upon their own resources. These arguments have also taken into account that agreement between the republics on their stabilization programs will take time and that funds are not likely to become available until the second half of the year. The recent experiences of Bulgaria and Romania are instructive in that both embarked on economic reform lacking the necessary reserves and foreign support.

Membership of the successor states was approved by the IMF Board at its annual meeting, 27-28 April 1992. Prior to this, Germany and the United States, acting in the name of the G-7, had announced a $24 billion package for Russia, comprising a $6 billion currency stabilization fund, a $4 billion standby credit from the IMF,[14] $1.5 billion from the IBRD, other cash from the EBRD, a $2.5 billion deferral of debt payments to Paris Club members, and $11-12 billion in bilateral credits (the bulk of this appears to reflect existing commitments, on which more below).

Similar, but smaller packages will need to be assembled for the other republics. However, the exact form of the arrangements remains to be decided. One option involves the introduction of a common stabilization program based on maintaining the ruble as a single currency. Since a number of the republics intend to introduce their own currencies, it is probable that a stabilization program for the CIS (Georgia presumably being dealt with separately) as a whole would not succeed. If the republics fail to restrict national budget deficits the target for the central budget is likely to be missed as well. A system of individual currencies, with each republic assuming full responsibility for its own budget, may be a more workable arrangement for gaining control over inflation (UNECE 1992,

---

13. Internal flight into convertible currency by households and external flight have been estimated at $5-10 billion and $15-40 billion, respectively (see *Financial Times*, 26 February 1992). In early 1992, Russia announced measures to stem this outflow. Experience elsewhere, particularly in Latin America, has shown that only credible macroeconomic policies and more rational trade and payment systems are likely to be effective in this case.

14. Prospective borrowing from the IMF is based on Russia's agreed 3 percent quota in the fund, equivalent to SDR3.6 billion. Ukraine has agreed to a quota of 0.69 percent.

chapter 4). As in the case of maintaining the ruble zone, the solution of
separate currencies would then call for either of two arrangements, or
more likely a combination of the two. One would require that potential
surplus republics extend export credits, but this time through other means
than the financial mechanisms at the disposal of Russia's financial authorities. Another is that the republics adopt individual stabilization programs,
supported by separate stabilization funds and adequate national reserves,
and thus settle their imbalances in convertible currency. This solution is
likely to be very costly in terms of providing western assistance, however,
hence the suggested combination of methods. Other payments arrangements might be workable—a system of currency boards[15] or a payments
union among the republics—and perhaps help avoid the entrenchment of
bilateral trading in the area.

Types of Financial Assistance

In the course of 1990-1991, western financial commitments to the PETs
assumed a very significant magnitude—some $111 billion, excluding facili-
ties provided by the international financial institutions. One third of this
is pledged to Eastern Europe and the remainder to the former Soviet
Union. These magnitudes may give the impression that the assistance
needs of the East have been met. The discussion above has indicated that
this has not always been the case. The two positions can be reconciled
only by looking more closely at the overall magnitudes, country distribution, types, and various impediments to the flow of assistance—the topic
of this section.

Between January 1990 and the end of June 1991, G-24 commitments
cumulated to nearly $32 billion (ecu26 billion) as detailed in table 6.1.[16]

15. *Editor's note*: A currency board system presupposes an irrevocable link, usually on a
one-to-one basis, between the national currency and a country's foreign exchange reserves.
Because reserves in the republics are uniformly low, it would require a drastic cut in money
in circulation, hence severe deflationary policies to reach a level at which a currency board
system could function properly. An alternative, of course, would be that the international
system provides through credible guarantees the initial reserves to the republics. But that
would be even more expensive than the full financing of current-account deficits, including
in interrepublican trade. In any case, a currency board presupposes yielding sovereignty over
monetary policy, something that may well be politically unacceptable.
16. The EC compiles the data on commitments on a rolling 18 month basis. The previous

Poland and Hungary, the first countries to commence the transition process and request assistance, have received the greatest share of commitments (30 percent and 18 percent respectively). Yugoslavia (15 percent), Czechoslovakia (7 percent), and Bulgaria and Romania (5 percent each) trail further behind; and funds for regional programs and unspecified account for the remaining 20 percent. Of the donors, the EC (73 percent), Japan (9 percent), and the United States (8 percent) have made the highest nominal contributions.

Table 6.1: Assistance Committed by the G-24 to Some Eastern Countries
(January 1990-June 1991, billion dollars)

Recipients	Total	of which:					
		Economic restruc- turing	Trade credits and investment guarantees	Debt reorga- nization	Emer- gency aid	Macro- econom- ic assis- tance	of which: IMF lending
Bulgaria	1.6	0.2	0.7	-	0.1	0.6	0.6
Czechoslovakia	2.2	0.3	1.0	-	-	1.0	1.0
Hungary	5.9	0.6	1.9	-	-	3.4	0.5
Poland	9.7	1.2	3.8	2.8	0.5	1.4	-
Romania	1.7	0.4	0.3	-	0.3	0.7	0.7
Yugoslavia	4.7	0.4	2.8	-	-	-	-
Regional/ Unallocated	6.2	2.3	1.0	-	0.1	0.2	-
Total	31.9	5.8	11.5	2.8	1.0	7.1	2.9

Source: author's computations based on EC 1991c, d as published in UNECE 1992.

---

period used extended from July 1989 (when the G-24 effort was launched) to end-1990. The data are presented in UNECE 1991b.

The EC has estimated the grant component at $6.5 billion, or somewhat over 20 percent of total commitments. The full aid element is larger, but presently cannot be calculated because of insufficient information from western creditors on their concessionary lending. Trade credits and investment guarantees comprise the largest type (36 percent) of G-24 assistance, of which Poland is the largest beneficiary. The bulk of macroeconomic assistance consists of exceptional, untied balance-of-payments financing, which, as noted, was intended to complement IMF lending during 1991, although an ecu0.87 billion ($1.1 billion) structural adjustment loan pledged by the EC in 1990 to Hungary to help it meet its high debt-servicing obligations is included too. Commitments to Bulgaria and Romania of $0.6 billion and $0.7 billion, respectively, fell short of the initial targets of $0.8 billion and $1 billion, respectively, because several potential donors did not contribute as expected. This category also includes Poland's $1 billion currency stabilization fund established to provide support for internal convertibility and the new exchange rate of the złoty in early 1990.[17] It differs from other types of macroeconomic assistance in that the funds could only be drawn if the exchange rate of the złoty were threatened, and thus it was never considered part of the country's foreign exchange reserves. Nonetheless the very existence of the fund was undoubtedly an important stabilizing factor in 1990.

Debt reorganization has become an important source of assistance. The $2.8 billion reported in table 6.1 appears incomplete, since it is lower than the combined operations in favor of Bulgaria and Poland. Also the ex-GDR's claims (originally in rubles) on former CMEA trade partners taken over by Germany at reunification are absent (although, they are correctly recorded in the data on disbursements discussed below). The economic restructuring category comprises technical assistance and funds for specific projects, a considerable part of which is accounted for by EIB and ECSC loan commitments. The EIB has been authorized by the EC to lend a total of ecu1 billion to Hungary and Poland and ecu0.7 billion to Bulgaria, Czechoslovakia, and Romania.[18] In addition to the assistance committed by the G-24, substantial funds have been made available by the multilateral financial institutions (table 6.2).[19] IMF facilities totaled some

---

17. The $1 billion stabilization fund for Poland was assembled by the G-24 in late 1989 and has been administered through the Federal Reserve Bank in New York. The funds were not required in 1990 or 1991.

18. EIB and ECSC lending to Yugoslavia takes place under an earlier protocol.

19. EBRD's loans and investments of $0.5 billion through the end of 1991 (lending having

$8 billion, of which nearly half was disbursed in 1991, while the World Bank approved loans of some $5 billion during its 1990 and 1991 fiscal years, of which around $2 billion was disbursed in 1991 (see UNECE 1991b).

Recipients	Total	of which: G-24	International financial institutions	of which: IMF	IBRD
Bulgaria	2.2	1.6	0.5	0.5	-
Czechoslovakia	4.0	2.2	1.9	1.5	0.4
Hungary	9.1	5.9	3.2	2.2	1.0
Poland	14.6	9.7	4.9	2.8	2.1
Romania	2.8	1.7	1.1	1.0	0.2
Yugoslavia	5.9	4.7	1.2	0.1	1.1
Regional/Unallocated	6.2	6.2	-	-	-
Total	44.8	31.9	12.8	8.1	4.7

Table 6.2: Global Assistance Committed to Some Eastern Countries (January 1990-June 1991, billion dollars)

Source: see table 6.1.

Since donor countries attach various terms and conditions to assistance, recipients' access is not automatic and any disbursement may considerably lag the actual commitment. Practices restraining use of committed funds include the tying of credits to the purchase of specific goods and services; the need to obtain commercial banks' acceptance of the conditions attached to an official guarantee pertaining to the opening of a line of credit, which was important as the perceived creditworthiness of most

---

started in September 1991) are not reflected here.

PETs deteriorated in 1990 and private banks were no longer willing to accept normal guarantee conditions; access to loans being spread over several years; making acceptance of an IMF-approved stabilization program a precondition for disbursement of the first tranche and upon achieving program targets for the disbursement of subsequent tranches; insistence upon legislative approval in the donor country or lengthy bilateral negotiations over specific conditions; and the G-24's reported commitments include their capital subscriptions to the EBRD, at least part of which is recorded as grants, although this money will be available to the East only through eventual loans and investments. The recipient countries too may hold up disbursements if their programs are improperly prepared or encounter delays.

It should also be borne in mind that some types of commitments made so far, while considerably easing the balance-of-payments constraint of the recipient countries or promoting capital inflows, may not provide a good measure of the size of new direct flows that might result. These include debt restructuring and forgiveness, stabilization funds of the type set up for Poland, and investment guarantees, the latter intended to foster private investment. Taken together, such support accounts for a large share of G-24 commitments.

As regards the actual flows of financial assistance to the East, data have been arranged here according to the standard framework developed within the OECD for recording such flows and ODA to the developing countries.[20] In 1990, gross flows amounted to $9.7 billion (see table 6.3). Of this Poland accounts for over 40 percent, Hungary for one quarter, and the other countries about equally for the remainder. This distribution in part reflects the fact that Hungary and Poland were the first countries to benefit from G-24 programs and qualified for assistance from the beginning of 1990. The eligibility of the other Eastern countries was formalized only in the latter part of that year, with few actions being initiated. Indeed, aside from the restructuring of debt, financial inflows into these countries were marginal, the largest being humanitarian assistance for Romania.

---

20. The OECD secretariat has begun to collect data on financial flows to the East, using replies by member countries and multilateral agencies to standard questionnaires. The data for 1990 are incomplete.

Table 6.3: G-24 Disbursements and Other Financial Flows to Some Eastern Countries in 1990
(million dollars)

Type of aid	Bulgaria	CSFR	Hungary	Poland	Romania	Total
Official aid	12	21	64	1 295	240	1 710
of which:						
Grants	12	21	64	845	221	1 241
Loans	..	..	..	450	19	469
Other official flows:	770	1 021	1 579	2 744	741	6 865
of which:						
Export and other credits	26	37	776	263	-	1 101
Rescheduled debt to west	..	..	..	1 231	..	1 231
Rescheduled debt to ex-GDR	744	984	803	1 250	741	4 522
Multilateral (IBRD)	-	-	113	54	..	167
Total official flows	781	1 042	1 755	4 093	981	8 742
FDI and other private flows	45	26	428	37	..	925ª
Total resource flows (gross)	827	1 068	2 184	4 129	981	9 667ª

Source: author's computations based on OECD 1991c as published in UNECE 1992.

Note: for lack of data on gross disbursements and repayments, estimates of Germany's contributions are based on budgetary appropriations. The data may not reflect the full extent of support provided, in particular as regards debt rescheduling.

ª Total private flows as reported in the OECD source. Total resource flows for individual countries do not add to the reported total ($9.7 billion).

The bulk of this assistance, nearly $6 billion, was exceptional financing (rescheduled official and private debt), of which $4.5 billion represents Germany's refinancing of TR deficits of the Eastern countries in their trade with the former GDR in 1990.[21] Disbursed official aid totaled $1.7 billion, most of which is grants ($1.2 billion) and the remainder loans on

21. "Exceptional financing" consists of rescheduled principal and interest coming due and debt forgiveness. The incomplete data presented here understate the importance of assistance extended through the refinancing of debt in 1990.

concessional terms. This latter category includes reported commitments of $546 million to Poland's $1 billion stabilization fund.

The EC has estimated the value of G-24 (including EC) gross official resource flows to the five Eastern countries in 1990 at some $4 billion.[22] This represents a disbursement rate of about 20 percent in 1990 (calculated relative to G-24 commitments adjusted on a 12 months *pro rata* basis). If restructured debt ($1.1 billion) and the approximately $0.6 billion designated for Poland's stabilization fund are excluded, the flows amount to some $2.5 billion (reducing the disbursement rate to some 13 percent). The lower figure may give a better picture of new official funds available to the Eastern countries in 1990.

Preliminary estimates for 1991 indicate that gross financial resource flows into the East nearly doubled to $20 billion while new capital (that is, excluding debt restructuring) rose to $12 billion (UNECE 1992). Most international institutions and bilateral creditors boosted disbursements sharply, in general to provide macroeconomic support. Preliminary forecasts for 1992 point to a fall in total new capital to less than $10 billion. IMF and G-24 lending are slated to contract to more normal levels, following most of the East's adjustment to the energy price shocks in 1991. These will be only partially offset by higher disbursements from the development banks. Private lending (including guaranteed export credit) is to rise, in part because of a small increase in FDI.

In summary, the $32 billion G-24 commitment to the East other than the former Soviet Union is quite large, all of it potentially reducing balance-of-payments constraints and giving impetus to economic development. Since the figure includes very different types of assistance, it needs to be interpreted with caution. In particular, it should be borne in mind that rescheduled debt is included and that the various conditions attached to the resources are likely to preclude automatic disbursal. Moreover, it was only towards the end of 1990 and the beginning of 1991 that the process of implementation of assistance programs could get into full swing. As most of the programs, including PHARE, consist of or have important initial elements of technical assistance, the amounts of disbursement is expected to be small in relation to commitments over the first 2-3 years (EC 1991b).

---

22. The methodology used to achieve rough comparability between G-24 commitments and flows recorded by the OECD are discussed in EC 1991c. Private finance is excluded, however.

The bulk of the assistance to the East has been extended on a nonconcessional basis, and thus is debt creating. The amount of aid (grants and concessional loans) appears to be relatively small. Since the terms aid and assistance tend to be used interchangeably, the large commitments of assistance have led to misunderstandings about the magnitude of western aid to the East and concern about the diversion of aid from the developing world. Virtually all bilateral and multilateral loans—for example those extended by the G-24 and EC for macroeconomic support—have been offered at market conditions (that is, at cost to the creditor country/institution plus fees). Nonetheless, for the PETs these loans contain an implicit subsidy and are an important source of external support: Most Eastern countries lack access to private credit markets and those that do have access pay a large premium amounting to 2-3 percentage points over the benchmark rates for ecu and *deutschmark* bonds.

The most comprehensive source currently available on international assistance to the former Soviet Union is a compilation circulated by the EC at the Washington conference in January 1992 (table 6.4). Between September 1990 and 31 January 1992, financial commitments extended to the CIS states amounted to ecu63 billion (nearly $79 billion). Of this, the EC and its members represent 76 percent. Germany is the leading provider, accounting for 57 percent of the total (50 percent if the assistance to pay for the withdrawal of Soviet troops is excluded). These commitments may cover several years and the figures do not include debt rescheduling[23] or grants from private, chiefly German, sources.

The purposes of and conditions attached to these loans at the time of their original announcement include (see UNECE 1991a): export credits tied to the purchase of national goods, including a high component of guaranteed credits for food purchases; credits extended specifically for the purpose of settling arrears owed to domestic companies in the donor countries; and credits and grants to be made available over a period of several years, including some DM12 billion from Germany to the former

---

23. The Paris Club agreed to reschedule $3.3 billion in Soviet debt falling due in December 1991. An undisclosed amount was also restructured by commercial banks. The notes to the fact sheet do not specify whether the claims of the former GDR on the ex-Soviet Union, taken over by Germany, are included. It is also uncertain whether western countries have included the arrears incurred by the Soviet Union *vis-à-vis* their exporters (some $4.5 billion in 1990).

Soviet Union for disbursement through 1994 in conjunction with the repatriation of Soviet troops from the former GDR.

Table 6.4: International Assistance to the CIS States[a]
(million ECU)

Donors	A	B	C	D	E	F	G	Total
EC	453	-	1 750	-	-	885	-	3 088
Member states	1 249	5 942	18 849	8 402	8 353	312	1 671	44 777
of which:								
Germany	1 189	4 521	11 522	8 402	8 353	197	1 671	35 855
Italy	-	1 421	3 241	-	-	-	-	4 662
Spain	-	-	1 118	-	-	-	-	1 118
France	22	-	1 675	-	-	30	-	1 726
United Kingdom	31	-	391	-	-	80	-	503
EFTA countries	38	-	734	-	-	87	28	887
of which:								
Finland	6	-	80	-	-	26	-	111
Norway	4	-	94	-	-	39	4	140
Sweden	12	-	-	-	-	18	-	29
Other countries	288	746	9 066	373	298	196	3 366	14 332
of which:								
United States	224	-	2 982	-	298	168	384	4 057
Japan	22	-	1 938	-	-	1	-	1 961
South Korea	-	746	1 118	373	-	-	-	2 237
Total	2 028	6 687	30 398	8 776	8 651	1 480	5 065	63 084

Source: EC 1992b.

Legend: a food and medical aid (grants), B balance-of-payments support, C export credits and/or guarantees, d other credits, E strategic assistance for the withdrawal of Soviet troops and destruction of nuclear warheads, F technical assistance, G other assistance.

[a] September 1990-January 1992.

The actual disbursement of these funds has been affected by many of the factors noted earlier for the other Eastern countries. Recent press reports indicate that some of the pledges made in 1990 have not yet been lived up to. Several creditor countries suspended facilities during the political upheavals in the Soviet Union in 1991 and have only recently recommitted the loans. In consequence, only a fraction of commitments is likely to have been released during the past two years. Rough computations (UNECE 1992) suggest that actual inflows in 1990-1991 constituted one quarter to one third of the $79 billion in commitments. At the same time, the former Soviet Union repaid $16.4 billion, implying a net inflow of medium- and long-term capital of some $6.5 billion. However, this was not enough to compensate for the net outflow of nearly $16 billion in short-term credits. In other words, official assistance could not compensate for the action of private banks reducing their exposure *vis-à-vis* the ex-Soviet Union. The failure of certain ex-Soviet republics to adhere to agreement on the joint servicing of Soviet debt concluded last year has held up the release of loans in early 1992.

A positive transfer of resources into the PETs during the critical stages of economic reform would have been desirable, but in fact most of them, including the pacesetters, Hungary and Poland, experienced a net outflow in 1990 (table 6.5). In general this was due to the withdrawal of funds by commercial banks which more than offset new lending by the multilateral financial institutions and G-24 countries. The heavy interest obligations of Hungary (as well as its large repayment of medium- and long-term debt) and Poland were also a factor.

In 1991 the situation improved with Eastern Europe (exluding Yugoslavia) obtaining $5.1 billion inward transfer of resources. Only Poland continued to experience an outflow. Hungary and, to a lesser extent, Czechoslovakia benefited from operations in the international capital markets, greater FDI, and EC/G-24 credits. Excluding IMF lending—the $3.5 billion drawn was primarily intended to bolster foreign currency reserves—resource transfers amounted to a $1.6 billion inflow. For Romania IMF resources constituted a crucial part of its balance-of-payments financing and were not used to reconstitute reserves as had been planned. As regards the ex-Soviet Union, its resource transfer was significantly negative in both 1990 and 1991, owing to the strong outflow of short-term credits.

Table 6.5: Net Transfers of Financial Resources to the East, 1990-1991 (million dollars)						
Recipients	Interest payments	Capital flows	IMF lending	Exceptional financing	Total	Memorandum Reserves (net)[a]
Bulgaria						
1990	-688	-2 477	-	2 614	-551	888
1991	-825	-868	405	2 041	735	-358
Czechoslovakia[b]						
1990	-316	326	-	-	10	1 110
1991	-321	1 485	1 004	-	2 168	-1 990
Hungary						
1990	-1 438	-689	-145	-	-2 272	562
1991	-1363	2 453	793	-	1 883	-2 740
Poland[b]						
1990	-3 329	-6 678	509	7 803	-1 695	-2 153
1991	-2 343	-3 993	322	5 148	-866	819
Romania						
1990	137	47	-	-	184	1 664
1991	-25	488	772	-	1 235	789
Yugoslavia						
1990	-822	3 607	-266	-	2 519	-1 590
1991	-632[c]	..	-110	..	..	..
Soviet Union[d]						
1990	-4.0	-6.9	-	4.5	-6.4	8.4
1991	-3.7	0.4[e]	-	-0.5	-3.8	2.5

Source: author's estimates based on national statistics as published in UNECE 1992.

Note: all flows are net, in convertible currencies only. Official transfers are not included.

[a] a negative sign indicates an increase in reserves.
[b] January-November 1991.
[c] January-October 1991.
[e] billion dollars.
[f] includes $1.9 billion in grants.

Conclusions

Overall, the G-24 and the international financial institutions have adopted a fairly well-defined approach to aiding the PETs. Considerable progress has been made in a relatively short time, although the degree of implementation and the successes of these measures vary considerably among countries. All Eastern governments are implementing IMF-backed stabilization programs and reforms, and steps have been taken to reintroduce institutions and instruments essential for the functioning and management of market economies. There has been some headway made in restructuring, chiefly through the privatization of small businesses, but large-scale privatization is proving more difficult than expected. Key infrastructure projects have been initiated by the development banks. All of these activities have been underpinned by wide-ranging technical assistance provided by western governments and the multilateral institutions.

It is, however, open to question whether this adds up to a comprehensive and coherent strategy so essential for transformations that are far-reaching, complex, and long-term in nature. Numerous bilateral and multilateral initiatives, coordinated to various degrees, have been undertaken. All are undoubtedly valuable in their own right. However, from the scattered information available, it is difficult to obtain an overview of the assistance effort, gauge how programs fit together, and determine whether there are unnecessary overlaps or crucial gaps that are not being filled. There are persistent reports of conflicting advice being offered to the East by outside experts.

So far little attempt appears to have been made to formulate a comprehensive and integrated medium- to long-term blueprint for the transition incorporating political objectives; macroeconomic targets and perspectives, including the balance-of-payments implications of debt-creating foreign assistance; timetables for specific reforms required to complete the transition; identification of requirements for technical and other assistance, their costs, and estimates of amounts to be covered from abroad;[24] infrastruc-

---

24. Donor countries plan their assistance programs well in advance, given that requests for assistance may have to be written into budgets at an early stage and that budgetary processes are often protracted. The East could benefit from certain donors' willingness to make multi-year appropriations.

ture requirements; and an explicit integration of committed assistance
with the transition programs of the recipients. Drawing upon key elements of the Marshall Plan, the UNECE has advocated such a comprehensive approach to assisting the East (UNECE 1990, 1991b, 1992, among
others).

The task of constructing such a blueprint would necessarily fall upon
the recipient countries, although western governments and institutions
could assist in the process. For various reasons, however, Eastern governments generally have ceased to elaborate longer-term plans. Background
papers that they occasionally and voluntarily prepare for meetings of the
G-24 report only on recent progress with reform, macroeconomic developments, and short-term prospects, and, in certain cases contain requests for
emergency assistance. Only Poland has presented a fairly detailed blueprint of reforms and projects that the government intends to pursue, but
even this refers only to the coming year and does not address the issues
in a comprehensive framework.

No objective economic criteria appear to have been established for
determining the assistance needs of the PETs. Finance committed to them
has been determined by their place in the queue, with the latecomers
receiving less than needed. Given the overall scarcity of aid, distribution
according to some agreed criteria (particularly of bilateral assistance)
might help to avoid, among other things, unproductive competition
between the potential recipients, which is said to have intensified with
the aid requirements of the ex-Soviet republics.

Currently, the EC Commission coordinates the assistance of the G-24
and the international financial institutions for the East, except the CIS
members and Georgia. So far, no comparable arrangement has been made
to deal with the latter, chiefly because western governments are reluctant
to establish another international bureaucracy (*Financial Times*, 4 March
1992). Nonetheless, it is questionable whether, for example, the five working groups set up at the Washington conference can effectively coordinate
the numerous sources and types of assistance being offered.[25] The challenge may well exceed that facing the EC and G-24 in the rest of the East,
given the diversity of the recipients and the even larger number of possible donors. Whatever solution will be adopted, it should aim at establishing a coherent framework for transition, take greater account of regional

---

25. *Editor's note*: its inefficiency led to a revised approach to delivering assistance to the
successor states of the Soviet Union other than the Baltic states, as discussed in chapter 5.

interdependencies, and ensure that the valuable experience gained dealing with other PETs becomes available to the CIS states. Indeed, similar admonishments seem in order for the Balkan countries, given the experience of the past few years. Full implementation of stabilization programs should improve the domestic macroeconomic environment and establish the conditions necessary for sustained economic growth. However, a strong supply-side response and rapid structural change, including privatization, which is the aim of numerous initiatives, may take longer to materialize.

Some thought might also usefully be given to ways to deal with the possible sociopolitical repercussions of a deepening of the economic depression in the East. Further decline in economic activity and increasing unemployment are foreseen for the near-term. It is doubtful that the types of assistance and programs currently implemented in the East can be counted on soon to turn this situation around. If pressures on the population to emigrate continue to rise, labor-intensive projects, heavily oriented towards construction and dispersed throughout the countries, could be used to complement the infrastructure programs currently funded by the development banks. Foreign assistance—perhaps additional structural-adjustment type loans as extended by the World Bank—might be essential since constraints on budget deficits, imposed by stabilization programs, restrict the allocation of domestic resources.

Although most Eastern countries are still relatively early in the process of transition, inflows of private capital have generally been disappointing. Czechoslovakia and Hungary have been best off in this regard. Both have had access to the international bond markets and foreign investment has been encouraging, flows of the latter into Czechoslovakia and Hungary amounting to $0.6 and $1.5 billion, respectively, in 1991. But private banks have reduced their exposure *vis-à-vis* all PETs. These developments suggest that one of the cornerstones of the western approach to promoting structural change and development in the east—through large inflows of private capital—looks questionable for some time to come.

Barring a sharp pickup in private flows, the East will continue to require official resources to support economic transformation and stabilization policies, although these are likely to total less than the $24 billion package recently proposed for Russia. Balance-of-payments projections for Bulgaria and Romania for 1992 suggest that both countries will again be confronted with financing gaps and inadequate reserves.[25] In each case only a part of the shortfall will be met by the international financial institutions so western governments will be called upon to make up the difference. Continued debate about the financing of several international financial institutions, including IFC and IMF, at a time of risen demands on their resources, cannot but complicate matters. And thus far no acceptable formula for burden sharing among donor governments has been worked out. This issue is of immediate relevance in putting together the stabilization fund for Russia and, later, other successor states of the Soviet Union. Finding a solution cannot be easy, given that western governments feel constrained by their own budgetary problems and deteriorating short-term prospects for their economic growth. With rising unemployment and other pressing domestic needs, it is difficult to allot foreign economic assistance a high priority on the policy agenda.

---

25. At the meeting of G-24 in November 1991, Ministers drew attention to the fact that new pledges were still necessary for Bulgaria and Romania to support the continuing reform effort (EC, *Press Release*, IP 91 994).

7

Assistance to the Transition Economies and North-South Cooperation

Miklós Losoncz

As pointed out in the chapter by Joseph Smolik, western assistance to the PETs' transitions takes on many forms. In view of the effects and magnitudes of the assistance involved, there must be global implications, particularly for the resource flow to developing countries, which is the topic of this chapter. First I briefly look at financial flows, including from multilateral institutions, commercial banks, the debt positions, and FDI in PETs, and their implications for the developing world. Second, in assessing these impacts it is not only the volume of the transfer of financial and related flows that counts, but also their impact on the conditions, notably interest rates, at which developing countries can access money and capital markets. Third, I evaluate the impact of the tariff preferences provided by the industrial economies to the PETs for the developing world. At each point, a distinction is made between the diversion of resources and the creation of additional means. A distinction should also be drawn between commitments and disbursements, and indeed the conditions at which the resources are provided. These factors, as well as poor data, complicate the quantification of the implications. For all of these reasons, I shall engage mostly in qualitative assessments, if only because most of the useful data are compiled in chapter 6.

Senior economic adviser in the Ministry of Foreign Economic Relations, Budapest, Hungary.

Western Financial Assistance and Its Impacts

It is important to distinguish among a number of different flows, including assistance from the multilateral financial institutions, official development assistance (ODA), commercial bank lending, debt relief, and FDI.

Official Flows

Official flows comprise multilateral lending, support from export-credit agencies, and bilateral nonconcessional lending. Due to considerable risks, the high degree of external indebtedness as well as the uncertainties related to the political and economic transition, western commercial banks have been either reluctant to provide credits to the PETs or have done so (as in the cases of Czechoslovakia and Hungary) at a high risk premium. Under these circumstances, PETs have had to rely primarily on borrowing from the multilateral financial institutions, including the EBRD, EIB, IMF, and the World Bank Group. Accordingly, the share of these multilateral institutions in total borrowing of the PETs has grown significantly in recent years. Although all multilateral, and, of course, all bilateral loans have been offered at market conditions (that is, at the actual market cost to the creditor country or institution plus fees), because of the lack or high price of access to private credit markets, they contain an implicit subsidy for the PETs (UNECE 1992, p. 186).

The growing importance of the four PETs (Bulgaria, Czechoslovakia, Hungary, and Poland) with active programs with the Fund can be illustrated by the fact that their share in fiscal 1991 (ending as of 30 April) was two thirds of the new credit commitments of SDR5.1 billion. The actual volume of credits drawn by the PETs rose sixfold (*Neue Zürcher Zeitung*, 4 October 1991). Now that it is certain that the successor states of the Soviet Union will become active members of the Fund, the total demand on Fund resources from the East as a whole is likely to rise significantly in the near term. According to Michel Camdessus, the IMF's managing director, his organization is expected to invest $25-$30 billion in the former Soviet republics over the next four years (*Financial Times*, 16 April 1991, p. 18). It is also expected that the General Arrangements to Borrow (GAB) will be activated to provide the planned $6 billion stabilization fund for the ruble, which is part of the $24 billion package now being assembled by the IMF for Russia.

The Fund operates with a fixed pool of loanable assets that can only be raised through "quota reviews," meaning a rise in the Fund's capital base against which it can then borrow in financial markets. But this has been increasingly more difficult to agree to in recent years, witness the Ninth Review, which has been in suspended animation for several years now. Even though the role of the Fund in ensuring some order in the East's transitions has been acknowledged, it is far from certain that the Ninth Review will soon be ratified. Under these conditions, the Fund's commitment to the East cannot but have an adverse effect on financial flows allocated to developing countries (UNWES 1991, p. 112). With the sharply risen commitments to the former Soviet republics, it is now more important than before to implement the Ninth Review as soon as possible, a matter that has been in the hands of U.S. legislation, which has been reluctant to raise funds for development assistance, particularly during an election year. The suggestion to create a special account to subsidize the Fund's interest rates made several times by Camdessus has thus far been rejected. It is almost sure that the IMF will need further GAB financing to be able to meet the financial requirements of the East as a whole. But that channel too is not assured as the GAB was instituted in the 1960s for quite different purposes.

True, the Fund is not in a position to provide all the loans needed to ensure orderly transitions in the East. However, the Fund's commitment is critical as its seal of approval through an approved adjustment program imparts credibility to the reform and, as a rule, opens the door to private sources of finance. And these are critical in reconstructing the East: Investment companies, investment funds, and commercial banks have the financial strength to provide the credits necessary for the restructuring of Eastern Europe. These too have potential implications for developing countries.

The total credit commitment of the World Bank has grown from $15.2 billion in 1990 to $16.4 billion in 1991; including IDA loans, loan commitments of the World Bank Group represented $20.7 and $22.7 billion, respectively. For 1992, credit commitments valued at $17-19 billion are envisaged by the World Bank; IDA's may amount to another $6.4 billion. Actual loans provided to the East amounted to $1.8 billion in 1990 and $2.9 billion in 1991, accounting for 12 and 18 percent, respectively, of total disbursements, thus suggesting a discernible shift in World Bank lending in favor of the East. It is probably safe to assume that these transactions in 1992 will grow by at least the rate observed in the preceding year. In addition, the World Bank is expected to invest $12-15 billion in the republics of the former Soviet Union.

As does the Fund, the World Bank too operates with a fixed pool of loanable assets. But the institution's equity was raised recently and the leeway to raise funds in financial markets thus afforded has not yet been exhausted (another $61.3 billion could be borrowed against the total authorized capital of $152.3 billion). Credit facilities of this magnitude together with borrowing against other reserves that can be mobilized as collateral, would seem to be sufficient for a while to meet additional demand, even if the former Soviet republics were to obtain substantial loans. Nonetheless, in spite of this margin of flexibility, some voices have already urged expansion of the World Bank's statutory capital to facilitate borrowing and also to ease the potential problem of redistributing voting rights to accommodate notably the loans to be extended to the successor states of the Soviet Union.

More or less the same considerations apply to the EBRD, whose capital base amounts to ecu10 billion (some $12.5 billion), 30 percent of which has been or will be paid in and the rest can be borrowed in financial markets. For 1992, EBRD plans to raise $0.9 billion on international capital markets. Note that apart from industrial countries and some of their institutions, as well as the PETs themselves, also some developing countries shared in the bank's founding capital. This too may have implications, albeit small, for the diversion of financial resources to the East.

To the degree that there has been no additionality in several of these transfers, notably in multilateral financial institutions, the risk of crowding out resources for developing countries should not be ignored. As regards the rest of the capital raised or to be raised on international financial markets, the competition of institutions lending to the developing world seems to be rather weak. As a matter of fact, the EBRD provided loans and capital investment valued at ecu621 million ($770 million) to five Eastern countries. This is still a modest sum, but it was accompanied by contributions from other investors amounting to ecu1.5 billion.

In 1990, the EC approved ecu1 billion lending from the EIB to Hungary and Poland over a three-year period. Thus far, the EIB, which is not a competitor to the EBRD, has approved $2.25 billion in investment loans for Bulgaria, Czechoslovakia, Hungary, Poland, and Romania. As a matter of course, EIB is not as a rule involved in providing loans to developing countries, let alone countries that are not EC members, as its primary mission is to assist the less developed areas of the EC. So there will be little direct competition. But potential diversion might occur indirectly, as a result of the expanded demand in financial markets. Anyway, without extending existing credit facilities the risk of diversion of resources from the third world might materialize.

Neither are the budgetary implications of providing export-credit guarantees significantly constraining on lending to developing countries. Provision of export credits has been made on the basis of considerations of creditworthiness, which is country-specific. In addition, export credits are provided at actual market conditions, no concessional elements at all being factored in the deal. On the contrary, low- and middle-income countries receive export credits from the OECD countries at somewhat less favorable interest rates than richer ones. Aside from costs, due to the recession and limits to financing imports, the PETs have thus far utilized only a rather small proportion of the available facilities. Consequently, the risk of diversion of flows from the third world to the East has been negligible. Because of the rather modest magnitude of export credits, even a substantial shift towards the East could not signal a potentially significant diversion of capital flows from third world countries.

The effects of bilateral nonconcessional lending are less clear, but there does not appear to be any significant evidence of diversion in 1990-1991 (World Bank 1992, p. 11).

Official Development Assistance

ODA in principle is a type of resource flow that could lead to significant diversion in favor of the East. Because of the restrictive fiscal policies pursued in industrial countries, the supply constraints in terms of available funds have been most pronounced in this area. But in 1990, the competition between the PETs and developing countries for ODA was not marked as only $1.5 billion was allocated for the East, which equals less than 3 percent of the total ODA allocated to developing countries (*Neue Zürcher Zeitung*, 6 December 1991, p. 13).

There is presently little, if any, chance of earmarking ODA resources to assist the PETs. For one thing, it is unlikely that a national consensus can be reached in the industrial world to support these transitions by raising fiscal revenues, such as might be required in any emulation of the postwar Marshall Plan for Western Europe. Neither is it likely that the peace dividend eventually accruing from maintaining a lower military profile, thanks to the removal of east-west tensions, can be converted into assistance to the East.

There may arise some competition for resources that will be freed up because assistance previously earmarked under the label of ODA, even though meant in support of strategic considerations, will be redeployed from the erstwhile implicit tolerance for the abuse of political power, corruption, violation of human rights, and wasteful use of resources. Such a reevaluation of western policy regarding development assistance is still in its incipient phase. Over the medium term, however, it might result in some reduction of present flows in nominal terms to selected developing countries. But such freed resources will not necessarily be channeled to the East.

The changes in the East are having an undeniable direct impact on all kinds of assistance, including financial flows, that these countries themselves previously provided to the developing world. Although the traditional assistance policies of the CMEA countries had little to do with the purposes ostensibly served by ODA, these transfers in whatever form nevertheless tended to ease the foreign-exchange constraint, including notably by providing useful export outlets, imports at concessional prices, and exports at above world-market price levels. These facilities are simply no longer available in the changed East, partly due to the collapse of the institutional system of regional economic and political cooperation in the CMEA.

Commercial Lending

As far as private commercial flows are concerned, the impact of western assistance to the East depends importantly on the total potential lending by commercial channels to the south and the PETs, and the degree to which there may be competition for such funds. In light of recent experience and on present expectations, direct sovereign lending to either group of countries is likely to remain of a rather limited scope. This applies in the first instance to U.S. financial institutions, which in any case have had only a limited exposure in the East as compared to, say, German banks. Because of the intensity of trade between Germany and the East, however, the exposure of German banks might expand significantly, but only in an indirect way, namely through the financing requirements of German exporters. Such lending might become the most important driving force in raising the exposure of all those countries, particularly in Western Europe, that hope to extend their trade relations with the East. This might involve some diversion of resources, notably in the case of German banks, otherwise possibly available for financing trade with developing countries.

As to the interrelationship of lending to the two groups of countries, an inquiry (see Bogdanowicz-Bindert and Philips 1992) of a number of financial institutions in several industrial countries found that banks in Europe, Japan, and the United States do not consider the developing and transition economies as substitutes or interconnected in any significant way. There can, therefore, be little talk of a tradeoff.

Because of the difficulties encountered in obtaining commercial loans in recent years, some Eastern countries, particularly Hungary, have sought to shift their borrowing requirements through the international bond market, even though, since 1989, the costs of raising such funds have risen considerably. But there does not seem to be any direct competition between transition and developing countries in this market, the bond market for most developing countries having been closed since the onset of the debt crisis or for other reasons.

Debt Relief

One of the most crucial problems faced by most PETs is the management of the large debt overhang. This may have considerable implications on the debt management of the developing countries. At this point two kinds of effects should be taken into account. There is the possibility of substitution, such as the earmarking of funds from a fixed pool (for instance, in the context of the Brady Plan) in favor of the East. But it remains difficult to assess whether such a constraint has been operative at all and hindered plans of the south to obtain debt reduction. The other effect comes about as a result of setting precedents. It is widely feared that debt relief for the PETs would induce developing countries to solicit a similar accommodation with the north. And, of course, it might have its own bandwagon effects in the East.

Until 1990, in fact, the Paris Club ruled out debt reduction, except for some low-income countries. In March 1991, the creditor countries participating in the Paris Club allowed Poland to reschedule all payments resulting in a $16.5 billion reduction of official debts. Bulgaria was also allowed to reschedule and reduce its debt stock by $1.8 billion. Between January 1990 and June 1991, debt restructuring brought another $2.8 billion relief for Poland. Further elements of debt relief are the claims of the former GDR on Eastern countries, which were taken over by Germany as a result of German monetary and economic union. The Paris Club agreed to reschedule some $3.3 billion of Soviet debt falling due in December 1991 (UNECE 1992, p. 187). Since then, further negotiations have taken place on rescheduling between representatives of former Soviet republics and G-7 deputy finance ministers.

Several developing countries (including Chile, Mexico, and Venezuela) have in the past obtained some debt relief on condition of implementing substantial structural reforms and debt restructuring. Several other countries have since then obtained some form of debt relief (World Bank 1992, p. 42). According to the World Bank, there are several other middle-income developing countries (including the Congo, Côte d'Ivoire, Honduras, and Morocco) as well as the bulk of the poorest and most indebted low-income countries that deserve some debt relief. The G-7 summit in London in July 1991 affirmed its willingness to make further progress on debt relief for selected low- to middle-income countries on a case-by-case basis.

The above suggests that some competition for debt relief between developing and transition economies may be emerging. This involves in the first instance debt rescheduling but also additional financial sources, and it is here that the potential for diversion to the East might become a reality, particularly now that the substantial debt of the former Soviet Union will have to be managed in a different way than this had been envisaged until late 1990. But official creditors continue to emphasize that the Bulgarian and Polish debt-rescheduling and relief exercises should be considered *sui generis*; in any case, they cannot be construed as setting precedents.

Foreign Direct Investment

FDI is not, in fact, subject to supply constraints, except in the very short run. For one thing, resource availability is not hindered by budgetary limits or the restricted volume of existing funds. The real constraint is on identifying projects whose expected rate of return will be sufficiently high to persuade economic agents to save and perhaps even to invest. Consequently, no diversion of existing resources can take place from developing countries to PETs. But it cannot be denied that there is fierce competition for FDI in the world economy, and this includes both groups of countries. In the short run, with the risen demand for FDI, this may delay the financing of projects that would otherwise have been possible. The reme-

dy in this case is really for countries to offer attractive investment opportunities. However, to date the volume of FDI that has in effect been
transferred, and even in terms of commitments, has remained small.

As far as the future is concerned, privatization of SOEs may increase
the attractiveness of PETs to foreign investors. But there are significant
differences in the privatization campaigns in the various PETs and the
ways in which foreign investors are allowed to participate in them. Thus,
Hungary has by far the most liberal regime, as it allows access of foreign
investors to virtually all state-owned property earmarked for privatization
in part or in full. It should, therefore, not be surprising that Hungary has
attracted the bulk of FDI coming into the PETs.

Eastern governments have been offering a great number of incentives,
including a liberal treatment of profit and capital transfer and generous
tax holidays, to attract FDI. In addition, the PETs can offer comparatively
well-trained labor at rather low costs, with total unit labor cost amounting
to some \$2 per hour, as compared to \$15-23 in most OECD countries and
\$4-6 in the Asian newly industrializing developing economies (NIEs).
Some of this gap is eroded by lower levels of productivity in the East, but
even correcting for that leaves a sizable margin, at least as compared to
OECD countries, but not necessarily in comparison with the more dynamic NIEs. However, effective exploitation of this comparative advantage is
being hindered by the material- and energy-intensive structure of the
Eastern economies, where labor costs account for a rather small portion
(around 15-20 percent) of total production costs in industry. This might be
a marked obstacle to FDI in the region.

Another obstacle is that Eastern governments tend to favor equity
investments, in particular joint ventures, as the main form of attracting
foreign capital. One of the reasons for this is that these countries are
interested in obtaining factors of production that are linked to FDI, including technology, managerial skills, knowhow, training, and marketing.
The other reason is that domestic capital markets in the East are rather
underdeveloped; in most countries, they simply do not exist. As a result,
portfolio investment cannot attract foreign investment on any large scale,
at least for the time being. This has been amply underlined by the fact
that the various country funds established in the west have found it
difficult to invest in profitable activities according to western portfolio
investment criteria.

There has, as a result, been little competition to date. But that might
increase in the future. For that to occur, at the very least economic, politi-

cal, and social stability will have to be restored in the East. Moreover, it should be borne in mind that the PETs and the developing countries serve different markets. Thus, a PET may compete for a capital project that has been earmarked for Europe (or perhaps Eastern Europe) in any case. But it is unlikely to be in the running for a developing-country project, partly because it cannot compete in the medium to long run as compared to what developing countries can offer. And many PETs find it difficult for the time being to focus on exploiting technically sound comparative advantages. That will come into its own only once further experience with transition has been gathered.

Since it is improbable that the Eastern countries will rely extensively on portfolio investment in the near future, the sharpening of the competition for this sort of foreign investment and a subsequent diversion of flows from the third world to Eastern Europe is not expected to materialize in the medium term.

Interest Rates

Under present circumstances, future trends in interest rates in a global context are a function of the supply of and demand for financial capital. The supply depends on global savings. The overall demand for capital in turn is a function of the sharply risen demand for investments in some critical regions of the world, like the Middle East, the eastern part of Germany, and the PETs that have recently experienced radical changes with severe economic consequences.

The reconstruction of the Middle Eastern economies most affected by the Gulf War will be far less costly than it had been envisaged just after the conclusion of the war. In any case, the larger part of the total reconstruction costs will be financed from sources within the region, particularly the net oil-exporting countries. Thus, the postwar reconstruction of the Middle East will not put a significant additional burden on international capital markets and interest rates either in nominal or in real terms.[1]

---

1. *Editor's note*: Of course, the net savings of the oil-exporting countries that would otherwise have been available for global redistribution will now not be. By thus cutting into the supply of capital, there may still be an upward effect on global interest rates. But it is believed to be comparatively small.

The expected total costs of German unification are fairly well known. Similarly striking are the cost estimates of rebuilding the PETs, particularly the former Soviet Union. Those transitions cannot be fully financed from sources of savings within the region, but will have to come from private and official financial sources. Certainly for the first several years, the overwhelming part of this external finance will be in the form of loans, whose interest rates are always immediately and directly determined by actual supply and demand conditions.

If the propensity to save in the global economy remains nearly constant, it is most probable that the enormous costs and foreign capital requirements of the restructuring of the PETs will exert an upward push to long-term real interest rates in international money and capital markets. Global real interest rates in the 1980s were significantly above those observed during the 1970s. Due to the economic recession in 1990-1991, interest rates in the United States declined, but those in Japan continued to be rather high by international standards. Apart from the characteristics and state of the business cycle, a gauge on the costs of the East's transitions and reconstructions can be obtained from the experience with German monetary and economic union in mid-1990 and the subsequent massive transfer of capital within Germany.

Nominal interest rates will additionally be affected by inflationary expectations. They will also rise due to the increase of the risk premium on long-term bonds and credits as a consequence of greater uncertainties. Even this early into the transition, as already related, the majority of the PETs have access to credits, if at all, only at a higher interest rate than the normal commercial one because of rather high risk premia.

The additional external capital requirements of PETs and the eastern part of Germany may amount to an increment of some $100 billion annually for the next ten years (*Neue Zürcher Zeitung*, 1 November 1991, p. 17). As a rule-of-thumb, this *ex ante* gap between the supply of savings and the demand for investment funds could result in a 1 percentage point increase of real interest rates (World Bank 1992, p. 43). Of course, actual interest rates are determined by other factors too. And because of political uncertainties and low capital absorption capacities in the individual PETs, investments there may lag well behind expected requirements. This would ease the upward pressure on interest rates, but the duration of the pressure would be extended.

Any increase of the interest rates results in higher costs of borrowing and a higher debt-servicing burden. Since the developing countries are the largest borrowers and debtors, even a small rise in global interest rates has a negative impact on them. Furthermore, rising interest rates may be indicative of relative capital scarcity, which might lead with a lag to a reduction of development assistance. In that sense, the pressures on financial flows in the global economy because of the capital needs of the PETs might exert an indirect diversion of assistance.

Trade Preferences

In their efforts to promote the establishment of pluralistic, market-based economic systems in the East, governments of industrial countries introduced several trade-liberalization measures that, in fact, significantly improved market access for exports from the PETs (UNECE 1992, pp. 189-92). First of all, in 1990, the EC lifted specific discriminatory quantitative restrictions earlier imposed on the East's exports. It also eliminated all quantitative restrictions on exports of most manufactured goods originating in the East, excepting agriculture, textiles and clothing, and iron and steel, and extended treatment under the General System of Preferences (GSP) to the PETs as of 1991. Trade in agriculture, textiles and clothing, and iron and steel was regulated separately.

Other OECD countries, like the EFTA states and the United States, followed suit, and introduced liberalization measures aimed at easing market access of Eastern goods. The measures ranged from the elimination of existing quantitative restrictions on nonsensitive products to the provision of GSP. As of the end of 1991, all OECD countries granted most-favored nation (MFN) status to Bulgaria, Czechoslovakia, Hungary, and Poland. With the exception of the United States, the same treatment was meted out to Romania. The Baltic states have in the meantime obtained similar treatment.

In addition, Czechoslovakia, Hungary, and Poland in late 1991 concluded Europe Agreements with the EC, thus opening the way to the gradual elimination of reciprocal tariffs on manufactured goods. However, those imposed by the EC will be reduced and gradually eliminated first, thus discriminating in favor of the East. Although specific rules govern trade in agricultural products, textiles and clothing, and iron and steel, the common feature of the regulations is on balance that the Central European countries concerned will be entitled to raise the volume of their exports with progressive elimination of tariffs. Furthermore, a free trade agreements between EFTA and Czechoslovakia was recently concluded, and those with Hungary and Poland will follow soon. The United States continues to liberalize its trade restrictions *vis-à-vis* the three Central European countries.

Unfortunately, available data do not permit a more or less accurate assessment of the value of all of these trade concessions. It is, however, beyond doubt that the relative competitive position of all PETs has improved relative to that of the developing countries as a result of discriminatory adjustments in quantitative restrictions. Furthermore, the PETs have achieved more or less equal status with the third world since they also make use of the GSP. Also, liberalization measures for the PETs were introduced in sensitive sectors. Finally, the competitiveness of Czechoslovakia, Hungary, and Poland will grow on EC and EFTA markets as a result of the establishment of free trade in industrial goods and significant preferences in trade in agricultural products.

All these improvements will increase the competitive edge of the Central European countries, particularly in comparison to developing countries with a similar export profile. Though the advantages for other PETs are proportionately less significant, on balance they nonetheless disadvantage developing countries. As a result, one may expect a potentially significant diversion of trade and technology to the East at the expense of some developing countries.

The diversion of technology may in fact be enhanced by the relative improvement of the attractiveness of the East as an outlet for FDI. In spite of the strict rules of origin and the rather high local-content requirement (more than 50 percent of the products should be manufactured locally in general, but this ratio is above 60 percent in electronics and the motor industry) of exports benefiting from the free-trade arrangements, low unit labor costs and free access to EC and EFTA markets may be attractive also for overseas investors seeking to expand their exports to Europe.

The potential diversion of trade and technology from developing countries could be offset by granting them additional preferences. The Development Committee of the OECD recently noted the significant and costly trade protection that persists in many sectors, including agriculture and textiles and clothing, costing developing countries more than $100 billion annually (OECD 1991a, p. 18).

Conclusions

The capital requirements of the PETs, both to firmly root market economies and to restructure and modernize these economies, tend to be enormous over the medium term. Because indigenous resources are measurably insufficient to finance these transformation processes, western governments took the initiative to organize assistance through their national
agencies and international institutions. Due to the orders of magnitude,
this assistance to the East cannot but have global implications, including
on capital flows to the developing countries. In spite of the huge capital
requirements of the East's reconstruction, under present circumstances
there is unlikely to be a global capital shortage. The implications are more
likely to be in terms of a redirection of capital flows and a modification in
its composition, as well as a rise in real interest rates in the medium term.

The competition for funding has risen considerably for the sources of
all multilateral financial institutions. The impact on the lending abilities
of these institutions has not so far been in the nature of hurting the needs
of developing countries, at given conditions of lending by these institutions. As regards the EBRD, the lack of additionality for the contributions
of member governments to the capital fund, particularly the part paid in
cash, may crowd out new resources mainly for other multilateral organizations. As far as the remaining commercial and other capital flows are
concerned, the competition for funds from institutions lending to developing countries would seem to be rather weak and remain so for the foreseeable future. But there is potentially fierce competition between the
PETs and developing countries for rescheduling and, as a result, for
additional financial resources. In sum, then, the risk of diversion of capital
flows from the South to the East would appear to be rather small, though
not necessarily negligible, certainly for individual developing countries.

Trade preferences granted to PETs, on the other hand, may significantly weaken the relative competitive position of selected developing countries. The risk of trade diversion is greatest in trade and technology flows,
and through the latter in improving the relative attractiveness of the East
for FDI, including from non-European sources. But that impact is likely to
differ for various groups of developing countries. It is expected to be less
important for low-income and some of the middle-income developing
countries. For one thing, it is highly unlikely that ODA funding will be
cut in favor of the East. Likewise, these countries will remain the primary

beneficiaries of debt relief and they will continue to benefit from GSP treatment.

The competitive position of the NIEs will be more adversely affected by the trade concessions granted to the East. It should be noted, however, that these countries have been shifting their output profile to more technology-intensive products and they hardly export any agricultural products. As a result, the commodity composition of their export offer is becoming less and less similar to the East's.

Western assistance to the East is expected to have the most adverse impact on Latin America. The commodity composition of the region's exports is quite similar to the East's. Trade preferences to the East will result in the deterioration of the relative competitive position of Latin American exports in industrial markets. Latin American countries are most interested in debt relief as well and some are important ODA recipients. Furthermore, the whole continent is competing for lending by commercial banks and FDI.

I have not attempted to assess the impact of western assistance on migratory flows because these are being dealt with in the west through administratively channels. These conventional measures may, however, not suffice in the longer run. The threat of mass migration from the East makes it necessary to elaborate a strategy aiming at absorbing the population in the region by economic means.

As regards the impact of western assistance on the cost of capital, any gap between the demand for and the supply of capital will be bridged by rising interest rates, which is bound to affect developing countries. Real interest rates will remain rather high over the medium term, hence, raise the cost of borrowing and debt servicing. Some developing countries that are not considered creditworthy will have to confront more limited access to capital markets (World Bank 1992, p. 12).

It should be noted, however, that the persistence of high interest rates is not unavoidable. If the leading OECD countries reduce their huge budget deficits and raise their fairly low saving rates, interest rates could be brought down. For example, a rise in the U.S. saving rate by 1 percentage point would result in a $55 billion increase in global savings. Thus, the governments and central banks of the industrial countries should take policy measures to promote private and public savings. Budget deficits could be lowered primarily by reducing military expenditures and subsidies provided to industry and agriculture. The implicit potential savings could exceed $100 billion—the increment of the capital requirements for the reconstruction of the East.

To avoid crowding-out effects and adverse competition for aid and multilateral lending, it would be desirable to distinguish between the policy objectives of helping the East and assisting the developing world. Eastern countries have already reached a fairly high level of economic development and *per capita* income compared to the majority of the developing countries, particularly the least developed ones. The East needs assistance to correct external and internal disequilibria, to improve general economic stability, to modernize economic structures, and to move towards market-based economic systems. In the least developed countries, however, the primary task is alleviating mass poverty. If only on the basis of these quite different policy goals, it would be useful to treat funds for the East separately from those earmarked for developing countries both in national budgets as well as in the lending profiles of the multilateral financial institutions, with as much attention as possible given to additionality for the funds earmarked for the East. The removal of barriers to trade by developed countries would raise the revenue of developing countries by an amount equivalent to twice the value of ODA granted by OECD countries. The liberalization of the trade regime of the developing countries is essential (OECD 1991a, p. 18).

8

The West's Experience and the East

Wladimir Andreff

Whereas there can be little doubt that the west's economic experience offers valuable lessons for desirable economic policy making in the PETs, one should carefully differentiate what is transferable from what may be unique or inappropriate, given the situation in the PETs. Instances of transfer include aspects of macroeconomic policy, techniques of privatization (Andreff 1992a), scheduling industrial modernization, breathing life into market behavior, setting up new institutions and regulations, transferring technology and knowhow through joint ventures and FDI, fostering management and accounting techniques, improving banking services, creating new services, organizing various types of capital markets, raising interfirm cooperation, spreading the benefits of international assistance, vocational training and business education, data processing and automated control of production. One could expand this list almost without an end.

This chapter focuses on private sources of western assistance that may render the PETs increasingly capable of operating a full-fledged market economy. As such it complements the preceding chapter. But here I focus on the situation in the three Central European countries and the former Soviet Union. First, I identify the private sources of such assistance, which will stem mostly from TNCs. I consider a TNC to be any firm that spreads its business, whether industrial or not, in more than one country, with or

Professor of Economics, University of Paris 1, Panthéon-Sorbonne, Paris, France.

without investing in equity or in durable assets. In the following sections, I briefly sketch the type of TNC that is most likely to be involved in passing on various aspects of western experience to the PETs and transforming their economic environment.

Agents Involved in Transferring the West's Experience

At the latest since 1989, many western businessmen have perceived the business climate in the East to be very attractive. Regardless of their degree of commitment, all have become potential agents for the transfer of the west's experience. By the same token, they have become transnational. This means that we shall have to survey the general trends affecting the development of these agents, and the arrangements through which they can channel their experience, including to the newly privileged sectors of expansion.

A follow-the-leader strategy is often the most promising, least risky behavior for managers of small enterprises when they enter a risky and unstable market. It is, therefore, useful to briefly glance at the strategy of major TNCs. It should not be forgotten that some had already in the 1970s taken advantage of the legislative accommodation of FDI. Even earlier, some had engaged in profitable barter or compensation trade with the East (Gendarme 1981). The increased attention paid to the East by TNCs does not mean that they have ceased to evaluate the comparative advantages of alternative business locations, however, before deciding upon the type of activity to be transferred (Andreff 1990, UNCTC 1988).

The most striking trend that was started in the 1980s has been the growth of nonequity arrangements, meaning all international business operations that lie in a grey area between traditional trade (exports) and wholly or majority-owned foreign affiliates (Oman 1984). Increasingly, the TNC is not the sole owner of the project or enterprise abroad and, in fact, may take no equity position. It is of special importance to note that nonequity arrangements often mean a reduced exposure to commercial and political risks that ordinarily accompany FDI. This explains why such new forms of investment have developed mainly in host developing countries since the 1970s. Commercial and political risks in the East are sufficiently daunting to businessmen to pave the way for various kinds of new forms of investment in the East.

These new forms encompass alternative modes of international business (see Contractor and Lorange 1988), including companies cooperating by sharing control, technology, management, financial resources, and markets. Basically this model of behavior is appealing for host countries, especially if their enterprises strive to cooperate with TNCs. In the grey area between trade and majority-owned subsidiary lie several types of cooperative arrangements: technical training, startup assistance agreements, production sharing, assembly and buyback agreements, patent licensing, franchising, knowhow licensing, management and marketing services agreements, nonequity cooperative agreements in exploration, scientific research partnerships, development and coproduction, turnkey projects, and finally equity joint ventures. All types of countertrade, such as barter, counterpurchase; buyback; production sharing; industrial offsets[1]; and switches, are commonly included in this grey area (Lecraw 1988).

Such agreements are also appealing because a firm that expands abroad always faces a tradeoff between the cost of supervising a foreign wholly-owned affiliate and transaction costs of traditional foreign trade; all the above-mentioned nonequity arrangements entail lower supervisory costs than FDI and lower transaction costs than trade. A strategy playing on the cost mix is proper for enterprises operating on an unpredictable and unstable market like the East's, since transaction costs may well increase in a more decentralized economy with a greater number of foreign trade decision makers and a rising need of microeconomic information. Supervisory costs may also be very high in case of social unrest fueled by new mass unemployment, people's impoverishment, and emerging signs of disappointment about the momentum and path of the transformation. As to the tradeoff between various kinds of nonequity arrangements, no general behavior on the part of enterprises can be inferred from past experience. The answer mainly depends on the type of activity. For instance, marketing agreements, licenses, and cross-licensing agreements abound in precision control instruments and robotics, while deeper cooperation is necessary in factory automation (Harrigan 1986). Nonequity contractual relations are of particular importance in a number of service industries, such as hotels and fast-food restaurants; accounting, engineer-

---

1. These are requirements placed on the exporter by the importer or importing country to produce part of the product, source parts, or assemble the product in the importing country; exports from the importing country may also be required.

ing, and management assistance; after-sale service networks; data-process-
ing facilities; and transportation systems.

The second general trend both in FDI and in cooperative international
business is a radical change in its sectoral composition since the 1980s. By
the middle of the decade, over 40 percent of the world's total FDI stock
was in service industries, compared with less than 20 percent in the 1950s.
In the PETs, the contribution of services to the modernization of the
entire economy has been fully recognized because of their spillover effects
and their link to the information revolution. Because PETs are well-en-
dowed with human resources and possess large markets, they might
develop rather quickly comparative advantages in some service industries.
A precondition is that the lacking capital and expertise be provided by
foreign firms. Since many services are difficult to trade, a wide area of
expansion is open to nonequity arrangements between western firms and
those of PETs.

Such a transfer of modern service industries should not be considered
a panacea for all transition problems, however. Modern services are less
able than industrial TNCs to take advantage of lower wages in the East.
They are hence less likely to hedge against increasing unemployment in
these countries. This is due to the fact that service firms have fewer
opportunities than industrial enterprises to split up the production process
into labor-intensive and capital-intensive segments because most services
have to be produced where and when they are consumed. The direct and
indirect impact of imported services on the balance of payments may be
expected to be positive. Imports of services at one point in time can lead
to the export of goods later on, and the availability of certain services
increases the competitiveness of exports and the efficiency of imports. The
positive impact on the balance of payments may be compounded by using
nonequity arrangements because they provide less capital from abroad
than FDI and they may trigger as much outflows of fees, royalties, and
repatriated incomes as classical affiliates.

Services are linked to other sectors on the demand side because of
purchases by service industries in local markets and, on the supply side,
because of other industries. There may also be an indirect impact exerted
through the quality and prices of services on the efficiency of other
industries, largely by improving intermediation and lowering transaction
costs per unit of value added. Finally, service firms may usher into the
PETs new values, attitudes, and behavioral patterns, and, thus, influence
both culture and economic life, including its efficiency aspects.

Special attention should be paid to the third general trend in international business: the "financial globalization" (Aglietta, Brender and Coudert 1990) of the world economy. All actors in the global economy, including banks; finance-related affiliates of nonfinancial companies (particularly in the trading, manufacturing, and petroleum industries); securities and financial-service firms; and insurance companies, should help the East in setting up capital markets and easing the movement towards full currency convertibility. By the same token, international trade-related services, such as agency houses; general trading companies; commodity traders; retailers; and purchasing agents, may lay the ground for the operation of genuine commodity markets in the PETs. This should link the latter rapidly to the global economy through arbitrage operations. A similar effect can be expected from investment or nonequity arrangements in other service industries, such as real estate, hotels, tourism, transportation and communication, hospitals and health services, and in professional services themselves (such as advertising, accounting, engineering, data processing, and business consulting).

I did not emphasize the capacity of TNCs to transfer technology since it is not a new activity, even in the East. The transition has opened up more opportunities for technology transfer of all kinds, including notably management and marketing skills, however. All these could strengthen the foundations for the emergence of an autonomous entrepreneurial force in the East. National managers who are trained in local western firms will propagate in the PETs new habits in accounting practices, advertising and marketing, finance, labor discipline, and quality control, with or without leaving their job. In the latter case, the transfer will operate through relations with the managers of local suppliers and customers of the TNC, or even through business competition, negotiations, and transactions.

The Modernizing Capacity of Western Assistance

Proprietary technology is one of the most important competitive factors of TNCs (Bertin and Wyatt 1986). Until the late 1980s, the scope of trade in patents was rather limited by both restrictions on the transfer of western technology to the East, and, within this latter, the relatively large share of "nonnegotiable" transfers (Hanson 1981). From the point of view of western economic agents involved in technology transfer to the East, the main shortcomings were the fact that it took much longer to assimilate the transferred technology by the Eastern partner, due to the nonmarket environment. This is precisely what is now bound to change. Also, TNCs did not consider it so attractive to cooperate with Eastern firms in spite of the well-known high levels of research in some Eastern scientific institutes. The main reason was the lack of tight relationships between these institutes and manufacturing enterprises (Andreff 1978) so that a reverse technology transfer in favor of the TNCs was not even workable. This too will be transformed with the restructuring and privatization of SOEs.

Now that competitive technologies are so badly needed, when marketing links are crucial, or when alien organizational methods are required in the East, TNCs have become much more interested in providing new technologies (Marer and Zecchini 1991; UNWES 1991, 1992). Because they can form many different formats of commercial technology transfer, nonequity arrangements should be essential to implementing the modernizing capacity of western economic agents. But TNCs ought to stop transferring outdated technology to the East. The best incentive to arrest this behavior is the establishment of effective markets in the PETs. In an interrelated market economy, anyone can reject a bad-quality input but is compelled to supply a good-quality output: Eastern firm will have to learn from TNCs how to adjust to such a constraint. For this purpose, technological partnership with TNCs seems appropriate. In some cases, however, this may be a bumpy road towards acquiring western technology. In past experiences of such technological partnership, cultural distances, uncertainties, misunderstandings, and hidden agendas have poisoned relations (Doz 1988).

New information technologies are, of course, among the most likely to improve economic performance in the East since they will immerse these countries into transborder data flows that are so vital to becoming competitive in service sectors. By collapsing space and time, the new data-based technologies should make it possible for certain services to be produced in one place and consumed simultaneously in another. Gains will derive directly as well as indirectly from the transfer of infrastructure for the utilization of transborder data flows (mainly telecommunications and computers). In addition, local research expenditures should be reoriented towards the more commercial applications of computer science.

How about such transfers and traditional restrictions enacted by the Coordinating Committee for Multilateral Export Controls (CoCom)? In

June 1990, 38 of the 116 categories of controls on technology sales to the East were scrapped in a first stage towards reducing the list to core items (Warusfel 1990). This list includes the product categories of sensoring systems, advanced materials and machine tools, advanced telecommunications, navigational and aviation equipment, and some types of computers and propulsion systems. Although in May 1991, CoCom agreed to relax rules on the sale of double-use technology to ex-CMEA countries, thus confining controls to the core list of the most strategic items, it maintained differentiation among individual countries, discriminating particularly against the Soviet Union. For example, in May 1991, western firms aired their disappointment about the fact that the supply of advanced telecommunication equipment, computers, and fiber optics to the Soviet Union has remained restricted.

The modernizing capacity of international business is not, however, limited to transferring technology. Another channel of modernization consists in western firms' participating in the revamping of the East's economic structures, including through participation in privatization; but this topic transcends the boundaries of this chapter. The bulk of the restructuring with the west's experience, however, will continue through FDI, joint ventures, and takeovers.

Enterprise restructuring involves changes in a firm's technology and organization to raise efficiency and competitiveness, with a possible underlying transfer of technology; changes in a firm's products and markets; changes in management to improve productivity through retraining and retrenchment; acquisitions and divestitures; leveraged buyouts, recapitalization; and downsizing. There are also negative side effects of restructuring: layoffs and increasing local unemployment, factory closings, liquidations of assets, and temporary regional underdevelopment. Of course, the west has had experience with such changes, particularly since 1973, when the first oil shock revealed a need for restructuring industries in nearly all OECD countries. Even though confined to a few spectacular examples, takeovers by TNCs of PET firms have always entailed some restructuring, involving modernization of plant and equipment, layoffs of redundant labor, and changes in the quality and diversity of output.

Comprehensive industrial restructuring ought to include a rise in the number of small and medium-sized enterprises throughout the East, where traditionally this kind of economic agent was much less widespread than in the west. Small local enterprises may develop with the help of western capital. Through advising and consulting, in particular small firms operating in high-tech production and providing high quality and exportable products may emerge. Relying on new western-style company laws and pushed by privatization, a number of new small firms have emerged mainly in Central Europe. The west's experience can also back the creation of supporting institutions to small enterprise development or provide some advice to already existing institutions, such as the Hungarian Foundation for the Development of Small Enterprises, the Polish Department for the Promotion of Entrepreneurship, and the Bulgarian Overall Association of Small Enterprises.

Western banks could provide highly useful advice and experience in how to establish confidence and links between the revamped banking systems in the East and small, restructured, and privatized enterprises. They could in this respect transfer banking technology, technical knowledge, prudential rules, and employee training. Together with advice to nascent nonbanking financing institutions, such as insurance companies; pension funds; and investment funds, the west's experience in banking can engineer a leap forward in developing a capital market, including an active stock exchange. Some experience of this kind has already been passed on, including from France. Western consulting firms and international experts have been called upon for advice in these matters in all PETs. Either governments or Eastern enterprises have also approached western consulting agencies and advisers on preparing feasibility studies concerning industrial restructuring, technology transfer, privatization, computerization, setting up new banks, and modernizing infrastructures.

Three other undertakings are likely to improve the business environment in a period of modernization and restructuring: (i) developing international business centers; (ii) opening up free trade zones in some regions, where the bulk of the industry is to be restructured; and (iii) the business environment is heavily affected by the quality of infrastructure, notably the whole range of telecommunications (Bernard, Gaspard, and Harral 1991; Blaha and Kahn 1989; Reynaud and Poincelet, 1992).

Before raising the management issue, a word is needed about ecology. Large investments in the restructuring of heavy industry, including reducing the high-energy intensity of production, should be complemented with investment in cleaning up the environment insofar as new domestic and foreign firms intending to locate there would need clean and fresh air and water, no smog, less environmental risks, and simply a nicer environment for their employees. The west's experience in antipollution measures is far ahead of the PETs' attempts in this field, and some major

TNCs became aware long ago that antipollution offers a lucrative market. For the most polluting plants in the PETs, there is no alternative to closing them down, or at best planning their reconversion and the entailed layoffs, both topics of industrial restructuring. But the west's environmental experience may spread to training managers of water offices or cleaning stations. Generally speaking, management is obviously a major area, where the PETs can benefit from the west's experience.

Can the West Change Management Styles in the East?

Instead of having mainly to cope with a resource constraint, as under central planning (Kornai 1980), management in PETs will now have to face a great variety of demand as well as financial constraints. Marketing, product differentiation, discriminatory prices, advertising, sponsoring and selling techniques, business finance, leads and lags, hedging, asset valuation, and risk-premium calculation are among the basic requirements. These techniques can only be successfully used when an accurate accounting system, quite distinct from the one maintained under planning, is available. In helping the PETs switch, the west's experience is a *conditio sine qua non*, and the primary role in this transfer should fall on western consulting and auditing agencies. Many juridical and institutional preconditions for this change are beyond the scope of the present chapter. And it would take us too far afield to sketch all western management techniques. Instead, I shall select only a few examples of possible private assistance in consulting, accounting, and selling techniques.

The first step towards improving the management system at the micro level consists in erecting a stable and accurate juridical framework. It comprises laws and regulations, such as a company law; a law on commercializing SOEs; a law or a code to regulate FDI; a bankruptcy law; regulation of the banking business; an antitrust law; a new fiscal regime; and a decree enforcing new accounting practices according to a western-style accounting plan (Crane 1991). Much of this transfer is presently under way to both the private and public sectors from both private and public sources in the west. The successful introduction of such a new legal environment requires independent lawyers and notary publics.

Concerning the institutional environment of management, the west may provide experience for setting up employers' organizations. The specific interests of enterprise managers in the field of labor relations should increasingly be discussed within the chambers of commerce (or industry). In some PETs, such chambers have existed for some years, but their operations have been hampered by serious problems regarding their representativeness. Several western-style institutions representing employers have recently been set up. One of the main tasks of these organizations is now to develop collective bargaining with trade unions. Collective agreements reached in market economies may be referred to in the negotiations that the PETs cannot avoid in the near future because of the economic crisis built into the transition process. Wage policy and safety nets should be at the center of the debate.

Accounting is certainly a major tool that the PETs can borrow from the west. Once a western-style accounting plan has been integrated into the juridical framework, a long-run transfer of accounting techniques and knowhow is needed at the micro level and can only be gained from western accounting and consulting firms. In a market economy, the accountant's duties include the advisory and control functions on the basis of accounting information, and current money management of the enterprise. The control function is carried out with the aid of the older techniques of double-entry bookkeeping[2] and the new techniques of budgetary control and standard costing. These techniques should be transferred to PETs by western accountants and consulting agencies. But this is not enough. The full role of the accountant in a market economy and the roots of the accounting profession are less formal and more subtle experiences to be transmitted. This concerns first the crucial role of the accountant as a guardian of the firm's solvency. Second, double-entry bookkeeping serves as a data-classifying device and a basis for establishing methods of control, which has provided a solid ground upon which accountants have built up a position of influence in industry and commerce. The accounting profession has in addition acquired expertise in such areas as trusts, portfolio management, bankruptcy, company liquidation, restructuring, and mergers. All this expertise is required to make a capital market efficient and improve the business environment. In recent years, western accountants have come to assume responsibility for the

---

2. In the Soviet-type firm, this was primarily utilized as a device for classifying data. Whether it or some other classification was utilized continued to be largely a matter of administrative convenience in assembling data prior to their transmission to supervisory organs.

utilization of business computer systems; for preparation of the payroll; and for the elaboration of corporate planning, taxation planning, and operations research. Big accounting agencies have diversified into the direction of corporate-finance consulting and the use of data technologies.

Indeed, bookkeeping and accounting in big corporations are distinct functions. The (head) bookkeeper is exclusively concerned with the bookkeeping system. Accounting, generally joined to finance, comprises data processing (financial and cost accounting) and data analysis (financial and cost analysis). All the experience involved in these activities must be learned from western economic agents by new private firms and commercialized SOEs in the PETs. So far, however, it should be stressed that there is a lack of international accounting standards in the PETs and that basic audit regulations, as understood in the west, are not yet commonly used there (see Lindsay 1989 for the former Soviet Union). As pointed out by Derek Bailey (1988), accounting adapted itself to businessmen, but commercially minded businessmen were absent from the USSR (see also, Meyer 1990, Rahman 1991). This has left no choice but to adopt western practices. Learning by doing both techniques and prudential principle with the assistance or under the sponsorship of western accountants and consulting firms will complement, for the PET firms, the basic features of an accounting reform and the new rules for assessing the value of assets and liabilities advised by multilateral organizations and to some degree implemented by those in most advanced PETs (OECD 1991e). Most big western accounting agencies and management consulting firms are already settled in the PETs or involved in joint ventures, thus securing a transfer of norms, standards, and knowhow.

The organization of the profession is the last experience from the west to be channeled into PETs insofar as accounting is concerned. This would favor the development of the accountants' advising and consulting role as independent advisers staying outside the enterprise. National associations of accountants are now reorganized on the western model in some PETs and are members of the International Federation of Accountants. This includes an international committee entrusted with harmonizing accounting standards. The membership of accountants in PETs is a guarantee for transmitting to them western standards and practices.

PET enterprises must be accustomed to face a demand constraint in the future market economy and then to master selling and marketing knowhow. We can think first of techniques for financing so badly needed exports to convertible-currency markets such as switch operations, export leasing and factoring, forfeiting, and project financing. Most of them have been experienced in east-west trade (Zloch-Christy 1991) prior to the transition and only a fine-tuning in the choice between techniques might still be learned from the west.

A less common selling effort of the enterprises in PETs was advertising, either for foreign or domestic markets. Some of the largest western advertising agencies have expanded into management consultancy. Many advertising groups are now able to provide their clients with an integrated package of business services. They penetrate now the PET's advertising market for either their own business or in joint ventures with local agencies. This is not to categorize this advertising experience flowing into the East as an unmitigated blessing, however. Some serious mistakes have been made. This shows that PETs must be careful in separating the wheat from the chaff of the west's experience.

Developing Services in the PETs

An interrelated network of services is required in a well-functioning market economy. TNCs have found in such a cluster of finance-related, professional, and even tourist and travel services their most lucrative market. Some of these issues have already been touched upon. But others should be inquired into here. A first general remark is that the service industry is rather capital intensive. Moreover, workers who are now released from restructured industries in the PETs must be retrained before they can adequately perform in the service industry. As a result, such activities in the PETs should not be considered a strong remedy against unemployment.

The west's experience may be of some help in developing all services linked to domestic trade, even though retailing will need to emerge from petty privatization and new capital formation in the PETs themselves. But there is ample room to imitate the bigger western retail establishments. Wholesale deals and warehouses have to be modernized, and commodity markets should be organized in order to reduce shortages. An obvious precondition is that the PETs find their way out of their current economic crisis. Second, to ensure a continuous supply the transport sector must be capable of providing continuous and reliable service. Privatization and restructuring of certain transport services may follow the west's experience, though it is useful to be careful of negative externalities associated with having a transport network that is too widely privatized. But road haulage and taxi services, for example, should be privately run. This raises several issues for the west's experience to be transmitted: the improvement of the road network; drivers' training; a more severe highway code, particularly regarding the penalization of driving under influence; and car insurance (which is not yet compulsory in several PETs).

The insurance service sector remained underdeveloped in the former planned economies (Nestorovic 1991). Although some measure of self-contained insurance services has emerged since the administrative reforms of the 1960s throughout the PETs (Pardo 1991), prior to the revolutions of 1989 the general state of development of the insurance industry remained limited, basically because social insurance covered most risks, including accidents, health, disability, and pension.

With the transition towards a market economy, the insurance sector has obtained a new role to play. The liberalization of the economy creates new risks, particularly in terms of business risks for firms and unemployment risks for workers. This opens a new market for insurance companies. Restructuring the economy and the institutions paves the way in the PETs for such new business risks as terms of payment, insolvency, failure and bankruptcy. These are complemented for businessmen by political risk insofar as only a few transactions are now secure because of the future political uncertainty in the months, and perhaps years, ahead. The traditional risk-averse behavior of enterprise managers, however, hinders the meaning of insurance to them and thus puts a brake on their insurance expenditures. On the other hand, since no capital market was in operation, insurance companies used to invest in short-term deposits at the state bank. Now they are able to buy newly issued bonds and equities, and the new stock exchanges are likely to provide them with opportunities for diversifying their assets. In this respect, insurance companies start to transform savings into investments, much alike to what occurred at some point in the west. But for now this transformation is limited by the small size of the capital market in the East.

In any case, the insurance industry provides a promising market in the PETs for decades to come. It is not surprising that industry leaders in the west act as market makers, advisers, and investors in the revival of the insurance market insofar as the risks of domestic economic agents are concerned. Big western insurance companies must also follow their usual business partners and cover their specific risks in PETs, and this concerns namely foreign investors and traders. Major insurance TNCs are now cooperating with the state insurance companies still extant in the PETs.

Though not as crucial as the aforementioned services, the PETs can assimilate from the experience of market economies in hotels, travel agencies, car rentals, tourism, and more general leisure facilities. They are needed at least for providing a space for a western way of life to western TNC managers and employees working in the PETs. In the west's experience, such services are not only a pleasant way of spending business money. They also offer a way of accommodating business. There is no reason to expect that new entrepreneurs and managers of the PET enterprises would behave in a different way from their western counterparts. Last but not least, after forty years (and even seventy in the USSR) of the "iron curtain" preventing many western tourists from visiting the East, a flourishing market is now opening there for various kinds of travel agencies and hotel chains. For the time being, however, it will essentially be those specialized in business travel that stand to gain most.

As for many services already mentioned, the uncertain value of the local currency in the future and its inconvertibility still hamper the swift expansion of the tourist market in the PETs. The low capacity of hotels that meet western standards is an additional hindrance. But TNC hotel chains have recently invested in all Eastern capitals and other big cities. Retraining of personnel is a must. Business tourism remains for now the fastest expanding share of the market (Francèze 1990) for reasons that are endemic in the basic features of the transition.

The willingness of some PETs to have their country inserted into the international tourism market is quite understandable. A net inflow of tourist revenue is always good news for the balance of payments. But the domestic cost may be high: tourism is capital and technology intensive. Thus, a hotel built according to international standards is a heavy investment generally paid in foreign exchange to some TNC (Ascher 1985). New trends on the international market favor cultural and ecological tourism today. Cultural attractiveness makes the PETs appealing. However, from an ecological point of view, it will take a very long time, and indeed strenuous efforts, to transform the PETs into attractive tourist havens.[3]

---

3. *Editor's note*: even many developing countries with an advantageous climate have been shrinking away from placing too much emphasis on developing the tourist industry as a source of desperately needed foreign exchange.

Training and Molding New Economic Behavior

The type of activities highlighted in this chapter require skills that are in short supply in the PETs. This lack is particularly striking in banking and other service industries, especially for skilled managers. Training young workers and decision makers and retraining the old ones and those less acquainted with the west's work organization and management are, thus, among the most crucial issues to be tackled. I cannot detail all aspects of organization in factories and offices. Suffice it to say that in western enterprises work organization is more flexible than in classical Soviet-type firms (Bayou 1990), the division of labor is more efficient, and manpower can be more easily hired and fired.

The PETs should move towards more flexibility and it is up to labor economists to advise on the basis of case studies the kind of work organization that might best suit each industry or firm. It must be stressed that transferring the west's experience through advisory services would not suffice insofar as training is concerned. In this matter, the west cannot escape providing more direct assistance, closer to aid than to advisory services, building upon the generally well-educated and skilled workers. What is primarily required is technical knowledge and knowhow for jobs linked to high-tech and a new work ethic. A large part of this training can be acquired only on the job.

A second channel is vocational training specific to each industry, profession, or enterprise. The formal programs of vocational training are, then, depending on each profession's specificity. The content of these programs may imitate, with adaptation to local circumstances, the west's standard programs for the same profession. This does not mean that such programs would be perfectly adaptable, especially because changing each individual's behavior at the work place is not a matter of technical knowledge and local circumstances. Thus, the behavioral legacies of the planning environment may weigh heavily on the outcome of vocational training. The latter might only be an unavoidable second-best compared with training on the spot.

A third solution, particularly in a period of rising unemployment is to appeal to the expertise of western employment agencies.

What could be a standard formal management training program? In answering this question it is useful to bear in mind that many business schools, universities, and consulting firms have defined their own specific management training programs. In line with what was said before, the main elements should cover accounting and bookkeeping, business finance, banking, cost calculation, estimation techniques of asset values, feasibility assessment and programming of investment projects (including the utilization of a time discount in the calculation of expected investment profitability), budgeting, operations research, privatization techniques, western experiences of enterprise and industry restructuring, commercial law, business administration, theories of organization, marketing techniques, trading, advertising, pricing, product-differentiation techniques, inventory management, insurance, industrial relations and labor management, western experiences of collective bargaining, data processing and computer science, foreign-trade techniques, negotiating for the transfer of technology, and the key aspects of social costs, particularly as applied to pollution problems. To say the least, it would remain to adapt all these standard teachings to the presently prevailing, and, hopefully in due course, also the evolving, circumstances of the various PETs (Bourenine 1990).

In the background of professional training lies the need to change basically the behavior of all economic agents in the transition away from planning. During planning, the Eastern economies were characterized by a lack of entrepreneurship (see Brabant 1990, 1991e) and by a generalized risk aversion among managers complemented with some speculative businesses for those people operating in the underground economy. It will probably take at least a generation to alter this behavior, which remains a cornerstone of the economic system even in the early stages of the transition period.

Businessmen in the PETs, new as well as old, do not properly understand the essential traits of the market economy. Too frequently they confuse industrious profit making with quickly gained speculative earnings, free competition with the "law of the jungle" under which even dirty tricks are condoned, contracting with bargaining, accounting with cheating, fiscal duties with bribery, free pricing with client squeezing, and business fairness with innocence. A change in economic behavior will not occur in the PETs until a new business ethic emerges. What matters, then, is not only management training but the more general understanding of economics and consequently a widespread economic common sense. All this is ordinarily acquired in general education and everyday life when they are more geared towards market criteria and values as in the west.

This is the core of the west's experience that will take the longest to be transmitted to the PETs.

Conclusions

Emerging markets in PETs may take over a number of features of the west's experiences. Direct and indirect relations with western economic agents, including major TNCs, should provide more benefits than costs in the transition. The west's experience cannot, however, be regarded as an overall panacea to all economic problems emerging today in the PETs. Some mistakes have already been made, such as in advertising. Decision makers and advisers in PETs should separate the wheat from the chaff in the west's experiences. A new ethic of business management should back economic behavior, and this should not be confused with either the worst of the former socialist behavior or the fiercest tycoon's attitude of primitive capitalism.

In sum, the experience of western private economic agents would provide assistance and benefits to PET enterprises. Both public and private agents could take advantage of the west's experiences. Because it will take longer to create privately owned structures in the PETs than had at first been anticipated, the state-run sector, for now, must be considered the main recipient of the west's experience, especially in matters concerning restructuring, training, and management techniques. An efficient state-run sector would not be, as some liberal economists believe, a hindrance to progressing towards the market economy. On the contrary, it would provide a basic springboard to reach it. However, that topic lies beyond the purview of this chapter (but see Andreff 1992c).

9

Specialization for Eastern Europe and Access to EC Markets

Giovanni Graziani

Great expectations have been built around the current EC trade liberalization process in favor of the five Eastern European countries: Bulgaria, Czechoslovakia, Hungary, and Poland, and to a lesser extent Romania. In this chapter, I shall focus only on these countries, unless the context makes it clear that a broader geographical delineation of East is being discussed. I do so because measures in favor of the Baltic states and the successor states of the Soviet Union, when in place, have been enacted too recently to have affected trade flows in 1990-1991.

Trade performance in western markets in 1990-1991 is sometimes described as the one bright spot in an ocean of mounting difficulties due to the transition process (UNECE 1991b) and offered as evidence of the new intra-European trade climate. Unfortunately, the entry path into free trade with Europe is still marred by many obstacles and the results so far are rather contradictory. These difficulties can best be assessed by first analyzing the key features of traditional east-west trade flows. Once this is clearly laid out, one can examine and assess current trends in trade and protectionism. Consequently, I shall focus chiefly on various angles of the East's exports to the EC up to 1989. That should be taken as a unique watershed year because the impact of the EC trade liberalization measures

---

Professor at the University of Brescia, Brescia, Italy.

should have been felt to some degree beginning with 1990, and then more fully from 1991 onward.

Key Features of Traditional East-West Trade

Eastern European trade with the EC was characterized by strong asymmetries in the relative importance of reciprocal trade and the commodity composition of that commerce. The EC is by far more important to the East than the reverse relationship. Since the 1970s, the EC's share of the overall trade volume of the five Eastern countries has hovered around 14 percent, whereas the East's share in the EC has barely exceeded 2 percent (Graziani 1985, 1987). If anything, this asymmetry was exacerbated in the second half of the 1980s. The East's total market shares in the EC slowly declined up to 1980 and then rose slightly until 1984, whereafter it further declined until the end of the period. By 1989, more than one quarter of the exports of Eastern Europe was with the EC, with Bulgaria's share being as low as 9 percent, but that of the other countries ranging between 28 and 34 percent. At that time, only Hungary and Poland kept their position. The East's market share in the EC in 1989 was lower than what it had been fifteen years earlier. By contrast, major competitors from Asia all increased their market shares, in many cases doubling them. In 1989, the combined share of the "four tigers" (Hong Kong, Republic of Korea, Singapore, and Taiwan) was 2.7 percent as compared to 1.9 percent in 1984. Germany was undoubtedly the major outlet, a trading pole that has gained further attraction since unification. Next in line, but with a big gap, are France, Italy, and the United Kingdom. But Eastern markets accounted for only 1.1 percent of the EC's total exports. This enormous discrepancy cannot merely be explained by the different relative size of the two regions, a key fact to bear in mind when assessing the possible impact of any EC trade liberalization.

The above trends in the overall levels of the commodity composition of trade between the EC and the five Eastern countries can be further dissected by looking at the commodity composition of reciprocal trade.[1]

---

1. I am referring to the commodity composition of EC imports (and sometimes exports) organized, whenever possible, according to the Standard Industrial Trade Classification (SITC, rev. 3), utilizing the foreign trade statistics compiled by OECD as my basic source of

The EC's imports from the East are rather diversified, although primary products have for a long time accounted for the most important relative share. Within that group, the biggest role used to be played by mineral fuels (SITC 3), which accounted for over one fifth at the beginning of the 1980s. The importance of this group was particularly pronounced for Bulgarian, Polish, and Romanian exports. It should not be forgotten, however, that part of these exports were petroleum products processed from imported oil from the Soviet Union and the Organization of Petroleum Exporting Countries (OPEC). Notably the oil acquired from the Soviet Union at low prices and easy settlement conditions afforded the East a substantial windfall gain. This opportunity fully vanished with the introduction in 1990-1991 of world prices and the subsequent collapse of CMEA trade. In 1989, fuels represented 13 percent of the exports of the five countries to the EC, with a peak for Romania at 32 percent. Ores and metals (SITC 4) accounted for another 7 percent. Finally, roughly one quarter of Eastern exports to the EC consisted of foodstuffs, animals, and agricultural raw materials (SITC 0+1+2-27-28). However, this share was much higher in the case of Hungary (33 percent), Bulgaria (30 percent), and Poland (28 percent). All three countries are naturally bound to incur trade impediments, particularly on account of the CAP unless the EC relaxes that stance.

All in all, food and raw materials form a substantial component of EC imports from the East, whose share of 42.3 percent in 1989 was certainly much larger than in the equivalent flows from elsewhere into the EC (27.8 percent). The overall balance for primary products has always been negative for the EC. One notable exception concerns the category food and live animals since 1982, except with Bulgaria and Hungary.

Intermediate products also took a substantial share. Two thirds were represented by basic industrial goods (SITC 6 minus SITC 68), iron and steel and textile yarns and fabrics accounting for the bulk of them (18 percent on average, but 30 percent for Czechoslovakia). The EC, more than other distant western countries, is a natural market for bulky and transport-intensive products. However, already in 1977 their share began to decrease, the main reasons being the EC's import restrictions and the growing competition from NIEs (Graziani 1987). Similar features are discernible for chemicals (SITC 5), whose share has generally been on the

---

information. The detailed tabulated statistical materials on which the present writeup has been based are available from the author on request.

increase since the early 1970s. The share for Bulgaria, Czechoslovakia, and Hungary exceeded 10 percent. The industrial cooperation agreements as a trade promoter between the two areas seem to have been particularly important in this sector.

The sector of finished manufactured goods consists of two broad categories that exhibit different weights and patterns. Machinery and equipment (SITC 7), which has a growing negative balance for the East, accounts for relatively little, roughly one third if compared to intra-EC trade (11 percent as against 36 percent). Its relative weight follows the ranking of development among the Eastern countries: It was more important for Czechoslovakia (14 percent); at an intermediate level for Bulgaria (12 percent), Hungary (13 percent), and Poland (12 percent); and well under the average for Romania (6 percent). Such are the residual effects of past intra-CMEA specialization, which made some of the Eastern countries able to exploit economies of scale (for example, Czechoslovakia in metal-working machine tools; Poland in ship building, motor cars, and tractors; Hungary in buses and household appliances; Bulgaria in non-electrical machinery; Romania in ball bearings and motor-vehicle parts). The reduction of shares in the 1980s suggests growing difficulties in penetrating western markets. Apart from international competition, the Eastern countries, particularly in the case of some manufactured products, also competed among themselves in the EC, largely because of the parallelism in industrial structures (Graziani 1982). Other negative factors are represented by weaknesses of marketing, spare parts, and after-sales services; poor infrastructure and financial services; as well as the well-known technological lag.

Lastly, the relatively bright spot is the category of miscellaneous manufactured goods (SITC 8), which in 1989 accounted for 19 percent of total exports on average, but 32 percent for Romania and 20 percent for Hungary. Clothing, footwear, and furniture, all traditionally labor-intensive goods, contributed to a positive, but shrinking, balance in the 1980s. Here too, EC nontariff measures coupled with increased competition from the NIEs seem to have been at the root of this trend.

At a more disaggregated level (two-digit SITC) for manufactured products, only in a few instances has the share of any of the Eastern countries exceeded 4 percent. Such is the case for iron and steel and clothing (but rather evenly spread among the PETs), organic chemicals (Czechoslovakia and Hungary), textiles (Bulgaria and Czechoslovakia), general industrial machinery (Bulgaria), electrical machinery (Hungary), road vehicles

(Czechoslovakia and Poland), and furniture (Romania). There is a general trend, even at the one-digit level for the weight to be higher for cruder products or those with a comparatively small value-added component (including, organic versus inorganic chemicals and plastics in primary versus nonprimary forms), as illustrated in table 9.1.

Table 9.1: Sensitive Imports into EC in 1989 (in percentages)							
Products	World	Bulgaria	ČSFR	Hungary	Poland	East	EC
Food and agriculture	14.8	30.0	18.5	33.1	27.4	22.6	14.8
Chemicals	10.3	11.8	11.6	9.9	6.7	8.2	12.4
Iron and steel	3.5	10.5	12.5	4.9	5.3	6.9	4.4
Textiles	3.2	3.5	6.0	2.9	1.7	3.0	3.8
Clothing	3.3	7.4	4.6	11.7	8.8	10.0	2.8
Total	35.1	63.2	53.6	62.5	49.9	50.6	38.2

Source: author's calculations based on OECD foreign trade statistics.

The importance of the EC trade policy *vis-à-vis* the East can indirectly be gauged by the weight of the so-called "sensitive" sectors in exports to the EC. It is in those areas that tariff and particularly nontariff barriers continue to be relatively stronger. Taken together, food and agricultural materials, chemicals, iron and steel, textiles, and clothing account for 63 percent of total exports for Bulgaria and Hungary, 54 percent for Czechoslovakia, 50 percent for Poland, and 34 percent for Romania. The same group accounts for just over one third of EC imports from the world.

Eastern Exports by Resource Dependence and Factor Intensity

As demonstrated elsewhere (Graziani 1989), a better insight into the composition of the PETs' trade with the EC can be gained by distinguishing between resource-based and other exports, on the one hand, and nonresource-based manufactures classified according to capital or labor intensities as well as technology intensity and growth of import demand, on the other hand, as illustrated in table 9.2.

Table 9.2: EC Imports from East by Various Criteria in 1989
(in percentages)

Criterion	World	Bulgaria	ČSFR	Hungary	Poland	East	EC
Resource-based	34.8	51.1	39.2	48.5	56.8	49.5	29.2
Nonresource-based manufactures							
labor-intensive	56.1	60.7	53.1	72.4	59.7	64.8	52.2
capital-intensive	21.4	33.2	36.0	22.7	23.6	25.5	22.1
other	22.5	6.2	10.9	4.9	16.7	9.8	25.6
Import growth above average	40.7	25.6	28.0	32.3	27.7	30.7	48.7
R&D intensity							
High	21.7	9.6	3.5	10.9	7.4	6.3	17.9
Medium	48.2	42.0	41.9	38.4	42.6	38.0	53.0
Low	30.1	48.4	54.7	50.7	50.1	55.7	29.1

Source: see table 9.1.

Resource-based exports are most pronounced for Bulgaria and Poland. However, for all five PETs, this share (50 percent on average) is much larger than for world exports to the EC (35 percent), with Czechoslovakia's (39 percent) coming closest to that average. Taking manufactures not based on primary resources and classifying them by factor-intensity, labor-intensive products predominate (on average 65 percent, but 78 percent for Romania and 72 percent for Hungary), as against 25 percent for capital-intensive and 10 percent for goods otherwise classified; the corresponding shares for the world are 56, 21, and 23 percent, respectively. In addition, traditional labor-intensive industries, like clothing, footwear, and furniture, prevail over nontraditional ones, such as engineering. Furthermore, PET exports of such manufactures are concentrated in low-technology sectors (56 percent), followed by medium (38 percent) and high technology sectors (only 6 percent). The same sectors in world exports to the EC account for 30, 48, and 22 percent, respectively. Finally, these manufactures are mostly (69 percent) concentrated in sectors characterized by a slower than average growth in EC import demand. Although this is true also for world exports to the EC at large, the latter share has nonetheless remained lower (59 percent).

If we define goods as complementary when the composition of imports (exports) of one country matches the composition of exports (imports) of another, and these two partners are competitive otherwise, it is evident that a certain, but limited, complementarity exists in the sense that EC imports are more skewed towards primary goods than EC exports. However, a more interesting type of complementarity can be analyzed within each commodity group. Computing a complementarity index at the two-digit SITC level, in general, as expected, measured values are higher for primary products than for manufactured goods. For SITC 5-8, 19 out of 35 two-digit groups present a rather low (equal or lower than 0.3) index for at least one PET. A low index means a comparatively high degree of intra-industry trade. This applies most for Poland (11 times), followed by Hungary, Czechoslovakia, Romania, and Bulgaria—in that order. However, for all 19 groups except two (paper products for Poland and power-generating equipment for Czechoslovakia and Poland) the value of the index exceeds that for the world. That is to say, intra-industry trade is less developed than on average in EC trade with PETs than is the case for the EC's overall imports, with EC countries specializing in higher technology and/or value-added products.

Summing up, the PETs' composition of exports to the EC is relatively biased in favor of resource-based products, most of which require substantial investments. If we add this to the share of capital-intensive manufactures, the PETs' exports seem to be particularly biased towards products making heavy use of natural resources and capital. Given that these countries are not well endowed with natural resources and that capital is scarce, the trade pattern evidenced here suggests a substantial misallocation of resources caused largely by the well-known irrational system of prices and other features of the planning regime. Further, manufactures based on other than natural resources consist mostly of sectors intensive in labor, low-technology, and low-skills for which the demand in the EC has grown moderately at best, competition from the NIEs has been fierce, and EC protection continues to be quite pronounced and it has been increasing in some cases. Finally, some intra-industry trade does take place for manufactured goods, although on a much smaller scale than average. When it occurs, there appears to be a division of labor, with the exports of PETs consisting mostly of basic products (low-grade chemicals, common steel, low-profile machinery, common textiles, and ordinary footwear), while their imports from the EC exhibit mostly higher technology and/or value-added goods. Do these results reveal anything at all about the potential comparative advantages of the PETs, given the implantation of a market-based economy?

Identifying the East's Comparative Advantages

It is obviously difficult to identify products most suitable for promotion in global markets at a time of a rapid redirection of trade flows and of sweeping internal transformations. Under the circumstances, the best one can do is to determine in which sectors the region held its apparent comparative advantages with the EC just prior to the revolutions and then to discuss whether these sectors are viable at all, given factor endowments in these countries.

The erosion of the PETs' share in overall EC imports in the 1980s was matched by the erosion of market shares for manufactures, something that had started already in the 1970s; the only exception to this trend was Hungary, which maintained its position. This erosion was not limited to machinery and equipment, but extended to manufactures with a lower degree of processing, like textiles, iron and steel, other metal products, or even clothing. The only gains materialized in nonferrous metals and wood-based manufactured products or in subsectors characterized by a lower degree of processing. Even chemicals, for which successes were booked through the early 1980s, began to slide from 1983 onward. In all these sectors, the more dynamic Asian developing countries steadily expanded their market share (Graziani 1987). At the end of the 1980s, for very few commodity groups was the PETs' share significant at all. For manufactures, these include furniture (5 percent), mostly accounted for by Romania; and 2-3 percent about evenly spread among the five countries (fertilizers, nonferrous metals, iron and steel, cork and wood manufactures, travel goods, and footwear). Among the primary goods, a significant share was held for coal (5 percent), entirely due to Poland; and 2 to 3 percent for food and live animals, oil seeds, crude fertilizers (mostly Poland), and petroleum products. All in all, the PETs were gaining in relative market share particularly for resource-based goods, followed by labor-intensive, low-technology products.

An index of revealed comparative advantage (RCA)[2] for each PET in the EC market suggests that all PETs except Czechoslovakia specialized in food and agricultural products, other raw materials, and petroleum prod-

---

2. *Editor's note*: RCA index values above unity suggest that the country has a comparative advantage in product *i* and lower than unity a comparative disadvantage. A minus sign suggests that there is a negative balance in that trade.

ucts (see table 9.3). A second cluster of strong and common specialization manifests itself in the miscellaneous manufactured goods, followed in a more erratic way by resource-based manufactures. The same computation for manufactures at the two-digit level reveals a striking feature: the nearly complete absence of positive RCA indices in machinery and equipment, excepting Bulgaria in general industrial machinery and, together with Czechoslovakia, in metal-working machinery. But even in these three instances, the indices are very low and accompanied by large negative trade balances.

Table 9.3: Indexes of Revealed Comparative Advantage on EC Markets in 1989					
SITC codes	Bulgaria	ČSFR	Hungary	Poland	East
0+1+22+4	2.08	0.79	2.51	2.04	1.53
2-22-27-28	1.90	2.67	1.44	1.29	1.51
27+28+68	0.73	0.63	1.00	2.39	1.38
3	1.13	0.92	0.37	1.45	1.59
5	1.15	1.13	0.97	0.65	0.80
7	0.36	0.43	0.39	0.37	0.35
6-68	1.15	1.94	0.96	0.94	1.16
8	1.01	1.08	1.63	1.21	1.55
9	1.64	1.05	0.85	0.55	0.67

Source: see table 9.1.

Legend: 0+1+22+4 is food, beverages, tobacco, oilseeds and oleaginous fruit (22), oils and fats; 2-22-27-28 is raw materials minus 22, crude fertilizer and minerals (27), and metalliferous ore and metal scrap (28); 27+28+68 is 27 plus 28 plus nonferrous metals (68); 3 is fuels, 5 is chemical products; 7 is finished machinery; 6-68 is manufactures minus 68; 8 is other manufactures; and 9 is products not elsewhere classified.

One will also note that on average the comparative disadvantage in this commodity group is higher than in the other groups. At a more disaggregated level, one could find perhaps only a few other niches of comparative advantage, like Hungarian household electric and lighting equipment or Polish wires and cables and ships. Similar remarks can be made about some more refined products pertaining to other commodity groups. These results suggest that no PET has a comparative advantage in dyeing, plastics in nonprimary forms, chemical products, scientific instruments, photographic apparatus, and optical goods. In all these groups balances are generally negative. There are, on the other hand, five categories (furniture, clothing, cork and wood products, travel goods, and iron and steel in ascending order) in which for all PETs the index is positive and rather large. Excepting Czechoslovakia, the PETs exhibit an RCA also in fertilizers and, excepting Bulgaria, in footwear, where the balance is nevertheless negative. In the remaining product groups positive RCA indices are more scattered among countries.

This analysis of RCA values suggests that the PETs' specialization has thus far been mainly in the types of goods that constitute the bulk of exports, as noted earlier. But some differences among the countries deserve to be noted. As expected, Czechoslovakia presents the weaker disadvantages in the higher technology-intensive products, followed by Hungary, Poland, Bulgaria, and Romania. The last three are also relatively more specialized in resource-based goods, Hungary in labor-intensive manufactures, and Czechoslovakia in capital-intensive manufactures.

Clearly, RCA values cannot reveal much about underlying real comparative advantages of any country, particularly in the presence of a substantial resource misallocation. The question is even more complicated when one tries to infer evidence for future patterns of specialization, given the rapid structural change that the transition should be bringing about. For example, a general redeployment of labor from agriculture and industry to the service sector and industrial restructuring might substantially change the trade structure. Insights on that matter were recently presented by Gordon Hughes and Paul Hare (1991).[3] According to their computations of value-added by each industry at world prices for the four countries (notably Bulgaria, Czechoslovakia, Hungary, and Poland), 20 to 25 percent of manufacturing output is produced by branches with negative value added, particularly the food-processing industry, followed by energy-intensive branches. This suggests that all the industries in Bulgaria and Czechoslovakia with apparently negative value added at world prices

---

3. *Editor's note*: The types of estimates contained in Hughes and Hare (1991) essentially ask the question what sectors would have been uncompetitive if, in the observation year, they had been subject to world rather than prevailing prices. One must therefore be careful not to read too much into these data as guidelines for restructuring. For one thing, relative prices have changed dramatically since the observation year. Likewise, the economic recession has been differently affecting the various sectors. Also, what a sector may indicate is not necessarily applicable to the individual firms, and it is at that level that comparative advantages will need to be built up or expanded. Furthermore, the studies have all been beset with numerous measurement problems.

are those for which these PETs revealed a comparative disadvantage. The obverse holds for Hungary, where some of the food industry and iron and steel reveal a comparative advantage. The same can be said for food and nonferrous metals, or about half of the negative value added in Polish industry.

Likely Specialization Paths for PETs

Obviously, specialization is a dynamic process and the results in terms of trade will differ depending on the time horizon one is willing to consider. In the first instance, the PETs will have to work primarily with the existing factor endowment to correct the established patterns of specialization and the problems encountered in the sectors indicated above. That includes energy-intensive exports (such as oil-based petrochemicals and metallurgical products based on cheap iron ore and fuel imports from the Soviet Union), which will have to be first in line for drastic restructuring, hence, contraction in exports. In some instances, however, it might be rash to simply do away with entire sectors, parts of which could be viable. Such is the case, for example, of Bulgarian oil-processing capacities, which have undergone intensive renovation and might be used on a compensatory basis by processing crude imported from abroad and paid for in terms of petroleum products. But these cases are the exception rather than the rule for energy-intensive manufacturing.

As for agriculture, the pressure to earn foreign exchange might translate into an export push. This might be further enhanced by productivity gains due to a substantial release of the labor force from agriculture and a swift positive reaction to liberalization measures in rural production. The most suitable candidates for an export boost could be derived by comparing *per capita* output in the PETs with that in the world. On that measure, cereals, sunflowers, meat, milk, canned food products, beer, and refined sugar would seem to have on average the greatest potential (Collins and Rodrik 1991).

What about manufactures? Some analysts (CEPR 1990) have based their projections on human skill endowments, and suggested an above-average expansion in exports of more sophisticated, skill-intensive products. But there are problems with this approach when countries or whole sectors are simply averaged. More reliable hints as to the future patterns of trade may be gleaned from the levels of education and R&D, provided a strong relationship between educational and R&D flows, on the one hand, and the availability of skilled workers, on the other, can be posited. Using various data compilations for this purpose, the picture that emerges reveals some notable differences among individual PETs. Summarizing the findings, the situation does not seem to be uniform for the various PETs and among the different domains of education, scientific and technical manpower, and R&D efforts. At least two of the PETs have a substantial number of scientists, engineers, and technicians. But it is not clear whether this endowment corresponds to the requirements of the transition in the years ahead. Particularly for manufactures, the current skill level of Eastern employees does not seem to indicate relevant opportunities for export potential in skill-intensive goods in the near term. This seems also to be the perception of foreign investors (Collins and Rodrik 1991).

Meanwhile the PETs will be forced to concentrate on labor-intensive manufactures. In terms of full nominal labor compensation, cheap labor is still a reality of the PETs. This is even so once the data are corrected for differences in productivity. Though this would suggest that the PETs might be attractive as location for FDI, several caveats aside from productivity adjustments are required. Appreciation of the real exchange rate in these PETs has been a feature of the transition, as highlighted in chapter 3. Only Czechoslovakia has succeeded in keeping nominal wages under control, but nonetheless the koruna has appreciated markedly. Palpable unemployment might begin to exert downward pressure on nominal wages, but there clearly is a limit to how much the social package can be cut.

Although in some sectors, some noticeable headway could be carved ou on the basis of differential labor costs, the substantial productivity differentials between PETs and Western European countries, for example, suggest (see Poland as reported in Burzyński, Sadowska-Cieslak, and Zbytniewski 1991) that substantial opportunities for improving factor productivity in the PETs exist. In some cases, this will require the appropriation of additional resources. But substantial mileage can also be gained from pursuing greater X-efficiency, including through reorganization, streamlining of operations, and labor shedding. The experience with some joint ventures has underlined the potential that prevails in several of the PETs under consideration here.

Facing EC Protectionism

Restrictions on access to EC markets constitute the major external constraint to an export expansion of Eastern products, all the more so since they have been increasing in sectors for which these countries apparently enjoy the best prospects. Traditionally the East was at the bottom of the EC hierarchic system of preferential tariff arrangements and discriminated against through a variety of specific nontariff barriers. In the late 1970s, for example, 27 percent of the five countries' exports to the EC were subject to quantitative restrictions, as against 9 percent for the rest of the world (Olechowski and Yeats 1982). From 1989 onward, some progress towards removing those constraints has been made. But, as I shall show shortly, the actual situation is less rosy than what official declarations might suggest.

As for tariffs, trade and cooperation agreements concluded with these Eastern countries, except Romania, embody a provision for applying a nondiscriminatory tariff regime. Apart from MFN treatment, GSP benefits have been granted to Hungary, Poland, and Romania since 1 January 1989, and to the other two countries since 1 January 1991. For all countries, except Romania, they do not include coal and steel products and for Poland fishery products are excluded. In this respect the Eastern countries have ascended slightly on the ladder of the hierarchy of groups having obtained preferential access to EC markets. They find themselves near most developing countries, but behind the EFTA members, the 12 Mediterranean countries with preferential arrangements, and the 66 developing countries parties to the Lomé convention, who enjoy duty-free access for their manufactured exports, except coal, steel, and textiles.

However, both the general tariff level and that pertaining to particular sectors remain higher than the average value for OECD: 8 percent as against 5 percent. Considering only MFN rates (Messerlin 1991), particularly hard hit are sectors like food processing (17 percent), textiles and apparel (11 percent), and agriculture (9 percent). If we consider the MFN-GSP rates together, only food processing and agriculture seem to be relevant (13 and 8 percent, respectively). However, tariff abatement under the GSP schemes is applicable only to a comparatively small amount of imports and for a well-defined period of time. Some of the products, particularly in agriculture and textiles, are affected by quantitative limitations embedded in the GSP scheme. Textiles coming under the provisions of the Multi-fibre Arrangement (MFA) are subject to a quota allocation scheme among the EC members, which has to be respected and implies a limited amount of coverage for GSP. On the whole, if one compares the value of imports receiving GSP benefits to total imports from the East, in most cases the share is well below 10 percent. Estimates of the possible gains in export revenues on GSP items after the concession of full GSP status, considering current trade flows, are rather modest (14 percent for Hungary and 20 percent for Poland). This is particularly so if one considers the limitations and exclusions affecting the coverage (UNCTAD 1990).

Even if the tariff situation is not deemed to be such that it restricts exports from the East in a major way, nontariff barriers should remain a major concern. Here too some progress has been made. Already in the trade and cooperation agreements, the EC committed itself to the progressive removal of quantitative restrictions by 1995, although excluding the most important Eastern export items, like agriculture, steel, and textiles. Since March 1990, the EC has raised the textile quota allocations for Hungary and Poland, and the steel import quotas for all Eastern countries. However, due to the very high proportion of sensitive products in the East's export structure and to the application of selective nontariff barriers, the Eastern countries are still disadvantaged *vis-à-vis* other EC trading partners.

It bears to observe that in 1990 the share of Eastern exports (36 percent) covered by the main nontariff barriers is far higher than that of the developing countries (26 percent) or the developed ones (16 percent). Due to the commodity composition of their exports, Bulgaria (48 percent), Hungary (40 percent), and Romania (39 percent) are particularly affected. The figures would be even higher, if subsidies (equivalent to 2 percent of the EC countries' combined GDP) and national measures by individual EC members were added. If one separates out the sensitive sectors (Messerlin 1991), similar results can be obtained. As regards agriculture, the average level of protection surpasses 100 percent and was increasing in the second half of the 1980s. Apart from the CAP, some selective measures, like VER agreements for sheep and goat meat, affect the East. Equally important is the case of textiles and apparel coming under the current MFA (the fourth), for which the coverage varies between 43 percent for Bulgaria and 64 percent for Czechoslovakia. Another, but lower, estimate suggests that the average *ad valorem* equivalent of these restrictions for the five Eastern countries ranges between 25 and 50 percent (OECD 1991d). Here the Eastern countries have concluded bilateral restraint agreements with the EC. As regards trade in iron and steel, 487 out of 490 items are affected by nontariff barriers, mostly VERs. Minimum prices imposed bilaterally or through antidumping duties have also contributed. Finally, in chemicals, there has been extensive use of antidumping actions. In the decade prior to the end of 1990, some 80 cases were initiated against Eastern exports, Czechoslovakia taking almost a third of them, followed by Romania.

A new step forward to improved access to EC markets seems to have been set by the newly concluded Europe Agreements, which regulate the future EC relations with Czechoslovakia, Hungary, and Poland; other Eastern countries may join this circle as new agreements are negotiated (presently under way for Bulgaria and Romania). As from March 1992, a progressive liberalization of trade restrictions has been initiated. But even in these agreements, special treatment is reserved for trade in products from sensitive sectors. The remainder of trade in manufactures should be completely liberalized by 1996, with the Eastern countries reciprocating more slowly, usually over a five-year period extending until the end of the decade. In agriculture, liberalization is strictly limited to a few commodities and to certain quantities within broader quotas, which are allowed to grow 10 percent a year. Variable levies can be reduced by 60 percent at most over three years. Naturally, all tariffs and levies outside the quota limits have to be paid. Tariffs for imports of textiles and clothing from the East should be eliminated within six years, while quantitative restrictions should not disappear before the sixth year and anyway no sooner than half the delay forecast in the Uruguay Round (which has yet to be concluded). In iron and steel products other than those coming under the supervision of the ECSC, nontariff protection should be eliminated immediately and tariffs within six years. For other products like furniture, leather goods, footwear, glass, and so on, protection will be maintained for five to six years. Furthermore, by authorizing EC countries to look outside the Eastern exporting country for the calculation of the fair price, against which PET export prices will be compared, the Agreements offer new opportunities to the EC members to initiate and complete antidumping actions.[4] Finally, they add to the grey area of nontariff barriers by allowing safeguard measures in those cases that might be deemed threatening to EC domestic producers.

---

4. *Editor's note:* several cases, notably concerning steel products, were tabled in the course of 1992.

The East's Export Boom of 1990-1991

Data for Eastern exports to the EC in 1990-1991 are sometimes offered as evidence of the positive impact of the recent trade liberalization measures. Although actual trade has been affected by the recession in the EC, the East's internal supply problems, and national deflationary policies, it may nonetheless be useful to investigate to what extent trade-policy measures may have enhanced the East's exports during 1990-1991.

EC total imports from the five Eastern countries increased both in 1990 and in 1991, except from Romania, which experienced a contraction in both years, albeit a smaller cutback in 1991 than in 1990. As for the other Eastern countries, the positive growth rate shrank for Hungary and Poland and rose for Bulgaria and Czechoslovakia. On the whole, imports into the EC seemed to show more dynamism than the average into the OECD countries.

However, these data should not be taken at their face value, since EC imports include, as from 1991, the data for the former GDR.[5] Totals are thus noncomparable; likewise for the distortions that affect the data pertaining to the commodity composition of trade. For example, cursory calculations show that Germany increased its imports of machinery and transport equipment between 1990 and 1991 fivefold. Arguably, this apparent boom is largely due to the inclusion of statistics of the former GDR, whose import structure from the East was very different from the FRG's, while only a smaller part is attributable to import growth that would have occurred if the former FRG had been maintained.

Complete data on the commodity composition of trade are not yet available for all EC countries. Preliminary data for 1991, however, allow such an inference on the commodity composition of trade only for France, Italy, and the United Kingdom, here referred to as EC3. The data underline that between 1990 and 1991 either the growth rate of imports fell or a contraction was experienced, as was the case for Poland. Bulgaria was the least affected, keeping its rate of export growth at roughly 15 percent. As noted, the Romanian one was negative. Globally, then, in times of recession, EC liberalization measures do not seem to have been sufficient to offset other negative factors at work.

---

5. *Editor's note*: the GDR's trade with the FRG was never included in EC exports because of the special role of *Innerdeutscher Handel* as recognized in the Rome treaties.

Taking the four sensitive sectors together, the data for EC3 suggest that the loss is smaller than for total exports. As a result, their share in total imports slightly rose for Bulgaria, Poland, and Romania; it remained stable for Hungary; and contracted for Czechoslovakia. Taking individual sectors, however, agriculture and iron and steel lost one percentage point each as a share of global exports to the EC3. Comparing the growth rates of the different sectors, textiles and apparel was the only commodity group to increase its pace of expansion slightly (from 15 to 16 percent), while the pace of growth of chemical products was more than halved, from 38 to 18 percent, and the other two groups actually decreased absolutely (agriculture from 21 to -9 percent and iron and steel from 40 to -18 percent).

Conclusions

After the good start of 1990 (except for Romania), 1991 signaled a turnaround in some of the EC markets for most Eastern countries, particularly so for some key sensitive sectors (except textiles and apparel). This is all the more disappointing, since it is the first year when the full effects of the EC trade liberalization measures should have been felt by all countries. On the other hand, the data on the downward trends seem to be too large to be explained in terms of the EC's recession alone. Whatever little information we have on underlying comparative advantages of the Eastern countries should be considered as well.

All in all, as the analysis of RCA indicators has shown, the apparent specialization of the five Eastern countries singled out for analysis here manifests itself mostly in the types of products that make up the bulk of their exports: resource-based products and standard labor-intensive, low-skill manufactures.

In the near future, the East's composition of exports to the EC is not likely to change dramatically. Some rearrangement may take place within resource-based exports, agricultural products tending to get a bigger weight in comparison to energy-intensive goods. Keeping in mind that labor is bound to be relatively even more abundant, labor-intensive manufactures will continue to be the most viable export earner, especially if reinforced by a favorable exchange-rate policy. In the longer term, the results of the restructuring process and the expected inflow of FDI and technology might allow these PETs to concentrate on more sophisticated exports, for which some countries would seem to possess the right factor endowments.

What type of international division of labor emanates from such an analysis? Commercial relations between EC and the East will continue to be examples of how developed countries trade with economies at an intermediate level of development. A composition of trade that in key sectors reflects largely substitutable rather than complementary relations creates problems for competition because it cannot be replaced by intra-sectoral trade flows. To this one should add the place of the EC in the world division of labor. In the 1980s, the EC has gradually undergone a process of de-specialization relative to Japan and the United States in sectors characterized by strong and average international demand, while tending to specialize in the weak demand products.

As the analyses here have shown in some detail, the East's relative specialization often expresses itself in sectors where international demand is weaker, competition from the NIEs is strong, competition among the Eastern countries is rising, some of the EC countries tend also to concentrate their export specialization towards the other industrialized countries of the grouping, and an increasing overproduction and/or unemployment exists in the EC which is giving rise to protectionist pressures.

The EC reacted until 1989 by strongly discriminating against the East. Since then, it has promoted a process of progressive trade liberalization. The analyses reported on here, however, show that the Eastern countries are still facing a disproportionate burden of EC trade protectionism. The possible benefits of obtaining lower tariffs under the GSP program are limited by the exclusion of steel products and, for Poland, of fishery products. Moreover they apply only to a very minor part of the eligible goods. But above all, nontariff barriers, although decreasing for the last few years, are still very high in absolute terms as well as relative to other regions of the world. Preliminary data for 1991 imports into three major EC countries reveal that the measures already taken have not positively affected the majority of sectors involved. Hopes that the new association agreements would expedite swift and full access to EC markets have been dashed, at least for now, in view of the slow liberalization process in the sensitive sectors.

There is a danger that protectionist pressures might be mounting in the East themselves, often as a way of enticing foreign investors, who themselves may insist upon being offered such sheltered treatment. This would amount to reversing the very fast trade liberalization applied until now. It is exactly over the next five years that an immediate drastic removal of EC trade restrictions would allow those countries to reap the full benefits of a deeper integration into the world economy. But this, of course, would imply also that long-delayed structural adjustment policies in the EC countries would now be embraced. The outlook for this scenario to hold over the next several years is, unfortunately, not promising at all.

Bibliography

Adamović, Ljubisa S., "Yugoslavia," in *Currency convertibility in Eastern Europe*, edited by John Williamson (Washington, DC: Institute for International Economics, 1991), pp. 169-80.

Aglietta, Michel, Anton Brender, and Virginie Coudert, *Globalisation financière: l'aventure obligée* (Paris: Economica, 1990).

Andreff, Wladimir, "Structure de l'accumulation du capital et technologie en URSS," *Revue d'Etudes Comparatives Est-Ouest*, 1978:1, 47-88.

———, *Les multinationales* (Paris: La Découverte, 1990).

———, "French privatization techniques and experience: a model for Central-Eastern Europe?" in *Privatization in Europe: West and East European experiences*, edited by Ferdinando Targetti (Dartmouth: Aldershot, 1992a), forthcoming.

———, "System's constraints and foreign constraints in the privatization process" (paper prepared for the Third International Conference of the International Society for the Study of European Ideas, Aalborg University, August 1992b).

———, ed., *Privatisations et secteur public dans les pays de l'Est* (Paris: Centre Français du Commerce Extérieur, 1992c).

Ascher, François, *Transnational corporations and cultural identities* (Paris: UNESCO, 1985).

Ash, Timothy N., "Problems of ruble convertibility," *RFL/RL Research Report*, 1992:29, 26-32.

Assetto, Valerie J., *The Soviet bloc in the IMF and the IBRD* (Boulder, CO and London: Westview Press, 1988).

Bailey, Derek T., ed., *Accounting in socialist countries* (London: Routledge, 1988).

Balassa, Béla, "Comment," in *The economics of common currencies*, edited by Harry G. Johnson and Alexander K. Swoboda (Cambridge, MA: Harvard University Press, 1973), pp. 173-7.

Bayou, Céline and Alexandre Wolff, "Portrait des directeurs commerciaux soviétiques," *Le Courrier des Pays de l'Est*, No. 348 (1990), 49-58.

Bernard, Jean-Philippe, Michel Gaspard, and Clell Harral, "L'économie des transports dans l'ex-URSS: réseaux, trafic, gestion," *Le Courrier des Pays de l'Est*, No. 363 (1991), 3-41.

Bertin, Gilles Y. and Sally Wyatt, *Multinationales et propriété industrielle: le contrôle de la technologie mondiale* (Paris: Presses Universitaires de France, 1986).

Bhagwati, Jagdish, "Regionalism and multilateralism: an overview" (paper presented to the World Bank Conference on 2-3 April 1992, mimeographed).

BIS, *Assistance financière et technique fournie par la BRI aux banques centrales des pays d'Europe Centrale et Orientale* (Basle: Banque des Règlements Internationaux, 6 November 1991, mimeographed).

Blaha, Jaroslav and Michèle Kahn, "Les transports à l'Est: clé du commerce entre les deux Europes," *Le Courrier des Pays de l'Est*, No. 345 (1989), 4-31.

Blommestein, Hans J. and Michael Marrese, eds., *Transformation of planned economies: property rights reform and macroeconomic stability* (Paris: Organisation for Economic Co-operation and Development, 1991).

Bobinski, Christopher, "West hides behind Polish tariffs," *Financial Times*, 9 March 1992.

Bofinger, Peter, "The transition to convertibility in Eastern Europe: a monetary view," in *Convertibility in Eastern Europe*, edited by John Williamson (Washington, DC: Institute for International Economics, 1991), pp. 63-95.

_____, "Discussion," in *The economic consequences of the East* (London: Centre for Economic Policy Research, unedited and unpaged collection of papers, 1992).

_____ and Daniel Gros, "A Soviet payments union: why and how?" (paper prepared for the conference 'Eastern European Trade Policy Issues,' organized by the European Bank for Reconstruction and Development, London, 25-27 March 1992, mimeographed).

Bogdanowicz-Bindert, Christine and Richard Philips, "The implications of developments in the east for commercial capital flows to developing countries," *Journal of Development Planning*, No. 23 (1992), forthcoming.

Bourenine, Vladimir, "Stratégies des programmes de formation des cadres dans les économies en transition," *Le Courrier des Pays de l'Est*, No. 348 (1990), 59-68.

Brabant, Jozef M. van, *Bilateralism and structural bilateralism in intra-CMEA trade* (Rotterdam: Rotterdam University Press, 1973).

_____, *Adjustment, structural change, and economic efficiency—aspects of monetary cooperation in Eastern Europe* (Cambridge and New York: Cambridge University Press, 1987).

_____, *Economic integration in Eastern Europe—a reference book* (Hertforshire: Harvester Wheatsheaf, 1989).

_____, *Remaking Eastern Europe: on the political economy of transition* (Dordrecht-Boston-London, Kluwer Academic Publishers, 1990).

_____, *Integrating Eastern Europe into the global economy—convertibility through a payments union* (Dordrecht-Boston-London: Kluwer Academic Publishers, 1991a).

_____, "The demise of the CMEA—the agony of inaction," *Osteuropa-Wirtschaft*, 1991b:3, 234-54.

_____, *The planned economies and international economic organizations* (Cambridge and New York: Cambridge University Press, 1991c).

_____, "Convertibility in Eastern Europe through a payments union," in *Currency convertibility in Eastern Europe*, edited by John Williamson (Washington, DC: Institute for International Economics, 1991d), pp. 63-95.

_____, "Réforme des droits de propriété, performance macro-économique et bien-être," in *Transformation des economies planifiées—réforme du droit de propriété et stabilité macro-économique*, edited by Hans Blommestein and Michael Marrese (Paris: Organisation for Economic Co-operation and Development, 1991e), pp. 34-57.

_____, "The new East and its preferred trade regime—the impact of Soviet disintegration," in *The economies of the former Soviet Union*, edited by Joint Economic Committee, United States Congress (Washington, DC: Government Printing Office, 1992a), forthcoming.

_____, "Ruble convertibility and external and internal equilibrium," in *The economies of the former Soviet Union*, edited by Joint Economic Committee, United States Congress (Washington, DC: Government Printing Office, 1992b), forthcoming.

_____, *Ruble convertibility, external and internal equilibrium, and perestroyka* (Cologne, Berichte des Bundesinstituts für ostwissenschaftliche und internationale Studien, 1992c:6).

_____, "Alternative trade regimes and the economics of transition" (paper prepared for the Polish-American round-table, Kazimierz Dolny and Warsaw, Poland, 5-7 June 1992d).

_____, "The new East, preferred trade regimes, and designing the transition" (paper prepared for conference 'The economics of transition in the East,' Rungsted Kyst, Denmark, 10-12 June 1992e).

_____, *Unravelling the ruble regime* (London: European Policy Forum, 1992f).

_____, *Privatizing Eastern Europe—the role of markets and ownership in the transition* (Dordrecht-Boston-London: Kluwer Academic Publishers, 1992g).

Brada, Josef C., "The political economy of communist foreign trade institutions and policies," *Journal of Comparative Economics*, 1991:2, 211-38.

_____, "The mechanics of the voucher plan in Czechoslovakia," *RFE/RL Research Report*, 1992:17, 42-45.

Brown, Bess, "The CIS and the republics: Central Asia," *RFE/RL Research Report*, 1992:7, 17-21.

Burzyński, Wojciech, Ewa Sadowska-Cieslak, and Dariusz Zbytniewski, *Polish export capabilities in the 90s* (Paris: Organisation for Economic Co-operation and Development, document CCET/TD(91)93, 1992).

CEPR, *Monitoring European integration—the impact of Eastern Europe* (London: Centre for Economic Policy Research, 1990).

Collins, Susan M. and Dani Rodrik, *Eastern Europe and the Soviet Union in the world economy* (Washington, DC: Institute for International Economics, 1991).

Contractor, Farok J. and Peter Lorange, eds., *Cooperative strategies in international business* (Toronto: Lexington Books, 1988).

Corbo, V., "Lessons from Bank-supported adjustment programmes for Eastern Europe" (paper prepared for conference "The transition to a market economy in Central and Eastern Europe," organized by Centre for Co-operation with the European Economies in Transition and the World Bank, Paris, 28-30 November 1990).

Crane, Keith, "La réforme des droits de propriété: étude sur la Hongrie," in *Transformation des economies planifiées—réforme du droit de propriété et stabilité macroéconomique,* edited by Hans Blommestein and Michael Marrese (Paris: Organisation for Economic Co-operation and Development, 1991), pp. 81-108.

Csaba, László, "Post-comecon trade in convertible currencies," *Est-Ovest,* 1991:5, 39-56.

Dembinski, Paweł and Jacques Morriset, "Experiences of IMF stabilization policies in Latin America and in Eastern Europe," in *Systemic change and stabilization in Eastern Europe,* edited by László Csaba (Aldershot: Dartmouth, 1991), pp. 65-76.

Diebold, William, Jr., "Rethinking the problem of trade and payments: the Soviet Union and the process of reforming relations among industrialized market economies," in *The Soviet Union and the world economy* (New York: Council on Foreign Relations, 1979), pp. 17-29.

Długosz, Stanisław, "Za długie cugle," *Polityka (Import-Export),* 14 September 1991.

Dollar, David, "Outward oriented developing countries really do grow more rapidly: evidence from 95 LDCs, 1976-1985," *Economic Development and Cultural Change,* 1992:3, 523-44.

Dornbusch, Rudiger, "The case for trade liberalization in developing countries," *Journal of Economic Perspectives,* 1992a:1, 69-85.

_____, "A payments mechanism for the Soviet Union and Eastern Europe," in *Inter-state economic relations in the former Soviet Union,* edited by Daniel Gros, Jean Pisani-Ferry, and André Sapir (Brussels: Centre for European Policy Studies, Working Document No. 63, 1992b), pp. 31-39.

Doz, Yves L., "Technology partnership between larger and smaller firms: some critical issues," in *Cooperative strategies in international business,* edited by Farok J. Contractor and Peter Lorange (Toronto: Lexington Books, 1988), pp. 317-38.

Dziewulski, Kazimierz, "Kogo protegowac?" *Zycie Gospodarcze,* 1992:5, 6.

EC, *Rapport sur l'état d'avancement de l'assistance coordonnée des 24 à l'Europe Centrale et Orientale (addendum)* (Brussels: Commission of the European Communities, 30 October 1990).

_____, *Common guidelines for coordinated G-24 exceptional balance of payments assistance to Central and Eastern European countries* (Brussels: Commission of the European Communities, 14 June 1991a).

_____, *First annual report on the implementation of economic aid to CEEC (PHARE)* (Brussels: Commission of the European Communities, October 1991b).

_____, *Scoreboard of G-24 assistance: commentary* (Brussels: Commission of the European Communities, 30 October 1991c).

_____, *G-24 assistance to Central and Eastern Europe, summary tables* (Brussels: Commission of the European Communities, 11 November 1991d).

_____, *Operation PHARE, project summaries* (Brussels: Commission of the European Communities, revision of January 1992a).

_____, *Fact sheet* (Brussels: Commission of the European Communities, 31 January 1992b).

EIB, *Financing in Central and Eastern European countries: Bulgaria, CSFR, Hungary, Poland and Romania* (Luxembourg: European Investment Bank, April 1991, mimeographed).

Eichengreen, Barry, "One money for Europe? Lessons from the US currency union," *Economic Policy*, No. 10 (1990), 117-66.

Francèze, Alain, "Le tourisme en URSS: une industrie à développer," *Le Courrier des Pays de l'Est*, No. 351 (1990), 3-41.

Gendarme, René, *Des sorcières dans l'économie: les multinationales* (Paris: Cujas, 1991).

Graziani, Giovanni, *Comecon, domination et dépendances* (Paris: Maspero, 1982).

_____, "Complementarities in foreign trade between the EEC and the CMEA countries" (paper presented to the conference on 'East-West Trade and Financial Relations,' European University Institute, 4-6 June 1985).

_____, "La CEE e il Comecon: concorrenza e complementarieta," in *L'Europa e l'economia politica del sistema mondo*, edited by R. Parboni and I. Wallerstein (Milan: Franco Angeli, 1987).

_____, "Influence and policy implications of the major factors in intersystems trade, especially the East-South trade" (study prepared for the UNCTAD Secretariat, Geneva, UNCTAD/ITP/TSC/6, 1989).

Gros, Daniel, "Regional disintegration in the Soviet Union: economic costs and benefits," *Intereconomics*, 1991:5, 207-13.

_____, "A multilateral payments mechanism for the former republics of the Soviet Union and Eastern Europe," in *Inter-state economic relations in the former Soviet Union*, edited by Daniel Gros, Jean Pisani-Ferry, and André Sapir (Brussels: Centre for European Policy Studies, Working Document No. 63, 1992a), pp. 41-47.

_____ and Jean Pisani-Ferry, "The ruble zone: simple rules for today and principles for tomorrow," in *Inter-state economic relations in the former Soviet Union*, edited by Daniel Gros, Jean Pisani-Ferry, and André Sapir (Brussels: Centre for European Policy Studies, Working Document No. 63, 1992), pp. 78-88.

Grubel, Herbert G., "The theory of optimum regional associations," in *The economics of common currencies*, edited by Harry G. Johnson and Alexander K. Swoboda (Cambridge, MA: Harvard University Press, 1973), pp. 99-113.

Hanson, Philip, *Trade and technology in Soviet-Western relations* (London: Macmillan, 1981).

Harrigan, Kathryn R., *Managing for joint venture success* (New York: Lexington Books, 1986).

Havrylyshyn, Oleh, "Trade and payments options for Central and East Europe" (paper prepared for the conference 'Eastern European Trade Policy Issues,' organized by the European Bank for Reconstruction and Development, London, 25-27 March 1992a, mimeographed).

_____, "When and how new currencies?" in *Inter-state economic relations in the former Soviet Union*, edited by Daniel Gros, Jean Pisani-Ferry, and André Sapir (Brussels: Centre for European Policy Studies, Working Document No. 63, 1992b), pp. 72-77.

_____ and John Williamson, *From Soviet disUnion to Eastern economic community?* (Washington, DC: Institute for International Economics, 1991).

Hillman, Arye L., *The political economy of protection* (London-New York: Harwood Academic Publishers, 1989).

_____, "International trade policy in the transition from socialism" (paper presented at the conference on 'Whither Socialist Society?' Jerusalem, April 1991).

Holzman, Franklyn D., *The economics of Soviet bloc trade and finance* (Boulder, CO - and London: Westview Press, 1987).

Hughes, Gordon and Paul Hare, "The international competitiveness of industries in Bulgaria, Czechoslovakia, Hungary and Poland" (paper prepared for RES Conference, 10 April 1991).

Joint, *The economy of the USSR: summary and recommendations* (London, Paris, and Washingon, DC: European Bank for Reconstruction and Development, International Bank for Reconstruction and Development, International Monetary Fund, and Organisation for Economic Co-operation and Development, December 1990).

Kobylka, Jari, "Customs duties increase in Czechoslovakia," *Business in Eastern Europe*, 13 January 1992, 20.

Kornai, János, *Economics of shortage* (Amsterdam: North-Holland, 1980, 2 vols.).

_____, *The socialist system—the political economy of communism* (Princeton, NJ: Princeton University Press, 1992).

Köves, András and Paul Marer, eds., *Foreign economic liberalization: transformations in socialist and market economies* (Boulder, CO: Westview Press, 1991).

Langenecker, Juliane, "East Germany: traditional FTOs going, going...," *Business in Eastern Europe*, 13 January 1992, 16-17.

Lavigne, Marie, "Les pays de l'Est ont besoin de réaménager leurs échanges commerciaux," *Le Monde Diplomatique*, 1991:10, 6-7.

Lecraw, Donald J., "Countertrade: a form of cooperative international business arrangement," in *Cooperative strategies in international business* edited by Farok J. Contractor and Peter Lorange (Toronto: Lexington Books, 1988), pp. 425-42.

Levitas, Anthony and Piotr Strzalkowski, "What does 'uwlaszczenie nomenklatury' ('propertisation of the nomenklatura') really mean?" *Communist Economies*, 1990:4, 413-16.

Lindsay, Margie, *International business in Gorbachev's Soviet Union* (London: Pinter, 1989).

Losoncz, Miklós, "The impact of Hungarian economic reforms on the competitive position of the developing countries in the East," *Journal of Development Planning*, No. 23 (1992), forthcoming.

Lynn, Jonathan, "Hungary sees full convertibility of currency at end of 1993," *Reuters*, 5 February 1992.

Lyon, Alistair, "Tough tasks await new Moslem group," *Reuters*, 18 February 1992.

Marer, Paul and Salvatore Zecchini, eds., *The transition to a market economy*, (Paris: Organisation for Economic Co-operation and Development, 1991, 2 vols.).

Marrese, Michael, "Hungary emphasizes foreign partners," *RFE/RL Research Report*, 1992:17, 25-33.

Matejka, Harriet, "Central planning, trade policy instruments and centrally planned economies within the framework of the General Agreement on Tariffs and Trade," *Journal of Development Planning*, No. 20 (1991), 141-63.

_____, "East-west economic integration," in *The Soviet Union and Eastern Europe in the global economy*, edited by Marie Lavigne (Cambridge: Cambridge University Press, 1992), pp. 2-23.

McKinnon, Ronald I., "Liberalizing foreign trade in a socialist economy: the problem of negative value-added," in *Currency convertibility in Eastern Europe*, edited by John Williamson (Washington, DC: Institute for International Economics, 1991a), pp. 96-115.

_____, *The order of economic liberalization—financial control in the transition to a market economy* (Baltimore and London: The Johns Hopkins University Press, 1991b).

Meade, James, *The theory of customs unions* (Amsterdam: North-Holland, 1955).

Messerlin, Patrick A., "Trade barriers affecting Central and Eastern European countries on the western market" (Paris: Organisation for Economic Co-operation and Development, document TD/TC/WP(91)22/ADD1, 1991).

Meyer, Monique, "Quelques points de comparaison entre les plans comptables français et soviétique," *European Accounting*, 1990:1, 88-97.

Mundell, Robert A., "A plan for a European currency," in *The economics of common currencies*, edited by Harry G. Johnson and Alexander K. Swoboda (Cambridge, MA: Harvard University Press, 1973), pp. 143-72.

Nestorovic, Cedomir, "Les assurances à l'est: situation générale et par pays," *Le Courrier des Pays de l'Est*, No. 360 (1991), 3-24.

Niezgódka-Medvoda, Malgorzata, "Zmiany ustawy o działalności gospodarczej," *Firma*, 1991:12, 20-21.

OECD, *Development co-operation report* (Paris: Organisation for Economic Co-operation and Development, December 1991a).

_____, *OECD economic surveys: Hungary 1991* (Paris: Organisation for Economic Co-operation and Development, 1991b).

_____, *Flows to Central and Eastern Europe in 1990* (Paris: Organisation for Economic Co-operation and Development, October 1991c).

_____, "Trade barriers affecting Central and Eastern European countries on the western market, a preliminary appraisal" (Paris: Organisation for Economic Co-operation and Development, TD/TC/WP(91)22, 1991d).

_____, *Accounting reform in Central and Eastern Europe* (Paris: Organisation for Economic Co-operation and Development, 1991e).

Okolicsanyi, Karoly, "Hungarian foreign trade turns from east to west," *RFE/RL Research Report*, 1992:15, 34-36.

Olechowski, Andrzej and A. Yeats, "The incidence for non tariff barriers on socialist country exports," *Economia Internazionale*, 1982:2, 227-45.

Oman, Charles, *New forms of international investment in developing countries* (Paris: Organisation for Economic Co-operation and Development, 1984).

Pardo, Carlos, "La renaissance des assurances en Hongrie," in *Techniques financières et développement*, No. 22 (1991), 58-64.

PE, "Polish foreign trade in 1991 and early 1992," *PlanEcon Report*, 19 June 1992.

Polak, Jacques J., "Convertibility: an indispensable element in the transition process," in *Currency convertibility in Eastern Europe*, edited by John Williamson (Washington, DC: Institute for International Economics, 1991), 21-30.

Portes, Richard, "Introduction," in *The path of reform in Central and Eastern Europe*, *European Economy*, 1991:2, special edition, 3-15.

_____, "Is there a better way?" *International Economic Insights*, 1992:3, 18-22.

Rahman, M. Zubaidur, "East-West accounting differences and the accounting problems encountered by the western partners of Soviet joint ventures," in *Economic reform in the Soviet Union: some guidelines for business* (Leningrad: International Management Institute and Milan: Euromobiliare, occasional paper, March 1991), pp. 39-72.

Reynaud, Christian and Martine Poincelet, eds., *Quelles politiques de transport pour accompagner la transition?* (Caen: INRETS-DEST, Paradigme, 1992).

Robinson, Sherman, Laura d'Andrea Tyson, and Leyla Woods, "Conditionality and adjustment in Hungary and Yugoslavia," in *Economic adjustment and reform in Eastern Europe and the Soviet Union—essays in honor of Franklyn D. Holzman*, edited by Josef C. Brada, Ed A. Hewett, and Thomas A. Wolf (Durham, NC and London: Duke University Press, 1988), pp. 72-105.

Rosati, Dariusz, "The CMEA demise, trade restructuring and trade distruction (*sic!*) in Eastern Europe—initial assessment" (Warsaw: Instytut Koniunktur i Cen, 1991, mimeographed).

_____, "Problems of post-CMEA trade and payments" (paper prepared for the conference 'Eastern European Trade Policy Issues,' organized by the European Bank for Reconstruction and Development, London, 25-27 March 1992, mimeographed); apparently literally reproduced in several other sources, including *The economic consequences of the East* (London: Centre for Economic Policy Research, unedited and unpaged collection of papers, 1992).

Schill, Wolfgang, "East Germany," in *Currency convertibility in Eastern Europe*, edited by John Williamson (Washington, DC: Institute for International Economics, 1991), pp. 181-96.

Senior Nello, Susan, *The New Europe—changing economic relations between East and West* (London: Harvester-Wheatsheaf, 1991).

Slay, Ben, "Post-communist privatization: efficiency, justice and anti-trust issues," in *Industrial strategies and policies for economic growth in the 1990's* (Budapest: Research Institute of Industrial Economics, Hungarian Academy of Sciences, special issue of *Review of Industrial Economics*, 1991a), 93-102.

_____, "On the economics of interrepublican trade," *Report on the USSR*, 1991b:48, 1-8.

_____, "Privatization in Poland: an overview," *RFE/RL Research Report*, 1992a:17, 15-21.

_____, "Poland and the international economy in the 1980s: the failure of reforming socialist foreign trade and prospects for the future," in *Escape from socialism: the Polish route*, edited by Walter D. Connor and Piotr Ploszajski (Warsaw: IFiS Publishers, 1992b), pp. 29-57.

Staniszkis, Jadwiga, "'Political capitalism' in Poland," *East European Politics and Societies*, 1991:1, 127-41.

Stark, David, "Privatization in Hungary: from plan to market or from plan to clan?," *East European Politics and Societies*, 1990:3, 351-92.

Stefanski, Roman, "FSM dopłaca do cinquecento," *Gazeta Wyborcza*, 10 April 1992.

Summers, Lawrence H., "The next chapter," *International Economic Insights*, 1992a:3, 12-16.

_____, "Back to the future—the world economy in a nutshell," *The International Economy*, 1992:4, 40-44, 61-62.

Święcicki, "Cugle w sam raz," *Polityka (Export-Import)*, 23 November 1991.

Tanon, Laurence, "Les premiers pas des publicitaires occidentaux sur le marché soviétique," *Le Courrier des Pays de l'Est*, No. 352 (1990), 77-81.

Tökes, Rudolf L., "From Visegrad to Kraków: cooperation, competition and coexistence in Central Europe," *Problems of Communism*, 1991:6, 100-14.

UNCTAD, "Protectionism and structural adjustment" (Geneva, internal report of the UNCTAD secretariat, TD/B/1282, 1990).

UNCTC, *Transnational corporations in world development—trends and prospects* (New York: United Nations, sales publication, ST/CTC/89, June 1988).

UNECE, *Economic survey of Europe in 1989-1990* (New York: United Nations, sales publication No. E.90.II.E.1, 1990).

_____, *Economic survey of Europe in 1990-1991* (New York: United Nations, sales publication No. E.91.II.E.1, 1991a).

_____, *Economic Bulletin for Europe, Vol. 43* (New York: United Nations, sales publication No. E.91.II.E.39, 1991b).

_____, *Economic survey of Europe in 1991-1992* (New York: United Nations, sales publication No. E.92.II.E.1, 1992).

UNWES, *World economic survey, 1990* (New York: United Nations, sales publication No. E.90.II.C.1, 1990).

_____, *World economic survey, 1991* (New York: United Nations, sales publication No. E.91.II.C.1, 1991).

_____, *World economic survey, 1992* (New York: United Nations, sales publication No. E.92.II.C.1, 1992).

Vanek, Jaroslav, *General equilibrium of international discrimination: the case of customs unions* (Cambridge, MA: Harvard University Press, 1965).

Vavilov, Andrey and Oleg Vyugin, "Trade patterns of former Soviet republics after integration into the world economic system" (paper prepared for the conference 'Economic Consequences of Soviet Disintegration,' organized by Österreichische Nationalbank and the Institute for International Economics, Vienna, 20-22 April 1992).

Warusfel, Bertrand, "La libéralisation du contrôle des échanges technologiques est-ouest et ses implications internationales," *Le Courrier des Pays de l'Est*, No. 353 (1990), 27-38.

Williamson, John, *The economic opening of Eastern Europe* (Washington, DC: Institute for International Economics, 1991a).

_____, "Convertibility," in *The transition to a market economy—special issues vol. II*, edited by Paul Marer and Salvatore Zecchini (Paris: Organisation for Economic Co-operation and Development, 1991b), pp. 252-64.

World Bank, *World debt tables 1991-92* (Washington, DC: The World Bank, 1992).

Wright, Robin, "Report From Turkestan," *The New Yorker*, 6 April 1992, 53-75.

Yasilyev, S., "Russia" (paper prepared for the conference 'Economic Consequences of Soviet Disintegration,' organized by Österreichische Nationalbank and the Institute for International Economics, Vienna, 20-22 April 1992).

Zahradník, Jaromír, "Czechoslovakia," in *Currency convertibility in Eastern Europe*, edited by John Williamson (Washington, DC: Institute for International Economics, 1991), pp. 217-25.

Zloch-Christy, Iliana, *East-West financial relations* (Cambridge: Cambridge University Press, 1991).

About the Book and Editor

The unprecedented economic, political, and social changes that have followed the east European revolutions of late 1989 rank among the epochal events of the twentieth century. The end of the cold war has opened up far-reaching possibilities for international economic cooperation, which may be able to stimulate economic growth in the region and revive interactions with the global economy.

This collection of essays comes to grips with the problems of repositioning the new Eastern economies in the global arena. The contributors address four main themes: freeing up foreign economic sectors through trade liberalization, currency convertibility, and greater access to markets for international capital; the disintegration of the trade payment, pricing, and settlements systems based on the transferable ruble; active participation in the key organizations entrusted with international financial, monetary, and trading regimes; and strategies for using international economic assistance to alleviate adjustment costs with ongoing transition policies.

Jozef M. van Brabant is Principal Economic Affairs Officer for the Department of Economic and Social Development of the United Nations Secretariat.

Index

adjustment costs of transition, 3, 7, 9, 56, 93-9, 114
  see also assistance to the transition, economics of transition, trade liberalization
Adria-Alps initiative, 68
  see also Hexagonale
Afghanistan, 11
Albania, 11, 16, 50, 69, 94, 95, 119, 121
  and European Communities (EC), 68, 92, 111
  and international economic organizations (IEOs), 88, 89
anchors of transition, 24, 25, 46
Andreff, Wladimir, 10
Angola, 11
Armenia, 64, 69, 70, 89
  see also Commonwealth of Independent States (CIS), Soviet Union, successor states of Soviet Union
Asian-Pacific trading area, 35
assistance to transition, 9-10, 38, 41, 42, 73, 75, 77, 99-102, 105-9, 111-73
  Baltic states, 116
  banking, 143, 146-7, 157, 164
  bilateral, 117, 118
  comprehensive recovery program, 56, 103, 105-9, 137
  coordination, 105-9, 120-2, 137-40
  debt, 114, 133, 141, 142, 147-8

  to Eastern Europe, 116-22, 157-73
  economics of transition, 57-61
  environment, 115, 118, 164-5
  errors and their correction, 57-61, 105-9
  export-credit guarantees, 145
  financial, 59-60, 112-40, 141-56
  global economic framework, 94-5, 99, 102-5
  and interest rates, 150-2, 155
  and international economic organizations (IEOs), 75, 77, 79, 89, 93-109, 141
  and investment companies, 143
  and investment funds, 143, 149, 164
  and investment protection, 113, 114, 128, 141, 164
  macroeconomic stabilization, 112, 113, 114, 118, 120, 157
  management, 165-8, 171-3
  objectives of, 112-16
  regional economic cooperation, 58-61
  services, 157, 168-70
  and successor states of Soviet Union, 122-6, 157-73
  support for cooperative approach, 60-1
  technical assistance, 112, 113, 114, 115, 117, 118, 165-70
  and technology, 153, 154, 161-5

most-favored nation (MFN), 152, 187
Mozambique, 11
Multi-fibre Arrangement (MFA), 188
  see also protectionism, sensitive
    products, trade developments
    since 1980s, trade liberaliza-
    tion
multilateral economic organizations,
  v, 6, 8-9, 80-7
Multilateral Investment Guarantee
  Agency (MIGA), 116
  see also International Bank for
    Reconstruction and Develop-
    ment (IBRD)
multinational corporation, *see* transnational corporation (TNC)
multilateralism, 61, 80-7, 108

nationalism, 22, 23, 34
negative value-added enterprise, 48
newly industrializing developing
  economies (NIEs), 149, 155, 176,
  177, 181, 182, 192
Nicaragua, 11
North-American Free Trade Association, 35
Norway, 68, 134

observership in Council for Mutual
  Economic Assistance (CMEA), 11
official development assistance
  (ODA), 95, 130, 142, 145-6, 152,
  154-6
  see also assistance to transition,
    developing countries and
    east-west assistance
Okolicsanyi, Karoly, 13
Olszewski Government, 33
optimum currency area, 53-6
Organisation for Economic Co-operation and Development (OECD),
  95, 121, 130, 131, 132, 145, 152,
  153, 155, 156, 176

Organization of Petroleum Exporting Countries (OPEC), 177
Overall Association of Small Enterprises (Bulgaria), 164

Pakistan, 18, 69, 88
Paris Club, 124, 125, 133, 147-8
partnership agreement, 68, 92
  see also European Communities
    (EC)
payments facility, 21, 59-61, 69-70,
  106
payments union, 46, 58-61, 69-72, 74-
  5, 77, 126
PHARE (*Pologne/Hongrie: assistance à
  la restructuration économique*), 116,
  117, 118, 132
  see also assistance to transition,
    European Communities (EC)
planned economy in transition
  (PET), 2
planning and international economic organizations (IEOs), 82-7
Poland, 10, 17, 18, 19, 24, 31, 32, 33,
  34, 67, 69, 75, 118
  and assistance, 119, 120, 127, 128,
    129, 130, 132, 135, 136, 138,
    142, 144, 152
  and Baltic Council, 68
  and convertibility, 20, 21, 24-5,
    26, 28-9, 120
  debt, 115, 128, 147-8
  and European Communities
    (EC), 18, 22, 35, 68, 73, 91, 92,
    111, 152-3, 175, 178, 179, 180,
    183, 184, 187, 189, 190-2
  and European Free Trade Associ-
    ation (EFTA), 68, 91, 153
  and *Hexagonale*, 68
  in international economic organi-
    zations (IEOs), 6, 76, 86, 89,
    96
  and ruble affair, 25, 26, 27